Jung-Bong Choi

Digitalization of Television in Japan

Jung-Bong Choi

Digitalization of Television in Japan

State, Economy, and Discourse

VDM Verlag Dr. Müller

Impressum/Imprint (nur für Deutschland/ only for Germany)

Bibliografische Information der Deutschen Nationalbibliothek: Die Deutsche Nationalbibliothek verzeichnet diese Publikation in der Deutschen Nationalbibliografie; detaillierte bibliografische Daten sind im Internet über http://dnb.d-nb.de abrufbar.
Alle in diesem Buch genannten Marken und Produktnamen unterliegen warenzeichen-, marken- oder patentrechtlichem Schutz bzw. sind Warenzeichen oder eingetragene Warenzeichen der jeweiligen Inhaber. Die Wiedergabe von Marken, Produktnamen, Gebrauchsnamen, Handelsnamen, Warenbezeichnungen u.s.w. in diesem Werk berechtigt auch ohne besondere Kennzeichnung nicht zu der Annahme, dass solche Namen im Sinne der Warenzeichen- und Markenschutzgesetzgebung als frei zu betrachten wären und daher von jedermann benutzt werden dürften.

Coverbild: www.purestockx.com

Verlag: VDM Verlag Dr. Müller Aktiengesellschaft & Co. KG
Dudweiler Landstr. 125 a, 66123 Saarbrücken, Deutschland
Telefon +49 681 9100-698, Telefax +49 681 9100-988, Email: info@vdm-verlag.de
Zugl.: Iowa City, University of Iowa, Diss., 2005

Herstellung in Deutschland:
Schaltungsdienst Lange o.H.G., Zehrensdorfer Str. 11, D-12277 Berlin
Books on Demand GmbH, Gutenbergring 53, D-22848 Norderstedt
Reha GmbH, Dudweiler Landstr. 99, D- 66123 Saarbrücken
ISBN: 978-3-639-07834-3

Imprint (only for USA, GB)

Bibliographic information published by the Deutsche Nationalbibliothek: The Deutsche Nationalbibliothek lists this publication in the Deutsche Nationalbibliografie; detailed bibliographic data are available in the Internet at http://dnb.d-nb.de.
Any brand names and product names mentioned in this book are subject to trademark, brand or patent protection and are trademarks or registered trademarks of their respective holders. The use of brand names, product names, common names, trade names, product descriptions etc. even without
a particular marking in this works is in no way to be construed to mean that such names may be regarded as unrestricted in respect of trademark and brand protection legislation and could thus be used by anyone.

Cover image: www.purestockx.com

Publisher:
VDM Verlag Dr. Müller Aktiengesellschaft & Co. KG
Dudweiler Landstr. 125 a, 66123 Saarbrücken, Germany
Phone +49 681 9100-698, Fax +49 681 9100-988, Email: info@vdm-verlag.de

Copyright © 2008 VDM Verlag Dr. Müller Aktiengesellschaft & Co. KG and licensors
All rights reserved. Saarbrücken 2008

Produced in USA and UK by:
Lightning Source Inc., 1246 Heil Quaker Blvd., La Vergne, TN 37086, USA
Lightning Source UK Ltd., Chapter House, Pitfield, Kiln Farm, Milton Keynes, MK11 3LW, GB
BookSurge, 7290 B. Investment Drive, North Charleston, SC 29418, USA
ISBN: 978-3-639-07834-3

TABLE OF CONTENTS

LIST OF ABBREVIATIONS

Abbreviation

A-V: Audio-Visual

BS: (Digital) Broadcasting Satellite

CATV: Community Antenna Television

CCIS: Coaxial Cable Information System

CS: (Digital) Communication Satellite

DBS: Direct Broadcast Satellite

HDTV: High-Definition Television

ICT: Information Communication Technology

INS Integrated Network Services

ISDB: Integrated Services Digital Broadcasting

ISTV: Integrated Services Television

IT: Information Technology

MITI: Ministry of International Trade and Industry

MPHPT: Ministry of Public Management, Home Affairs, Post and
  Telecommunication

MPT: Ministry of Post and Telecommunications

MTR: Mobile Terrestrial Reception

NHK: *Nippon Hoho Kyokai*

NTT: *Nippon* Telegraph and Telephone

NVOD: Near Video On Demand

PSB: Public Service Broadcasting

R&D: Research & Development

T-Commerce: Television-based Commerce

VOD: Video On Demand

CHAPTER I

INTRODUCTION

Digital HDTV in a Post Office, Tokyo, 2001

It was a hot, bustling day in Tokyo. I walked into a small post office to send off some packages, where I saw the sleek body of a digital Hi-Definition TV standing in the center of the office foyer. I was dumbstruck by its sophisticated design and the breathtaking clarity of the image on the approximately fifty-inch screen. By today's standard, digital HDTV is almost a technological cliché, but it was quite a stunner, at least to me, just a few years ago. But why had this awe-inspiring technology novelty been showcased in this run-down post office?

The mysterious presence of the digital HDTV was explained a couple of weeks later when I spoke with a worker at NHK. According the NHK staff, it was the Ministry of Post and Telecommunications[1] who masterminded the public exhibit of digital HDTV sets in numerous post offices and other public spaces across the country. They also informed me that the public display began in July 2000 (during the G-8 summit held in Okinawa) as a twofold attempt to give a boost to HDTV sales and to herald the launch of Japan's digital broadcasting television service slated for December 2000.

My curiosity was piqued. Why would a ministry of the government, known principally for its administrative competence and bureaucratic command, become a huckster for HDTVs? What were the motivations for the venerable ministry rolling up its sleeves and jumping into TV sales? What is at stake in promoting digital HDTV and launching digital broadcasting television in Japan? What is the relationship (and difference) between business and the state? More specifically, what is the identity of the

---

[1] The MPT was merged with other ministries into the Ministry of Public Management, Home Affairs, Post and Telecommunications (MPHPT). The MPHPT changed its English name to the Ministry of Internal Affairs and Communications (MIC) as of September 2004.

1

Japanese state in this unsettling time of global info-capitalism spearheaded by neo-liberalist principles? Gripped by a barrage of questions, I decided to jettison the topic that I had previously proposed for my dissertation.

Digital TV, Digitization, and *Digitalization*

Digital television is becoming a global trend with a startling velocity. Following the lead of North America and Western Europe, a host of countries in East/South Asia, South America, and Eastern Europe are also hastening the epic shift from analog to digital television. It is predicted that approximately 350 million people will be viewing digital broadcast television by the end of this year. At the current pace, nearly 38 percent of the world's TV households will be receiving digital signals by 2010 (Informa Telecoms & Media, 2002, p. 2). Underlying this technological gold rush is an array of remarkable features that digital broadcasting presents: interactivity, multichannel capacity, immunity to interference by other signals, superb audio-visual qualities, and quasi-universal interoperability with other media that recognize digital language.

These outstanding qualities are founded upon the quintessence of digital technology: the binary codification (comparable to the dots and dashes of the telegraph code), which converts data into "a bitstream of zeros and ones" (Owen, 1999, p. 151). Since digital technology can break down virtually any type of information (print, painting, music, sound, photography) into a uniform code of bits and bytes, it is now possible to establish universal compatibility among various media. As Timothy Todreas (1999) observes, "text, graphics, audio and video used to be within the purview of separate industries: print, radio, and television respectively. Once digitized . . . bits can commingle effortlessly. Content can travel down the same distribution path and can be used interchangeably" (pp. 78-79). Paradoxically, the atomize-ability of digital technology precipitates digital convergence, in which all the sophisticated traditional media taxonomies and typologies will become muddied and eventually obsolete. This

2

convergence effect—on which I will elaborate in chapter two—is central to Japan's struggle to promote digital television as the hub of all digital devices.

Aside from the universal connectivity of digital television with neighboring media, there are a few other properties of digital television that are pertinent to my research: audio/visual excellence, multichannel capacity, and interactivity. The digital television is capable of delivering superior audio/video quality compared to its analog counterpart. However, the enhanced audio/visual fidelity of digital television is best exploited in a combined use with the Hi-Definition television system, an advanced method of injecting televisual signals onto the screen in a much more precise fashion than that of its predecessors, the NTSC and PAL systems. Contrary to common belief, HDTV is not an immediate offspring of the digital television system, although electronics makers, broadcasters, and policymakers of the digital television excitedly promote it as digital television's headliner. There are multiple, significant reasons behind the deliberate "passing" of HDTV as *the* figurehead of digital television, especially in a Japanese context, on which I elaborate in chapter three.

Compared to analog signals, digitized information takes much less bandwidth, i.e., much less channel capacity to distribute content per unit of time. This technical "thriftiness" is an end result of the compression technology that can filter out redundant data and squeeze more data into a given bandwidth. The economic use of bandwidth means greater space to fit more channels, which ends the "distribution bottleneck" (Todreas, 1999, p. 79) common to analog formats. The sudden abundance of bandwidth leads to an explosion of channel outlets, metamorphosing the topography of Japanese television in terms of ownership structure, revenue sources, cultural diversification, content provision and distribution, etc. I address this subject in both chapter four and five from two different angles.

The interactive function of digital television is yet another benefit of the efficient use of bandwidth. A broadened bandwidth not only increases the volume of channels and

3

the velocity of information but also enables "two-way" traffic. With expanded two-way interactions between sender and receiver, digital television could transform the modality of broadcasting from a linear, unilateral communication to a cyclical, bilateral one. Apparently, the level of control for the user is strictly limited by the choices provided by the software programmer. However, the interactivity of television will incrementally open new modes of socio-economic and cultural interactions (Video-On-Demand and T-commerce, for instance) among the user. I shall touch upon this subject in my conclusion in conjunction with Japan's proposed template for Integrated Services Digital Broadcasting (ISDB).

Still, all the perks of digital television don't come without costs and shortcomings. The multiple channels of digital television could inspire program diversification and perhaps contribute to a socio-cultural diversification. However, the mind-blowing channel wealth in Japan's digital broadcasting satellites (BS) and communication satellite (CS) could trigger the contrary as well. In fact, critics and viewers have already become disillusioned by the promise of channel multiplication, for it has impoverished, rather than improved, the program quality and originality in a way similar to what cable television did in the U.S. Likewise, the interactive functions of digital television could turn into a blight rather than a blessing. Tony Feldman (1997) posits that interactivity "runs the risk of giving them [the users] so much power in determining their own experiences of content that the only message conveyed is the one the user chooses to receive. The freedom to chart your own course, therefore, can emasculate as readily as it can liberate" (p. 18).

Like any technology, the introduction of digital television in and of itself does not animate "social" changes. In other words, it does not necessarily encourage particular types of cultural subjectivities or orders, and is much less likely to guarantee felicitous social realities. It is, precisely, the socially determined ways of using the digital television rather than the technology itself that could engender or suspend meaningful social

4

changes. Therefore, what matters is the social engineering of digital television. I shall call the social engineering now unfolding in the post-technical production of digital television a *digitalization* of television, a process in which the technological novelty is articulated with specific social values and objectives, discursively and materially.

Government, State, and Para-state

My project centers on the *digitalization* of television in the context of Japan. Unlike the digitization of television, which refers to the technical shift from an analog to a digital system of television, the *digitalization* of television intrinsically concerns the *social making* of digital television. It wrestles with an ongoing process by which the values and functions of digital television are pronounced and negotiated within specific political, economic, cultural, and technological environments. At the same time, the *digitalization* of television stands for a mode of inquiry that I employ in my research. It aims to denaturalize the rise and adoption of digital television, historicize the socio-economic demand/desire for technological novelty, politicize the institutional and discursive endeavors to popularize the medium, and critically interpret both acclaims for and oppositions against the establishment of the digital television system. In my project, the notion of digitalization is a major vehicle of exploring the multi-layered social actions involved in the realization of Japan's digital broadcasting system, social actions that implicate power dynamics, cultural sensibilities, and institutional propensities, which are also situated within a larger, transnational techno-economic matrix.

In the process of *digitalizing* television in Japan, the state has been the undisputable nodal point. Generally speaking, the relationship between technology and society is mediated by the state, which can not only assist or deter technological innovation but also affect the overall socio-cultural milieu in which the development and dissemination of particular technologies are determined. Today, information technologies comprise a strategic sector, a cluster of core capabilities that affect the economic structure

5

and competitiveness of each nation-state. Since virtually all nations see their future linked to new information technologies, governments' involvement in the field has never been ambiguous. The American government, as Herbert Schiller (1995) notes, has decisively endeavored to "assure the promotion of the ever-expanding communication sector" (p. 17), which has now become a backbone of the national economy. Similarly, the astounding growth of the Japanese economy between the1960s and 1980s was achieved by virtue of undivided support from the government to develop ICTs concentrating on audio-visual electronics, computer memory chips, and telecommunications equipment.

Of course, the government's involvement in ICT industries varies in intensity and method according to time and space differentials. Since the late 1980s, signs suggesting the state's retreat from the direct management of the communication and information industries have grown salient in major industrialized countries, as the tie between ICT and transnational capitalism becomes ever-tightened and as deregulationist doctrines gain global currency. Kaarle Nordenstreng (2001) observes, "we are witnessing some confusing cases in which the state is actively advocating a denial of state involvement in the media" (p. 159). In Japan, the Ministry of Post and Telecommunications privatized NTT (Nippon Telegraph and Telephone)[2] and, presently, Prime Minister Junichiro Koizumi is primed to privatize national postal services.

But the general tendency in which governments self-consciously step back from the private sphere is not the dominant current in the information and communication industry, at least in the case of Japan. The Japanese government's commitment to ICT remains unflagging to date, as instantiated by the ongoing process of *digitalizing*

---

[2] Nippon Telegraph and Telephone (NTT) had been Japan's largest company owned and operated by the state since its formation in 1952 until 1985. It had monopolized the domestic provision of telecommunications services and equipment. Although it was converted into a private corporation in April 1985, the first shares were not sold to private investors until February 1987. In addition, the MPT gradually regained its influence over the management and business strategies of NTT during the early and mid 1990s.

6

television. With *digitalization*, TV in Japan ceases to be a mere entertainment medium and transforms into the nucleus of all ICT (Information Communication Technology). It will be reborn, as claimed by the MPT and NHK officials, as the informational portal, to which other digital devices such as mobile phones and computers will be adjusted and subordinated. Given this gravity, the Japanese government's fervent intervention into the *digitalization* of television is hardly surprising.

The scope of my research, however, stretches beyond the involvement of the Japanese government in the *digitalization* of television. I differentiate the "Japanese state" from the "Japanese government," which normally denotes the bureaucratized nerve center that makes and enforces law and policy. In my project, the Japanese state refers to an institutional tapestry that networks various social agents, such as research institutions, public organizations, critics, and business associations, who participate in the shaping of nationwide protocols relevant to the *digitalization* of television. The government and the state in the context of Japan used to be synonymous before the early 1980s, when the degree to which public and private organizations exerted their influence in the procedure of constructing national communication policies was negligible. But after some twenty years of steady political decentralization and organizational deregulation, the relationship between the Japanese government and the state became something akin to Siamese twins: physically united by their tissues but disjoined in their souls and identities.

My research, therefore, does not focus solely on the governmental bureaus and their policies but attends to the roles played by such social actors as NHK, public intellectuals, and trade organizations. I shall call these "para-state" bodies. A number of para-state organizations have formed fluid and non-permanent quorums that spelled out the value of digital HDTV, constructed the purpose of digital broadcasting, and executed tasks conducive to the rollout of digital television services. Together with governmental units, they assume a major place in the national decision-making process of *digitalizing* television, thereby constituting an arc of "shared state sovereignty."

The notion of the (Japanese) state, thus conceived, necessitates an examination of various expressions of its institutional power beyond the narrow purview of "policy." For example, a wide range of public events and exhibitions, large-scale construction of digital infrastructures, propagation of ideas about information society and the digital divide, publication of data and reports, as well as legislative routines, are all integral parts of my analysis. I classify the visual, performative, intellectual, and constructional undertakings of the Japanese state as a domain of discursive acts, both distinct from and entwined with the province of policymaking. Throughout the main body of my dissertation, I emphasize the synchronization of the state's policy and discourse based on two interrelated reasons. The first is the variegated composition and functions of the Japanese state, as I mentioned above. The second is derived from my judgment that the triumphant wave of deregulation forces the redefinition of the interface between state and business, and the consequent change in the modus operandi of the state. Japan is not immune from this shift, and its impact is expressed in the form of a growing overlap between policy and discourse.

Deregulating the Boundary between Policy and Discourse

It seems necessary for me to unpack some political economic assumptions I bring to bear on my analyses of the Japanese state's participation in *digitalizing* television. Many suppose that the ferocious expansion of deregulationism resulted in the shrinkage of the state. I disagree, but neither do I believe that deregulation augments state power. The kind of change brought about by deregulation is not manifest in the intensity of state power, but in the types and methods of exercising power.

My argument is that deregulation does not represent an annulment or invalidation of state intervention; instead, it embodies an encouragement for new patterns of state intervention, and new modes of interaction between state and private organizations in the market and other socio-public arenas. Particular types of state intervention were animated, as deregulation rose to be a dominant system of connecting, *not severing,* the

8

private sector with the state. Under the ascendancy of deregulationism, conventional patterns of the Japanese state's interference with business and the market—such as controlling prices, breaking monopolies, moderating supply, etc.—have slowly dissipated.[3] But the state participates in the private sector not only as a police but also as a guarantor. In effect, the dominance of deregulatory principles reins in the state's "controlling hand," while allowing it to stretch out a "helping hand." The fact that the Japanese state hustled to promote digital HDTV sales is just one of many examples. I contend that the Japanese state's contribution to the *digitalization* of television is catalyzed via, *not despite*, deregulation.

This is not to deny that deregulation reduces the conventional terra firma and grasp of the *government*. But the reduction of the *government*'s clutch is only a partial— if not incorrect—representation of deregulation. Coupled with the retraction of government from the private sphere is the advance of non-governmental organizations into what had formerly been the inviolable realm of bureaucratic management. Deregulation facilitates—though it does not guarantee—a greater leap forward of non-governmental (both public and private) entities into the regime of national/local administration through various channels. This transformation is often dubbed a political "decentralization," since the higher involvement of non-governmental bodies in political decision-making results in the redistribution of state power.

Evidently, the redistribution of state power is an uneven process, destined in many cases for the empowerment of capital at the expense of labor. For example, the Japanese government set up an IT Strategy Headquarters based on the so-called IT Basic Law in January 2001. Headed by the Prime Minister, the headquarters consists of the cabinet with experts from the private and academic sectors. Many of the private sector experts

---

[3] I discuss this tendency in chapter one.

were from *Keidanren* (Japan Federation of Economic Organizations), the largest and strongest business organization in Japan. The corporate tilt of the state power structure is also evidenced by the fact that the *Keidanren* has been regularly posting "policy recommendations" to various departments of the government, including the Ministry of International Trade and Industry (MITI), a hallmark of the Japanese government's bureaucratic supremacy until the early 1990s. One doesn't have to dig deeply to find evidence of the reversed flow of policy-making—now flowing from business to government. A document titled "Policy Recommendations and Priority Requests to the Japanese Government on the Promotion of Regulatory Reform" (2000) issued by *Keidanren* underlines the inversion clearly:

> In order to demonstrate both domestically and internationally that there has not been the slightest change in its approach to regulatory reform, the government should further strengthen its arrangements for tackling regulatory reform and clearly state as early as possible that it will be formulating a new program. We strongly hope for the prime minister's leadership in this respect (p. 2).

For better or for worse, deregulation destabilizes the rigid division between the state and the private sphere, and stimulates a tighter coupling of business and government, lawmaking and lobbying, public affairs and private initiatives, policy and discourse. While the bureaucratic control of the Japanese government diminishes, the vacuum is filled by corporate leadership, which now constitutes the major axis of the Japanese state power geometry. Moreover, the bureaucratic and regulative energy of the Japanese government does not simply evaporate but mutates into a relatively unautocratic and liberal momentum that synergizes with corporate initiatives. The MPT, for example, funnels its effort into R&D supports for digital HDTV, the organization of symposiums on digital broadcasting, public exhibitions of digital televisions, installation of digital infrastructures, and institutional networking across academic, business, and public institutions. These emergent roles of the government are performed both in combination with the hitherto-dominant functions of government (various regulations, stimulations,

10

legislation, etc.) and in concert with the private/public organizations who now densely populate the Japanese state.

Deregulation and the subsequent organizational and functional dispersion of the state is not an isolated phenomenon. It has been encouraged by the theoretical narrative of a historical shift from a society based on an industrial economy to a post-industrial model. As Daniel Bell (1999), one of the leading theorists of this transition, perceptively noted, the post-industrial society is characterized by "the rise of new axial structures and axial principles" (p. 487). By "the rise of new axial structures," Bell hints at the emergence of a social order, wherein the intensive mobilization of technologies and various forms of knowledge employed by the loosely and flexibly connected "creative classes" (Toffler, 1990) surpasses and eventually supplants the leadership assumed by the centralized bureaucratic bodies of the government.

As the organizational deregulation has intensified over the past couple of decades, the Japanese state (like many other states) has become visibly amphibious. As an institutional compound that encompasses the government, business associations, and other private/public organizations, it regulates business while running businesses of its own right; it alternates the roles of umpire, manager, commissioner of the private sector on the one hand and the duties of the market's liaison, outpost, and deputy on the other hand. While treating the Japanese state as an amphibious entity, I do not mean to overstate its potency. Quite the contrary, I am alluding to the rapid dissimulation and disembodiment of the rigid bureaucratic citadel that many scholars have traditionally considered emblematic of the Japanese state. Unlike the past, when it was virtually indistinguishable from the Japanese government, the Japanese state today is rapidly losing a solid geo-cognitive definition, as a result of its promiscuous intermingling with other public and private organizations. The promiscuity certainly expands the scope of the state, but not necessarily its strength. Ironically, its loss of definite institutional

11

habitat, organizational unity, and structural integrity feeds its ubiquity. The Japanese state is both in flux and at overflow simultaneously.

Syndromes of the Great Convergence

In many important ways, the deregulation—not only of the market but more importantly of the government itself—is an institutional manifestation congruent with what might be called the "syndromes of the great convergence" occurring around the globe in discrete instances: economy wedded to culture, socialist politics espousing market values, broadcasting merged with telecommunications, machines internalizing human values, private enterprises sustaining public affairs, military endeavors nourishing the entertainment industry, Christianity preached by rock music and Hollywood movies, Humanities' agendas set by Natural Sciences, and so forth. This great convergence compels the political economy of media to critically evaluate its stagnant focus on "government policy." Institutional and political economic approaches to media can no longer comfortably bypass the ill-treated equation between the state and the government in the age of deregulation. Likewise, addressing governmental policies in isolation from the various types of discursive acts—visual, verbal, architectural, etc—of the state comes as an equally vexing practice.

Policies assume narratives and rhetorical tropes, while discourses seek the agent of officiation and the structure of fomularization. The state speaks, performs, builds, and displays, as much as it plans, governs, decrees, and legislates. The symbiotic rapport and the porous boundary between policy and discourse should be actively re/searched, as much as the complex relationships—i.e., correspondence, coordination, or convergence—between the government and the state need to be elucidated. Policy and discourse develop into an "assemblage" in Gilles Deleuze's (1987) word, a nexus at which an abstract purpose intersects with material practices (Crary, 1999, p. 31). They are mutual vehicles, corollaries, and often a dissociative ensemble.

12

My study tries to demonstrate both the discursive and performative aspects of policy on the one hand and the managerial, governmental dimensions of discourse on the other, as appeared in the drive for *digitalizing* television in Japan. As the syndromes of the great convergence tend to beget new research programs and methods, the organizational permeability and functional transmutation of the Japanese state demand an approach that juxtaposes the realm of policy and the domain of discourse. I submit that these all point to the necessity for an amalgamation of critical/cultural/interpretive approaches and institutional/political economic approaches in media studies.

<u>Chapter Outline</u>

Individual chapters are rather loosely clustered around four key questions: 1) what is the significance of the digital television system and the *digitalization* of television in Japan? 2) in what specific ways has the Japanese state contributed to the establishment of digital broadcasting in Japan? 3) in what capacity have non-governmental, para-state apparatuses joined forces with the Japanese government in sculpting the architecture of digital television broadcasting? 4) finally, in what sorts of ways are the discursive acts of the Japanese state convergent and often transposable with the policy generated by the government?

In the first chapter, I narrate the history of the roles played by the Japanese state in the development of the nation's information and communication industry. During the last four decades, the Japanese state's function has changed by degrees from one that focuses on planning and direct ownership/management, through financing, R&D, and the construction of legislative and technological infrastructures, to one that focuses on the creation of cultural and discursive environments propitious to the long-term development of the industry. I maintain that this shift in focus coincides with the expansion of deregulatory norms and the growing influence of both private and public organizations in state affairs.

In my second chapter, I analyze the Japanese state's discursive and legislative efforts to mobilize the digital television as a means to rejuvenate the national economy that had plummeted into a deep recession during the 1990s. Japanese power elites (bureaucrats, media conglomerates, electronics manufacturers, and other business leaders) have promoted digital television as the nucleus around which other digital information devices come together and, more importantly, as the driving engine for the advancement of Japan info-capitalism. I argue that digital television is to Japan's culture and economy as the personal computer is to the U.S. culture and economy. Hence, the Japanese method of *digitalizing* television exhibits characteristics congruous with its cultural milieu and material condition, which are distinct from those of the U.S.

The third chapter examines the meaning and place of digital HDTV within the overall structure of digital broadcasting in Japan. I trace the checkered trajectory of Japan's HDTV (Hi-Vision), which during the 1970s and 1980s epitomized the nation's obsession with technological supremacy in the thick of economic and cultural animosity between Japan and the U.S. Currently, digital HDTV is being mobilized as the dazzling corridor that shepherds the viewer into the cosmos of digital broadcasting. In this chapter, I reflect on the significance of NHK not only in developing Japan's superb HDTV technologies but also in drafting the blueprint of Japan's digital broadcasting system. As a public service broadcasting and committed partner of the MPT, NHK is a national para-state organization par excellence.

My central objective in chapter four is to delve into the international nexus of Japan's digital television, especially in the field of digital communication satellite television (CS). Digital CS is the main gateway through which transnational media capital break into the hitherto tightly sealed market of Japan's television. Rupert Murdoch's Sky and GE's DirecTV ventured into Japan's CS only to retreat, mainly due to Japan's cultural hostility blended with legal and economic xenophobia. I discuss a tacit yet exquisite division of labor between the Japanese state and Japan-based media corporations in extracting capital and business know-how from Murdoch's Sky and eventually expelling it from Japan's national television sphere.

The last chapter engages with the angst over digital television broadcasting enunciated from the perspective of Public Service Broadcasting (PSB). Some espouse digital broadcasting as a gift, while others see it as a threat to the values upheld by PSB. One of the most contentious issues is the channel multiplication capacity of digital broadcasting. I criticize the discourse of crisis, which claims that the unbridled channel multiplication will breed the "vices" of commercialism, such as fragmentation of audience, expansion of subscription systems, and deterioration of program quality. I argue that digital broadcasting positively forces public service broadcasters to redefine their identities and missions, while presenting opportunities to revitalize and expand the *public nature* of broadcasting beyond the decrepit and fictitious divide between public and commercial broadcasting.

CHAPTER II

STATE, PARA-STATE, AND

THE INFORMATION INDUSTRY

Deregulation and the State

Shortly after the dismantling of the Berlin wall, Francis Fukuyama (1992) postulated that the relentless expansion of liberal democracy-capitalism left the modern political system with no competing heterodoxies, internally and externally. Indeed, nearly two decades of neo-liberalist campaigns from the onset of the Reagan-Thatcher era have triggered a far-reaching reorganization of global orders: the decline of the transcontinental socialist alliance, and the subsequent absorption of Eastern Europe, the former Soviet Union, and China into the circuit of global info-capitalism. Central to the triumph of neo-liberalism is the canonization of deregulation, a protocol that has altered the meaning and place of national economies, cultures, and identities on a global scale.

Kees van der Pijl (1989) observes that the proliferation of deregulation dogma has compelled the redefinition of the state-society nexus, prompting what he calls a transition from a Hobbesian model to a Lockean model. According to van der Pijl, the Lockean state-civil society model has supplanted Hobbesian political economies, ones that are more state-centered and regulation-intensive, triggering the reorganization of the link between the state and business, as well as the redefinition of the identity and function of the state. Not only did the preponderance of deregulationist mantra spur the collapse of state socialism of various kinds, as Stephen Gill (1997) argues, but also it rapidly incapacitated the state-centered structure of domestic and international market across the industrialized nations (p. 86). Global civil societies, too, are looking to Anglo-American self-regulating principles as the primary model for emulation.

Some scholars in media studies assert that the hegemony of deregulationism begets the corrosion of fraternity and the mortgaging of social equity at the whims of the few. Ali Mohammadi (1997) interprets deregulation as an outright establishment of the corporate agenda within the political system of government (p. 70). Similarly, Gerald Sussman (1997) sees it as skewing politics to the "supply side" at the sacrifice of distributional equity (p. 246). Cees Hamelink (1994) reports that the quasi-universalization of laissez-faire not only engendered economic instability of the vulnerable but also posed a formidable threat to human rights. As a result, a host of deleterious repercussions followed: the concentration of wealth has spiraled as antitrust and monopoly laws are lifted; public supports for healthcare and education are cut while structural unemployment and stagflation are rampant; subsidies for public broadcasting have been ruthlessly jettisoned while financially frail local media have been devoured by transnational media giants.

As deregulation has become a favorite term among politicians, economic leaders, and NGOs/NPOs, there arises a tendency that places the state squarely opposed to the market, resurrecting the deep-seated dichotomy between state and society in liberal normative philosophy. Rhetorical assaults on the state as an obsolete, counter-democratic entity cropped up with enormous belligerence. As self-proclaimed liberitarian Jan Narveson (1999) states,

> Business . . . is what makes the world go around, providing people with the things they want in life more than any other identifiable source. Insofar as it does just that, people become better off. On the other hand, insofar as the state tries to step in and 'help' it along, business, and consequently people, do worse. Thus the state is redundant at best, counterproductive at worst—its normal condition (p. 18).

Under this political and economic climate, states become incapable of maintaining a balance between economic efficiency and social equality, and their interventions into the market with reasons other than enhancing business efficiency face steep resistance. Industrial policies and state ownership of public infrastructures are perceived as a political bête noire, as the oversized body of the state is increasingly construed as an institutional dinosaur that has outlived its service. Narveson (1999)

17

continues, "the state may at one time have served a good purpose, but that it no longer does: it has overstayed its leave. There is room, though, to doubt that it ever did that in the first place. Perhaps the State has always been nothing more than an expensive nuisance" (p. 3). In Japan, too, similar voices have been raised. Hirotaka Takeuchi and Mariko Sakakibara (2000) render a scathing critique of the state's involvement in the market. "[T]he core of the problem is that the government mistrusts competition and therefore is prone to intervene in the economy in the ways that harm the nation's productivity and prosperity" (p. 203).

But the political assault on the state as an institutional nuisance communicates an analytically and ideologically distorted assumption. By separating state and business diametrically, it hints that the state at its normal condition is a disinterested yet meddlesome watchdog of socio-economic interaction. Jeffrey Hart (1992) maintains that the state-societal dichotomy is rooted in liberal political philosophy and premised on the notion that the power of the state is limited to prevent unjust obstruction in the actions of individuals and selected collectivities. He states,

> In an ideal free enterprise economy, all business corporations
> would be private and relatively independent of state agencies and
> thus part of civil society. No capitalist country meets this liberal
> ideal; all use state-owned enterprises to perform certain functions
> of government and limit the autonomy of private firms through
> regulations (Hart, 1992, p. 2-3).

It should also be mentioned that suspicion and aversion toward the state is a frame of mind that is articulated predominantly in the Western, industrialized society. In many parts of the world, the state continues to command an unsurpassed weight as the de/centralized headquarters of national decision-making processes. Kaarle Nordenstreng (2001) maintains,

> Indeed, in the view of some interest groups, it has overreached
> itself and should be rolled back, with civil society and the so-called
> third sector assuming a greater role in the management of society.
> But the developing countries are far from ready for this. In these
> countries . . . relying on civil society or NGOs would be largely
> wishful thinking (p. 160).

18

Furthermore, the state is highly valued by some as an organizing and distributive core of social energies such as labor, capital, technologies, and other resources. Collective identity and exert the democratic aspirations of the citizenry still revolve around the state system (Waisbord & Morris, 2001), even in many Western industrialized nations. While non-state bodies are undoubtedly expanding their parameters, the assumption that their growth would make the state superfluous is plainly misleading. It is an optical illusion caused by an overestimation of civil organizations' maturity and the misconception of the state as a hindrance to the self-governance of market. To the contrary, the strong leadership of the state could be a prerequisite for the growth of laissez faire in business.

Karl Polanyi (1957) has long refuted the dichotomous thinking by claiming that, in the case of Britain, the creation of a self-regulating market society was an outcome of a strong state endeavor. "Laissez-faire itself was," asserts Polanyi, "enforced by the state and enormous increase in the administrative functions of the state, which was now endowed with a central bureaucracy able to fulfill the tasks set by the adherents of liberalism" (as cited in Gill, 1997, pp. 81-82). Even the ferocious rise of market deregulation during Thatcher and Reagan administrations was made possible to a great extent by the supreme leadership of the states. Immanuel Wallerstein (1999) posits, "capitalists depend on the intervention of the states in such a multitude of ways that any true weakening of state authority is disastrous [for them]" (p. 33). Therefore, the deregulationist current cannot and should not be deemed an unambiguous indicator of the decline of the state; rather, it is at once a cause and outcome of the shift in its modes of operation and organizational patterns.

Neither Volatility nor Stability: Reconstruction of State

Across disciplines in the humanities and social sciences, discussion on the fate of state in the wake of global deregulation has long shown an acute polarity patterned into the "already-frail-state" versus "still-robust-state" binary. In the field of media studies,

too, assertions of the shrinking state (Noam, 1987; Rosenau, 1997) are sharply

contravened by claims of continuing relevance (Golding & Harris, 1997; Curran, 2000;

Morris & Waisbord, 2001). Recently, however, the voice from the camp endorsing the

abiding significance and vigor of the state is overtaking those who hint at the decline of

the state. Oliver Boyd-Barrett (1998) contends, "substantial powers are still invested in

issues of sovereignty, whether in domains of trade, culture or politics, and the mapping of

the place of media with respect to such issues is a live and legitimate topic for

investigation" (p. 167). James Curran (2000) suggests that tales of the state's downfall

have been greatly exaggerated. He goes on to argue that the concept and theory of

globalization tend to underplay the lasting potency of the nation state as a political form

and economic entity. Waisbord and Morris (2001) maintain in a similar vein:

> States remain important agents in shaping the global media order
> and the structure of media markets. They perform different
> functions that aren't equally threatened or obliterated by
> globalization, and they have tools for taming globalizing forces.
> States remain the locus for decision making on domestic policies,
> and they concentrate technical administrative capacities that are
> not currently replicated by any other institutional arrangement (p.
> xvi).

However, the contentions that underscore the vitality of states could not

encourage a paradigmatic shift. Rather, they hurled the entire debate on the status of the

state into an aporetic suspension by failing to provide persuasive methods of analysis or

new axes of inquiry. One of the many factors that drove the debate to an impasse was the

immeasurably multifarious nature of the state, which baffles any attempt to speak of it in

its entirety. Some functions of the state are significantly weakened by deregulation, while

other aspects of the state have been discernibly reinvigorated even in the wake of

globalization. In fact, globalization has endowed the state with ample opportunities to

reassert its singular authority in bargaining with an increasing number of supranational

and transnational organizations. On the other hand, it grip on manufacturers and financial

20

institutions has eroded measurably, as international markets constantly change the mode of distributing goods and information, as well as the loci of production in geographic space.

Anderson, Brook, and Cochrane (1995) have been attentive to ways in which states adapt to and influence the newly emerging economic geometry. They posit, "Rather than disappearing into a melting pot of global mixing, states have responded by stretching and overlapping their relations, and by combining with other states as well as non-state bodies, to produce increasingly complex and often fluid political arrangements" (1995, p. 3). This view resonates with what Aihwa Ong (1999) called "a new, more flexible and complex relationship between capital and governments" (p. 21). Ong maintains, "transnationality induced by accelerated flows of capital, people, cultures, and knowledge does not simply reduce state power, as many have claimed, but also stimulates a new, more flexible and complex relationship between capital and governments" (p. 21).

This erratic and versatile nature of the state intensifies, albeit disproportionately, when examined with a comparative institutional approach on a trans-geographical basis. Inasmuch as there are diverse forms of the state—welfare, liberal, socialist, developmental, authoritarian, etc.—the extent to which each state is affected by the deregulationist wave differs dramatically. Michael Mann (1997) points out that while globalization may "weaken the most advanced nation states of the North, successful economic development has served to strengthen nation-states elsewhere" (p. 494). The asymmetry between the North and the NICs (Newly Industrializing Countries) states is also complicated by the fact that the governments of stronger nations debilitate and disrupt the system of other states (Boyd-Barret, 1998). In addition, the particulars of each state vary immensely, conditional on the historical formation of the socio-cultural and politico-economic configurations specific to each nation-state.

What this multi-dimensional unevenness amounts to is, irrespective of the validity of "enduring importance" and "increasing irrelevance" theses, the impossibility of addressing *the state* in totality. In lieu of making broad-brush statements about *the state*, researcher need to attend to tangible issues of a state/or states that are periodically specific and geopolitically identifiable. Hence, it is important to formulate a set of questions by which past and present, rupture and continuity of state's functions are historicized and by which modes of state intervention in civil affairs can be interrogated in a particular local context. Additionally, states should be understood in plural forms not simply because of the peculiarity of national conditions but more importantly because that they no longer maintain physical coherence and operational consistency. In other words, the centralized bureaucratic body of the government is no longer the sole bastion of state power. Rather, states are in a massive exodus. At the same time, they are in flux, occupied and populated by non-state or para-state tenants. Disembodied, disorganized, and blended into different sites, spheres, and organizations of civil society, states may form a grand alliance with trade unions, academic institutions, NGOs (Non Governmental Organizations), NPOs (Non Profit Organizations), and various forms of supranational organizations, accelerating and intensifying the formation of the arc of shared sovereignty. Concurrently, the conventional functions as well as the modus operandi of exercising state authority have progressively altered from the "governmental" ones that are control, ownership, and planning-intensive to the "catalytic" ones that facilitate concerted actions among different sectors of civil society, from giving birth to certain initiatives to smoothing the progress of social trafficking. In the following, I shall discuss the shifting characteristics of the Japanese state with respect to industrial policies in the area of information technologies.

The Japanese State: Critique of State-centric Approach

Mapping the Japanese state-society connection has long been dominated by the state-centric approach. The state-centric approach by and large suggests that the Japanese state holds the ultimate power in defining national interests and in shepherding the flow of socio-economic energies. This view is premised upon a clear divide, and a stable hierarchy for that matter, between society and state. Ezra Vogel (1979), who pioneered the "discipline" of studying the Japanese state-business nexus from a state-centric perspective, ascribes the successful construction of post-industrial settings to the competence of the Japanese government and bureaucracy. He states that "for over a hundred years . . . the Japanese government had to assume leadership in dealing with broad issues in planning, restructuring, modernizing, and phasing out declining industries, a leadership America is only now beginning to consider desirable" (p. ix).

Vogel's analysis of Japan as a bureaucrat-orchestrated economic machinery has been echoed and further elaborated by many. Dazzled by the strong administrative leadership, Henry Rosovsky (1972) depicted Japan as "the only capitalist country in the world in which the Government decides how many firms should be in a given industry, and sets about to arrange the desired number" (p. 233). Similarly, Brian Woodall (1996) recently portrayed Japan's bureaucrats at MITI (Ministry of International Trade and Industry) as omnipotent civil servants, who exercise unrivaled power "in the form of formal legal authorizations and informal 'administrative guidance,' to develop whatever industries it deemed critical to the health of the national economy" (p. 3).

It was Chalmers Johnson (1982) who refurbished the plain state-centric approach to the relationship between Japanese state and business by bringing cultural issues to the fore. He suggests that the Japanese preeminence in high-tech industries is a result of the nation's cultural legacies that bestow upon the state the prerogative to orchestrate

23

industrial and technological policies. Johnson, renowned for characterizing Japan as a "developmental state,"[4] maintains that Japan has a "plan-rationale system," wherein the government acts as the conductor of national economy. Johnson describes the plan-rationale system in a way that runs contrary to the "market-rationale system" of the U.S., wherein the role of the government is reduced to a referee of the civil economy.[5] The paramount leadership granted to the state in Japan, according to Johnson, is based on the nation's quest for social consensus and harmony to be maintained by the authority of the political center.

Blended with cultural particularism, the state-centric approach proliferated and was often adopted as a celebratory narrative of the nation's uniqueness by Japanese scholars and business leaders. Theories of Japanese uniqueness (*Nihonjin-ron*), for instance, explain the nation's robust economic growth in terms of its propensity for strong societal consensus and group-oriented values. Different versions of *Nihonjin-ron* accentuate the virtue of *Wa* (harmony), as responsible for the social stability and cooperative relationship between political and civil entities. At the same time, however, the state-centric accounts were employed by the U.S. and European governments to force the Japanese government to loosen the protection of domestic industries and interference with international free trade protocols. During the 1980s, when trade disputes between the U.S. and Japan flared up, U.S. economists, corporate leaders, and congressional representatives coined the term "Japan Inc." to pejoratively denote the indivisible bond between the state and business in Japan. Beneath the notion of Japan Inc. is an assumption that the ascendancy of the Japanese state in determining industrial dynamics violates the self-governance of civil economy as a whole and will eventually suffocate

---

[4] This is opposed to a "regulatory state" model of the U.S. Chalmers Johnson (1982), p. 34.

[5] According to Johnson, individual buyers and sellers assume control in the market-rationale system of the U.S.

the market's autonomous creativity. Other cognate concepts like "mercantile state" "developmental state" ensued in the Western academy, adding even more disdain to the unequaled leadership of the Japanese state.

Yasosake Murakami (1987) critiques "Japan Inc." as a pseudo-concept that portrays the Japanese society as a totality controlled by bureaucratic strategists. "According to this notion," contends Murakami, "Japanese society is monolithic and tightly regulated and thus resembles a single corporation run by a group of clever leaders, who mobilized the postwar Japanese populace for the sake of economic growth. Any closer examination, however, show this to be a crude and simplistic stereotype" (p. 39). As Murakami states, Japan Inc. and other comparable concepts fail to capture colliding interests and policies among different ministries by picturing Japanese government as an organic unity. These concepts are byproducts of the statist approach's inherent limitation, which overlooks that the state must confer with other societal actors to negotiate and alter policies, like many other states in advanced industrial societies (Hart, 1992, p. 33). Subscribing to an ideal image of consensual authoritarianism in which diverse social interests are graciously harmonized by and subordinated to the supremacy of the state, the state-centric approach elides power struggles/alliances in and out of the state, and the friction/collaboration between various divisions of the state and business.

The state-centric approach was systematically critiqued by Daniel Okimoto (1989), who unraveled the complex mode of articulation between state and business by bringing to light the significance of advisory councils (*Shingikai*) and consultative committees (*Shimoniinkai*) operative in the state's policy making. Okimoto defines them as para-state agents by which differing interests and positions of corporate owners, bureaucrats, technicians, researchers, marketers are brought together and negotiated. In line with Okimoto's framework, Hiroyuki Odagiri and Akira Goto (1996) later elaborated the operation and function of advisory councils as the epitome of how the Japanese state is run. They observe that the (Japanese) state is no more than a site and mechanism of

25

hammering out preliminary social consensus, which is "reached as the result of the accumulation of the extremely delicate and time-consuming efforts to adjust the many differing opinions"(p. 43). Odagiri and Goto's claim that the advisory and consultative council system is a "typical Japanese way of obtaining consensus" is questionable. Nor can the Japanese state be understood as a disinterested apparatus of manufacturing consensus. However, understanding the way in which these councils operate can certainly illuminate the interlocking mechanism between state and civil society, and more importantly the changing roles and organizational modalities of the Japanese state with regards to the mobilization of information technologies and the developmental strategies of information industries.

From State to Para-state

Setting up temporary advisory councils and study groups has long been a common practice in virtually all ministries in the Japanese government. This tendency is growing progressively more salient since the mid 1970s. In the MPT, numerous committees— such as the Committee on Reception Difficulty of TV broadcasting, the Multiplex Broadcasting Committee, the University of the Air Preparation Committee, etc.—have been formed and dissolved. This type of consultative committee is usually composed of experts across information and communication industries, such as representatives from NHK, National Association of Commercial Broadcasters, Japan Newspaper Publishers and Editors Association, Dentsu Inc. (an influential advertising company), as well as other professionals in the fields of engineering, laws, and economics.

Belying their humble appellations, advisory councils, consultative committees, and study groups exert enormous influence on government decisions and guidelines. Fewer and fewer policies are crafted by state officials alone, as more and more decisions are handled by the civilian and business delegates. The government officials, of course, do participate in these council activities as a pacesetter of the organizations and as an

26

arbitrator that settles disagreements within the group. The intermediary role of the state bureaucrats within these ad-hoc assemblies was well demonstrated when MPT officials successfully resolved conflicts among commercial terrestrial broadcasters, local network affiliates, cable companies, and NHK with regard to the right to participate in the DBS (Direct Broadcast Satellite) project (Goto, 1983, p. 43).

But the delegation of the state's authority to the outsourced commissions does not always come with an even distribution of participatory rights across different sectors of civil society. In most cases, the government offers large corporations privileged access to public resources in various forms. In turn, the privileged conglomerates conform to the macro-economic principles pressed by the state. For instance, a systematic inclusion of corporate forces within the process of governmental decision-making has visibly accelerated over the last couple of decades. So-called "fixed-term employment," which allows the Japanese government to hire current or retired business leaders in administrative positions, has been well underway. The tendency is often publicly acknowledged, as former Japanese Prime Minster Mori once mentioned, "I believe that it is important to incorporate the knowledge and insight of the private sector into the administrative process at both the central and local government levels."[6]

The degree to which the state relies upon the participation of the business sector has increased in line with the need of business for the state's support. This internalization of corporate input in various state apparati further obscures the distinction between business interests and national economic policies. In the worse case, it could lead to a hardnosed tilting of public policy toward the satisfaction of capital and to the detriment of labor and common civilian interests. However, the inflow of the corporate personnel in the state mechanism does not necessarily bring about a crude interpolation of corporate

---

[6] Full Text of Prime Minister's Speech to the Diet. (2000, September 22). *The Japan Times*. http://www.japantimes.co.jp/cgi-bin/getarticle.p15?nn20000922a4.htm

sensibility into political judgment or a patent privatization of the state propitious only to capital. More often than not, the committees and study groups would exercise a substantial degree of autonomy, a freedom from both business interests and even political orientation of the government. At times, they would introduce plans at variance with the interest of mainstream industry and adverse to administrative interventions. For example, a council for CCIS's (Coaxial Cable Information System) in the mid 1970s strongly contested the broadcasting and newspaper enterprises' attempt to monopolize CCIS and frustrated the MPT's plan to launch a state-owned public corporation, on the ground that CCIS is an information service to be managed by local communities (Shiono, 1978, p. 9).

Erik Swyngedouw (1997) observes that this institutional bargaining reflects "the temporal crystallization of particular (allied) and often diffuse class interests within the state apparatus and creates rules and regularities that operate almost in a semiautomatic form" (p. 152). The para-state bodies, too, can be perceived as an aggregate of privileged social and economic actors, who share long-term interests and yet whose immediate interests are subject to compromise at the stage of pre-market modulation. Binding the private and the public, and state and business together, these councils operate as the site at which negotiation among different business sectors takes place and the consolidation of the economic and the political materializes. They epitomize an "interregnum" (Gill, 1997) equipped with administrative and executive entitlements over civil, public, and business affairs, while representing an institutional prescription to ascertain the legitimacy of state authority.

That the councils act as the key engineer of public policy suggests that contemporary states are not as autonomous from societal influence as state-centric theories suggest. Rather, as Peter Hall (1986) argues, the state can be better understood as "a network of institutions, deeply embedded within a constellation of ancillary institutions associated with society and the economic system" (p. 17). The intensive and extensive use of the intermediary regime results simultaneously in the reproduction of state authority and in the expansion of the organizational perimeter of the state. In other words, not only is the power of Japanese state mediated by para-state polities but also the configuration of the state itself is transforming into a cluster of decentralized networks consisting of quasi-public institutions that participate in the process of decision-making over national, public, and civilian affairs.

The rise and preeminence of para-state bodies is but one aspect of the many changes that the Japanese state has undergone since the 1960s. There are other striking and less conspicuous transformations in the manner by which the Japanese state operates and is organized, which are worthy of a close look. The following is a concise historical sketch of the shifting and continuing characteristics of the Japanese state demonstrated in the area of information and communication industries, starting from the 1960s and stretching to the very recent. During the last forty years, the purpose and utility of the Japanese state have steadily moved from an overt and thorough management of the market, financing, and legislation to a tactful and delicate engagement with the private sector through discursive and organizational maneuvers. The overall transition is observable even with a cursory glance, but not tightly congruent with the three periods (the 1960s - the mid 1970s, the late 1970s - the 1980s, and the 1990s - present) I employ here. There are overlaps, revivals of old traditions, and enduring practices across the three epochs, as much as outright ruptures and chasms. Hence, the progressive shift should be seen as a general tendency, which always includes many of exceptions and anomalies. Nevertheless, a historical survey of the modes by which the Japanese state has engaged in the field of information and communication industries is critical to understanding of the manifold roles it plays in the course of digitalizing television today.

Omnipotent State and Para-state Bodies:

The 1960s – the Early 1970s

Like many other countries, Japan put information and communication sectors
under strict governmental control during World War II and harnessed them as political
and military instruments. Modeled after Britain, postwar telecommunications and
broadcasting policies of Japan also enforced various forms of administrative control over
communication enterprises. Managerial and supervisory power was assumed solely by
the MPT (Minister of the Post and Telecommunication) and MITI (Ministry of
International Trade and Industry),[7] and no other local governments or organizations
could exert influence on broadcasting and other telecommunications services (Shiono
1978, p. 9).

Direct ownership and operation of information-related industry by the state was
most acutely pronounced in the telecommunication sector. The Wire
Telecommunications Law enacted in 1953 prohibited the operation of non-broadcasting
services such as two-way communications via coaxial cable by any business
organizations other than two state-owned telecommunication giants, the Nippon
Telegraph and Telephone Public Corporation (NTT) and the Kokusai Denshin Denwa
Corporation (KDD) (Shiono, 1978, p. 31). The main reason for the tight state control was
that communication services constitute the backbone of social infrastructure, which must
insure such public interests as "universal access" and "freedom of speech." Hideo Nakasa
(1978), a chief researcher at NTT, defends the rationale as follows:

> [The] nationwide monopoly of the network of subscriber telephone
> and of telex is inevitable from technical necessity. The function of
> the telephone network and the telex network is that conversation
> and communication can be made freely and indiscriminately from
> anywhere to any place within the country and the secrecy of
> conversation must be maintained and the network must spread

---

[7] MITI was reorganized as the Ministry of Economy, Trade and Industry (METI) in 2001.

equally to any place even where it does not bring about much
profit (p. 77).

As postwar Japan's economy shifted from light-industry (food, textile, ceramics,
etc.) to heavy industry (metal, machinery, and chemicals), audio-visual equipment,
together with other consumer electronics, gained momentum as a strategic sector capable
of competing in the international marketplace (Kash, 1989). Hence, the 1960s and the
early 1970s mark an era where Japan's primordial information industry grew on the
strength of audio-visual equipment and other electronics industries. Despite the fact that
state's direct ownership of and control over information facilities did not drastically abate
during this period, basic information-processing industries in tandem with
communication device manufacturing in the private sector saw a brisk growth. The
audio-visual equipment industry in particular was given precedence according to the
economic principles of comparative advantage in the international market, and was
systematically brought up as the kernel of massive industrial restructuring under the
banner of information society.

The government's decision in prioritizing particular business sectors was
legitimized by the exigency of postwar rehabilitation and later Japan's scarce national
endowment. But Shinichi Ichimura (1998) maintains that designating strategic industry
had been an undisputable prerogative of the Japanese government since the beginning of
modernization in the late nineteenth century until the 1990s:

> The Japanese industrial restructuring policies were adopted first as
> rather protective measures as if Japan was an underdeveloped
> economy to protect its infant industries and modernize the old or
> small enterprises . . . . The Japanese government has been anxious
> to push up certain industries as those to be given priority in
> restructuring and further development (Ichimura, 1998, p. 166).

The formidable leap of the strategic industries hinged largely upon the competent
orchestration of overall industrial policies by the bureaucrats at MITI and MPT (Johnson,
1982). Their planning and steering skills in promoting key industries and frontier
technologies and in phasing-out less competent and unprofitable fields played a crucial

31

role in uplifting Japan's competitive edge in information and communication industries (Hein, 1990).

Apart from nominating strategic industries, there are five key functions that the Japanese state performed during this period, which were manifest in the process of fostering audio-visual equipment and information-processing industries in their infancy. First, chief officials in the MITI nurtured them by using government purchases to invigorate production and by sheltering the domestic market from foreign competition (Woodall, 1996). Second, they provided extensive and intensive financial support, including government aids, subsidies, and tax benefits. Third, the state agencies functioned as comprehensive research departments pressing for new product developments and for innovations in system-type products (Rosovsky, 1972). Fourth, in collaboration with other business organizations, the state operated as national consulting agencies for Japanese industries, offering informed guidance to the private sector and instructing excellent methods of solving financial and managerial problems (Odagiri & Goto, 1996). Finally, it was also MPT and MITI who spurred new trends in the mass communication businesses and the electronic equipment industries. An array of large-scale initiatives was launched, stimulating synergistic development in neighboring industries. For example, the new national network development program was promulgated in 1968 with the goal of creating national communication networks that link remote processing system of information with national communication and computer circuits.

By 1970, with the growing influence and participation of enterprises in what was formerly steered by the government, however, criticism towards the counter-productivity of regulations and the inefficiency of state owned-and-operated corporations surfaced. Demands for legislative reforms consistent with the speedy expansion of audio-visual and information-processing industries were expressed from the business sector, government-sponsored institutes, public symposiums, and even from within public corporations such

32

as NTT.[8] The government did actively attend to the private sector's calls, replacing dated laws with new ones and introducing a series of supportive measures that would benefit those engaged in the information industry. While initial stimulants were unleashed from the government in many cases, the interplay between the business sector and the decision-making bodies of the state formed a circuit of bilateral response. That is, the government animated the private sector in ways that entrepreneurs could vigorously seek their specific needs from the government by consistently releasing packages of policy guidelines and research data (Murakami, 1981).

Although the government's leading position in the establishment of early information industry and social infrastructures is irrefutable, the multifaceted and often elusive relationships between the government and the private sector cannot be adequately captured by the typified terminology of "state industrial policy." It was during this period that para-state institutions and bureaus emerged as a nucleus of molding communication and industrial policies. Much of the national plans and policies were proposed, examined, and adopted by numerous quasi-governmental commissions: partially autonomous, pro tem assemblies consisting of civilian experts and representatives, housed under and funded by government ministries, and entrusted with varying degrees/types of jurisdictional authorities. In 1968, for instance, the Industrial Structure Council submitted its report to the Diet, requesting that the government foster the communication/information processing service and liberalize telecommunication circuit for that purpose. The government promptly reacted to this by revising the Public Telecommunications law in 1971, both liberalizing data communication and authorizing governmental aids to the multipurpose use of CATV.

---

[8] Shiono (1985). The Development of the System of Telecommunications Law in Japan. p. 34.

Shortly after the enactment of the Information Technology Promotion Law in 1970, a number of semi-juridical bodies engaged in a variety of activities including policymaking, developing plans for the hardware and software of computer, and subsidizing particular projects. For example, the introduction of multipurpose cable broadcasting in September 1971 was proposed and carried out by an investigation committee under the supervision of the MPT. The committee, composed of industrial experts, technicians, and urban planners, launched a project dubbed "Wired City," which harnessed CATV as a new multipurpose information media, which subsequently stimulated Japanese broadcasting and other communication businesses. Other para-state committees and councils, such as Information–Technology Promotion Agency, Living-visual Information System Development council, and Japan Computer Usage Development Institute, played no smaller role in bridging state initiatives with the civil economy.

The Information–Technology Promotion Agency drafted one of the most foundational blueprints for the future course of Japan's information sector entitled "The plan for an information society: a national goal toward the year 2000," which was published in 1971 and widely circulated among Japanese businessmen and policymakers in foreign countries. These ad-hoc councils also functioned as inter-ministerial liaisons. The Living-Visual Information System Development Council was established in 1973 by merging two juridical bodies affiliated respectively with the Ministry of Post and Telecommunications and the Ministry of Trade and Industry. The council operated as the consultative hub networking business firms, research institutes, and relevant government bodies.

One of the most crucial and yet often neglected dimensions of the para-state organizations is that they served as the mouthpiece and engineer of major social discourses. Various branches of the state and affiliated institutions were responsible for imbuing the society with non-material forms of energy and stimuli by organizing public

34

hearings, conventions, press conferences, and by distributing publicity booklets and research outcomes. While drafting, examining, and proposing policies to the government, the para-state institutions also actively engaged in shaping the cultural environment and social consciousness propitious to the development of information industry and technologies, as instantiated by the theory of information society (*Joho Shakai Ron*).

Information Society Discourse and
the Growth of A-V Industry

The root of the information society idea[9] is variegated (Lyon, 1995). It is comprised of a range of heterogeneous and yet interlaced threads: government policies, futuristic speculations, academic inquiries, and lived social experiences. In Japan, the rise of information society theory (*Joho Shakai Ron*) is intrinsically tied to the structural vulnerability of Japanese industrial capitalism that has been heavily reliant on an export-led economy. Government officials, business elites, and leading intellectuals had to plot long-term strategies to protect the nation from the fluctuation of the international economic system by enhancing technological self-sufficiency and overcoming the structural handicaps of the national economy, including scarce natural resources, aging demographic composition, frequent natural disasters, etc. However, *Joho Shakai Ron* was more than a body of organized economic strategies; it was the crystallization of the cross-institutional effort that brought together industrial policy, scholarly research, popular imagination, and political yearning to overcome the nation's socio-economic weakness and to hasten the exodus from an industrial society based on materials and energies to an information-oriented society.

---

[9] The notion of the Information Society was a Japanese invention proposed for the first time by Tadao Umesao in 1963.

International and domestic economic conditions during the late 1960s and early 1970s gave strong impetus to the vision of the information society. When a recession struck shortly after the Tokyo Olympics in 1964, the notion of the information society became a central catchphrase among the planning units in MITI and leading businessmen alike, who sought out a new business enterprise less vulnerable to the caprices of international trade and economy (Nakasa, 1978). With falling profits and a high rate of unemployment during the recession, Japan's economy as a whole ventured boldly into the burgeoning information sector. The dollar shock in 1971 and the oil crisis in 1973, which caused tremendous anxiety about energy resources, reassured the relevance of *Joho Shakai Ron*. Hence, the policy-cum-discourse of *Joho Shakai Ron* functioned as a rallying cry that united Japanese businessmen, scholars/researchers, technicians, civilians, and bureaucrats toward a goal of building a society and an economy founded upon an intensive use of information and communication technologies.

Although much of the social imagination about the information society in Japan was shaped by the government's strategic effort to sustain sound economic growth, it was also anointed with a philosophical veneer of social evolutionism. Keiji Tachikawa (1983), an expert in applied science working for a state-funded research laboratory, deftly captures the mindset fascinated with the promise of the information society. He states,

> In order to enjoy a more affluent life in the future and to efficiently manage their social and economical activities on a global basis, human beings must shift from an industrialized society based on materials and energies to an information oriented society. We have to construct, as soon as possible, a new society where the production, processing and distribution of information will create more value than that of material things in the past (p. 54).

The idea that the value created by information is far superior in quality to that based on materials and energies exemplifies how the scenario of economic transformation dovetails with a narrative of social evolutionism. Tachikawa draws on what might be called an economic teleology spelled out by Michio Kitahara (1991), who charted the four-step trajectory of human evolution—acquisition of language, writing

36

systems, printing, and telecommunications—in relation to the progress of economic and political structures. He adds, "the existence of the human race in the future may depend on an efficient information system which can totally support its activities" (Kitahara, 1991, p. 54). Such ideas not only rendered inevitable the path towards the information society but also reified information technologies as intrinsically bearing socially empowering qualities.

Not surprisingly, voices of concern and dissension sprang up. Tetsuo Tomita (1978), who headed the Communications Policy Division under the MPT Minister's Secretariat, rang the wake-up call. Tomita critiqued policymakers and entrepreneurs spellbound by the prospect that information technologies would emancipate the nation from such challenges as labor shortages, rising wages, aging population, a crisis of cultural identity, etc. "Too great expectations have been placed on the coming of the information-oriented society for the purpose of solving various problems which have come to confront the present industrialized society" (p. 38), says Tomita. Since the information society is, for him, not a cure-all for social problems but a blueprint for national communication policies, Tomita calls attention to the peril of surrendering to the narratives of futurology in which "various wishes and expectations have wrongly been taken for potentialities among the people concerned" (p. 39). Manuel Castells (1996) is also unsympathetic to the way in which an information society is envisioned by Japanese ideologues.

> Japan built a new mythology around a futurological view of the information society, which actually tried to replace social thinking and political projects with images of a computerized/ telecommunicated society, to which were added some humanistic pseudo-philosophical platitudes (p. 243).

Despite these critical responses, the aura of an information society barely deflated; instead, it compelled some major construction, real estate, transportation, trading, and banking companies to plunge into growing information and A-V electronics industries. During and after the oil crisis years, audio-visual equipment makers and many other corporations in neighboring industries rushed ahead with automaton production, which in turn augmented production capacity to a considerable degree.

Alongside the discursive crusade toward an information society, a number of financial measures that the government introduced, such as tax breaks, R&D subsidies, long-term, low-interest funding, etc. spurred a rapid growth of the audio-visual equipment industry. The hegemony of information society discourses also encouraged an exponential expansion of the domestic media market both in hardware and software. As the production of audio-visual appliances industry has repeatedly shifted its core item—black-and-white TVs, color TVs, cassette-tape recorders, portable radio/TVs, faxes, VCRs, etc.—most Japanese households were equipped with diverse audio-visual devices. Even when the domestic household penetration rate for most key items approached the saturation point around the mid-seventies, the industry successfully sparked demand by unveiling an array of new products, new technological features, and competitive pricing policies (Yoshimi, 1999). Technological innovations in the electronics industry in turn stimulated enterprises centering on new technologies such as data communication, telephone fax, electrical transmission of text, multi-purpose cable TV, etc.

The diversification and diffusion of information technologies concurred with a leapfrogging in the production and consumption of mass media. Although the maturation of national media and communication environment cannot be ascribed solely to the diffusion of information technologies, the state's proactive industrial policy and discursive maneuvers wielded some measurable impacts on the formation of Japanese communicative and informational spheres. The phenomenal success of Japanese color TV and then-emerging production of home VCRs, equipped with automatized functionality, was often used to validate Japan's headlong rush toward an information society.

> In an information society, it is said that a man acquires most of his information through his visual sense rather than through his auditory sense, and that communications between man and

38

machine, machine and machine, increase, in addition to man-to-
man communications . . . . [I]t is essential . . . to fully develop
automatized visual communication devices (Tachikawa, 1983, p.
56).

As of March 1982, 98.9 percent of households in Japan owned color TV sets. The

sharp increase of color TV sets between 1968 and 1980 was followed by a commensurate

increase in the number of commercial broadcasting companies from 50 in 1968 to 97 in

1981 (Shimizu, 1983, p. 121). In the same period, seven nation-wide television networks

reached almost 94 percent of Japan's total population, and the average daily viewing time

swelled to three hours per person, an increase of thirty minutes. Advertising revenue for

television increased nearly eight times (from 11 million yen to 84 million yen) between

1965 and 1980 (Shimizu, 1983, p. 126). CATV also grew into a mainstay of two-way

communication businesses involving such services as teleshopping, telemetering or

security services. In 1982, the daily circulation of Japanese newspapers totaled 68

millions—exceeding that of 62 millions in the U.S, whose population then was two times

as large as that of Japan. Those who read a newspaper on a regular basis reached nearly

58 percent of all population in sharp contrast with 27 percent of the U.S, and 42 percent

of U.K. (Tamura, 1987). As a result, combined total output of communication products

in Japan had jumped nearly 200 times between 1955 and 1979, posting significant gains

during the country's high-growth era, an era symbolized by the audio-visual and other

home electronics industry.

Oblique Management: Deregulatory Legislation and
R&D in the Mid 1970s – the Late 1980s

Between the mid 1970s and the late 1980s, deregulation arose as a key issue

across telecommunications, broadcasting, and other multimedia industries. The

blossoming of new media technologies during this period necessitated an introduction of

new legal foundations accommodating such changes. Additionally, the intensification in

economic and technological global interconnectivity forced Japan to lift regulations and monopolistic measures imposed by the government. Ill-trained for the complex and volatile matrices of global capitalism, state bureaucrats had to reduce their role as the mastermind behind cross-industrial policies and, instead, stepped up their effort to streamline relevant laws and regulations. The overhauling of statutes and by-laws was facilitated by a multitude of para-state committees, who skillfully monitored and conveyed demands from the business quarter to the administration. Another noticeable shift made during this time in the function of the Japanese state is the augmentation of indirect patronage. This includes the construction of national information infrastructures and various incentives to R&D endeavors, which helped alleviate the private sector's enormous cost burden. All in all, it can be said that during this period the state repositioned itself as an organizer, as well as generator, of various forms of socio-cultural energy and capital, reducing by degrees its previous identity as the controller, regulator, and master designer of overall industrial dynamics. Such adjustment was compelled by a number of political and economic factors, on which I shall expand below.

Since the mid 1970s the mutual dependence between information technology and advanced financial capitalism began to deepen noticeably. Information technologies prompted a commensurate change in the nature of financial capitalism by catalyzing the flow of cash, merchandise, and data across geographic and institutional boundaries. Castells (1996) posits,

> Financial capital needs . . . to rely for its operation and competition
> on knowledge and information generated and enhanced by
> information technology. This is the concrete meaning of the
> articulation between the capitalist mode of production and the
> information mode of development (p. 472).

During this period Japan saw a fast expansion of private data communication thanks to the proliferation of the banking system for credit transfers. Although the service began in 1968, a full-fledged development began emerging in the mid 1970s. In 1973 merely 470 computers were connected for data transfer, but in 1978 approximately 5000 computers were in operation in 1978, making a ten-fold increase in five years (Akatsuka

& Yoshida, 1999, p. 14). The increase of value added network (VAN) services demanded relaxation on the use of leased telecommunication circuits, as the data communication and data-based services became the backbone of domestic commercial and financial traffic. Hence, financial circles as well as computer and data equipment manufacturers raised their voice for policy reform. With the mounting pressure from financial spheres, a significant move toward deregulation occurred on October 23, 1982 when a revised Public Telecommunications Law came into effect. This law permitted medium and small enterprises to enter the business of value added network (VAN) services, making free use of leased telecommunication circuits possible.

Other new media technologies introduced from the mid 1970s unsettled the existing doctrines and organizational formations of broadcasting and telecommunication. Different forms of utilizing the radio spectrum—traditional over-the-air broadcasting, direct satellite broadcasting, digital cellular telephony, and so forth—were brought into play. Also a number of versatile transmission technologies, such as coaxial cable and fiber optics, came forward, precipitating the shaping of formerly scattered individual media into new, multimedia compounds. The diversified means of communication left the legal system based on a set of binary codes antiquated: public/private, wire/wireless, and one-way/two-way. Furthermore, the spread of multiplex broadcasting, broadcasting satellites, facsimiles, and optical fiber communications disrupted the categorical clarity among print, broadcasting, and telecommunication. The fact that an order of the MPT classified facsimile transmission as a type of broadcasting proves the confusion wrought by the sudden deluge of new media.[10]

---

[10] Facsimile transmission became extremely popular in Japan both at home and at work. The telephone network for private facsimile communications saw a hundred-fold growth between 1972 and 1980, from 1,300 terminals in 1972 to 140, 000 in 1980.

The advent of hybrid media technologies demanded both swift legal reforms appropriate for the rapidly changing industrial dynamics and for an establishment of new information networks that can integrate diversified communication and information media. However, neither function could be handled properly and efficiently by the private sector alone. The MPT had to step in to draw up national communication policies stitching together broadcasting, telecommunications, cables, satellites, datacasting, etc. Kazuhito Goto (1983) submits,

> As new technologies and new media are accepted as applicable to communications, the need for an integrated policy for the nation's communication system has come to be strongly acknowledged among the interested parties. In other words, they have come to realize that leaving the new communication technologies and media to their spontaneous development may eventually rebound against the national interest (p. 25).

The state undertook a bimodal task of tightening its grasp on new technologies and relaxing existing laws to put the technologies into operation. In response to the transformation of technological climates, the MPT revised the Broadcast Law in 1982 to allow new entrants in telecommunication business to make use of broadcasting infrastructures. Heralding the imminent coalescence of telecommunication and broadcasting, the revision introduced a so-called multiplex broadcasting service, which required existing broadcasters to share their broadcasting facilities for multiplex broadcasting, including data transmission. (Shiono, 1985, p. 38).

Following this path, an interim report submitted in December, 1983 by the Information Industry Committee of the Industrial Structure Council to the MITI made a number of momentous proposals regarding the future development of information industry in Japan. Above all, it called for at once the lifting of state control in order to maximize the private sector's initiative and the shifting of the governmental supports from planning and funding toward establishing a national informational infrastructure. It states,

The present telecommunication-related systems should be totally
reviewed to ensure the three categories of freedom, i.e., freedom of
participation, freedom of business activities, and freedom of use. A
necessary communication infrastructure should be developed to
build an Advanced Information Society (Shimizu, 1985, p. 128).

This report set up a template for the new roles to be played by the government in

correspondence to the shifting kinetics of the information industry, domestically and

internationally. These proposals resonated with another policy guideline titled "Road to

an Advanced Information Society" submitted to Prime Minister Nakasone in 1984.

Drafted by a government-commissioned committee, this report highlighted legal and

societal arrangements essential to realizing an advanced information society, in addition

to the necessity of national information infrastructures (Shimizu, 1985, p.130). A number

of similar actions followed suit. On July 30, 1984, the director general of the Broadcast

Administration Bureau in MPT said at a news conference that the Ministry plans to

conduct a re-examination of the Broadcast law in compliance with public needs arising in

the age of new media (Shimizu, 1985, p129), which was materialized by a proposal

drafted by the Ministerial Advisory Commission on Broadcasting Policy in the Age of

New Media in 1987. The advisory council strongly urged the government to minimize

restrictions, on the bases of the increasing irrelevance of spectrum scarcity and the new

broadcasting climates of diversification and convergence. The Broadcast Law was

revised in 1989 once again, introducing new services that were conventionally classified

as telecommunication business, thereby permitting non-conventional broadcasters to

participate in the broadcast marketplace (Komatsubara, 1989, p. 83).

It must be emphasized, however, that the import of deregulation in this period is

not synonymous with the transfer of state power to the business quarter; it meant the shift

in government's responsibility from the enforcement of established rules to the

rearrangement of legal setups congruent with the transformations in industrial and

technological environments. While the primary function of the state in this period

revolves around the legal reordering conducive to the operation of new technologies and industries, the Japanese government did not entirely do away with traditional roles such as proclaiming industry-wide strategies. Okimoto (1989) points to the cause by which the Japanese government's unrelenting grasp on national industrial strategy was vindicated:

> If the composition of the emerging economy is left entirely in the hands of the market, the government runs the risk that finite resources will be diverted from key industries like semi-conductors, computers, and telecommunications—on which Japan's future competitiveness hinges—and invested in sectors of less importance for the industrial economy (restaurants, coffee houses, and real estate speculation, for example) (p. 50).

Moreover, the role of the state as designer and bankroller of technological innovation has seldom diminished in spite of the acceleration in deregulatory actions. In another place, Okimoto (1986) notes, "Japan was self-consciously seeking to carry out a range of radical innovations in such areas as biotechnology, electronics, and materials, thereby capturing large segments of world markets in such sophisticated technologies as very large scale integrated circuit (VLSI) memory chips and fiber optics" (p. 35). Under the charismatic command of MITI (Ministry of International Trades and Industries), information technologies, micro-electronics, robotics, and the like were the favorite sons of Japan's strategic industries. The shift toward ICTs corresponded to the change in the demand composition of world trade and had rewarded the nation with supremacy in the global economic race. The impact of this change on Japan's technology mix was reflected in the application of advances in the technologies of information, telecommunications, and computers to the development of flexible manufacturing systems (FMS) based on computer numerically controlled (CNC) machine tools and computer integrated manufacturing (CIM) (Kudo, 1998, p. 134).

The Japanese state's involvement with technological innovation during this period came to pass in different guises. Financial assistance for R&D expenditure of the private sector in such forms as subsidies and tax breaks became salient. Universities and private research institutes were financed for developing new technologies, for modernizing production and inspection facilities, and for joint projects that would further strengthen

44

the industry-academic nexus. Big corporations in telecommunications and communication industries were indirectly aided by ready loans from banks, together with government grants, subsidies, public corporation procurement, credit allocation, and special tax benefits (Doane, 1999, pp. 43-44). Also various branches of the government conducted a variety of projects that involved huge financial risks in-house or in cooperation with public corporations, such as NHK and NTT. The development of broadcasting and communication satellites, GPS (Global Positioning System), space communications, and ultra LSI (Large Scale Integration) in computer chips are cases in point.

As Daniel Bell (1973) avers, in the post-industrial society "the crucial decisions regarding the growth of the economy and its balance will come from government, but they will be based on the government's sponsorship of research and development" (p. 344). Unlike the common perception, however, the Japanese government expended a relatively small amount on technology on behalf of the private sector. In 1975, government support for research activities of the private sector accounted for 40.9 percent of the government science and technology budget. Around the mid 1980s, the figure rose to 47.8 percent (Doane, 1999, p. 48). On the other hand, the ratio of government to total national R&D spending in Japan throughout the 1980s was lower than in other advanced industrial economies. While the U.S. and France exceeded 45 percent, U.K and Germany nearly 40 percent, Japan was as low as 20 percent (Ichimura, 1998). This was partly due to the enormous growth of Japanese private sector R&D, which overtook that of U.S. during the 1980s. R&D expenditures of U.S companies— General Electric (3.4 percent), Xerox (6.6 percent), RCA (2.4 percent), and Texas Instruments (6.6 percent)—were far lower than those of Japanese companies—Hitachi (7.9 percent), Matsushita (7.2 percent), and NEC (13.0 percent) (Kash, 1989, p. 198).

This trend, nevertheless, should not be interpreted as a decline in the Japanese government's funding for the information industry; it has consistently encouraged the

45

private sector to increase R& D expenditure by providing incentives such as lower bank-loan rates and tax-breaks for private sector R&D spending. Besides these indirect financial supports, the government set aside extra/supplementary budgets under the Fiscal Investment and Loan Program (FILP) throughout the 1980s until the present. In 1995, for example, the supplementary budget and R&D expenditures under the Fiscal Investment and Loan Program (FILP) amounted to 16.8 billion dollars, approximately 70 percent of the initial budget (Genther Yoshida & O'Neill-Brown, 1996, p. 48). Four out of nine public corporations that received FILP funds in 1995 are information and communication-related corporations: Telecommunications Satellite Corp. of Japan, Information technology Promotion Agency, Japan Information Center for Science and Technology, etc. (Genther Yoshida & O'Neill-Brown, 1996, p. 57).

<u>Building Cultural Infrastructure</u>

With augmented industrial capacity and social fervor toward technological advance, there unfolded discourses of a second stage of the information society, often dubbed the "advanced information society." Castells (1996) posits that the advanced information society can be characterized as an "extension of the concept of informationalism to the overall economy and society, calling for a profound transformation of Japan through the diffusion of information technology" (p. 242). Even though the basic tenor of the advanced information society concept sounds virtually identical with that of its precursor, the information society idea (*Joho Shakai Ron*), more emphasis was placed this time on substantial tasks, such as development of integrated network infrastructure, social and legal reform, and the nation-wide diffusion of ICTs (Information and Communication Technologies).

Much of the narrative of the advanced information society highlights the significance of building a national information infrastructure in particular. Yoneji

Masuda (1985), whose concept of "computopia" stands at the forefront of the rhetorical crusade, maintains,

> In industrial society, the modern factory, consisting of machines and equipment, became the society symbol and was the production center for goods. In the information society the information utility (a computer-based public infrastructure) consisting of information networks and data banks will replace the factory as the societal symbol, and become the production and distribution center for information goods (p. 621).

He goes on to assert that the network infrastructure is a collective asset vital to the elevation of life quality and social intellect. But the notion of infrastructure stretches beyond physical foundations and entails mental frameworks (public consciousness) and intellectual capability to mobilize both material and non-material sources.

> The socioeconomic system will be a voluntary civil society characterized by the superiority of its infrastructure, as a type of both public capital and knowledge-oriented human capital, and by a fundamental framework that embodies *the principle of synergy and social benefit* (emphasis in original, Masuda, 1985, p. 623).

David Lyon (1995) critiques Masuda and other Japanese proponents of the advanced information society for underhandedly replacing the threadbare hypothesis of post-industrial utopia with a smartened visage of computopia—old wine in new bottles. Lyon is not flawed in this assessment, especially given that the preceding discussions of the advanced information society by many technocrats such as Nakasa, Akutsu, and Ito cultivated a near theological faith in new information technologies. Nakasa (1978) stated that the network society would bring about "the progress of human society and to the enhancement of civilization" and give "more leadership to ordinary citizens" (p. 83), a claim loudly echoed by Masuda: "the goal . . . is a society that brings about a general flourishing state of human intellectual creativity, instead of affluent material consumption" (as cited in Lyon, 1995, p. 58).

Yet the social imagination of an advanced information society is not helplessly utopian; instead, it has several rather sensible and practical concerns. It would not be mistaken to say that the discussion of the advanced information society was sparked

47

largely by the rise of network technologies such as coaxial cable and ISDN. According to

Yoshinaga Ishii (1985), the idea of the advanced information society concerns the

changing modalities of public and private communication made possible by network

media and multilateral information processing devices (p. 7). Ishii predicts that the

change in the mode of communication would trigger similar changes in social

organization and power dynamics. Nakasa, too, hails the arrival of coaxial cable and

ISDN for their capability to speed up two-way social communications, whereby "the

receiver can simultaneously become a sender, . . . or the receiver's intention can be

reflected more exactly on the sender's information content and on the arrangement of the

content" (Nakasa, 1978, p. 84). Social empowerment through networks of lateral

solidarity, and reformation in the organization of power through democratic technological

infrastructure are central to Masuda's vision. He observes,

> In the political system, democracy based on participation of the
> citizens will be the general mode of policy-making, rather than the
> indirect democracy of the parliamentary system. The technological
> base to support this participatory democracy will consist of (1)
> information networks made possible by the development of
> computer-communications technology; (2) simulation of policy
> models; and (3) feedback loops of individual opinions; with the
> result that policy-making will change from policy-making based on
> majority versus minority rule to policy-making based on the
> balance of gain and loss to individuals in the spectrum of their
> areas of concern, both in the present and in future time. In policy-
> making by this means, the feedback and accumulation of opinions
> will be repeated many times until agreement is reached, to insure
> the impartial balance of merits and demerits of the policy decision
> as it affects individuals and groups with conflicting interests
> (Masuda, 1985, p. 630).

In response to mounting demand for national information infrastructure, the MPT

embarked on a project called "Tama New Town" in the late 1970s. The Tama project was

a groundbreaking undertaking in that it introduced a coaxial cable information system

(CCIS) for two-way visual conferencing and was later emulated by Canada's Telidon

program and Sweden's Terese project. The large-scale infrastructural investment carried

on well into the 1980s. In August 1983, the MITI and the MPT separately announced plans to build model advanced information cities in an effort to present the public with a vivid picture of what the society was bound for. The MITI's plan was called the "new media community," while the MPT's was named "teletopia." About ten cities throughout the country were designated as model areas, where an integrated new media system composed of the INS (Integrated Network Services), urban CATV, and videodex was supplied. It is noteworthy that the projects were financed and carried out by public and private institutions together. Tama New Town, for instance, was jointly funded at the request of the MPT by a characteristic industrial mix of two leading newspapers, a broadcast enterprise, a bank, and government subsidies (Hiroshi 1978, p. 33). Also, NTT (Nippon Telegraph and Telephone), a public telecommunication company owned and operated by the government, chipped in by installing the cable wire in all the cities.

Wallerstein (1999) gives an interesting angle on the state's commitment to so-called national economic infrastructure, especially National Information Infrastructure (NII):

> The state can distort the market very easily . . . . More importantly, it can build so-called infrastructure, which of course means that given entrepreneurs do not have to assume those costs. This is usually justified on the grounds that the costs are too high for any single entrepreneur and that such state expenditure represents a collective sharing of the cost that benefits everyone . . . . In any case, the costs of the infrastructure are not usually imposed on the collectivity of beneficiaries but on all taxpayers, and even disproportionately on non-users (Wallerstein, 1999, pp. 25-26).

Wallerstein's illuminating account, however, is limited in understanding the cultural aspects of building a national information infrastructure. Although the policies a state introduces are by no means neutral, they must address the needs of the general public in one way or another to win the public support and to attain institutional validity. Hence, the state would hesitate to exhibit a crude and overtly capitalist tilt to the detriment of the interest of other social classes. The leadership of a state, as Gramsci suggests, rests upon its ability to elicit the consent of the governed and the ability to synchronize the interest of the dominant group with that of the subordinate. Above and

49

beyond economic factors, in this regard, one has to bring to light the cultural and performative value of initiating such construction works.

The model city projects were more than a technological hotbed or an economic springboard. They were visual-discursive campaigns in which different forms of social energies and capital were aligned for the common goal of building a paragon of the future information society. The much-touted consortium consisting of various state institutions, public companies, and private enterprises was a political demonstration that eloquently displayed to the general public the need for societal collaboration in the proposed journey toward technotopia. That is, while the model town projects themselves were physical infrastructures of an advanced information society, they were also employed as a means for constructing the cultural, psychological infrastructures of an advanced information society.

In this large-scale "performance," where an abstract idea of information society is visualized in a material spectacle, the lines that separate state from civil society, technology from psychology, policy from discourse curiously collapse. As such, the model city projects exemplified both an exhibition room that seduced the public's interest and enthusiasm for advanced information society and a powerful discourse inculcating the idea that the general public is the true beneficiary of the technological dividends. In fact, the detailed process of constructing the model cities was publicized at great length by the mainstream media, and the daily routines of the inhabitants in the techno-towns were televised to the national audience at regular intervals (Tamura, 1987, p. 23). In this respect, they served as a cultural infrastructure that would form the ideological foundation for the steady and sturdy growth of information industry in its entirety.

Between the mid 1970 and the late 1980s, the Japanese state had steadily established new interfaces with information and communication businesses, while slowly easing off of the conventional patterns of engagement. But the change was by no means a drastic one. As stated above, the state continued to define overall industrial strategies,

50

promote the development of basic technologies, encourage commercial applications of technologies, provide development funds, and hammer out comprehensive legal bases. However, the gradual shift from a management and planning-intensive mode to an organizational and discourse-centered configuration cannot be underestimated, for the latter tendency grew much more salient during the 1990s.

In the next chapter, I shall examine how the state (primarily para-state institutions) participated in the reconfiguration of information/communication technologies amid the intensifying economic crisis started from the early 1990s. The focal point of this chapter will be the ways in which a new identity of digital television, as the home-based informational hub, is constructed through discursive, technological, and legislative projects undertaken by the state in cooperation with leading business institutions.

CHAPTER III:

MAKING DIGITAL TELEVISION:

STATE, ECONOMY AND DISCOURSE

Introduction

It has become a ritual to roll out the red carpet for a newly arrived technology.

Recently, cries of hosanna have greeted digital technologies as the digital code

increasingly assumes the status of a technological lingua franca. Clinton once extolled the

information superhighway as the telematic destiny of America, Bill Gates espoused the

global web of digital satellites as a boon to humanity, and Gore pronounced digital

interactivity as the next step in human evolution. In the same vein, the imminent digital

conversion of TV in many countries is being met with hearty acclaim. Digital TV in the

U.S., for example, is hailed as enhancing "the quality of governance, intelligence of

political discourse, diversity of free expression, vitality of local communities,

opportunities for education and instruction, and many other dimensions of American life"

(The Advisory Committee on Public Interest Obligations of Digital Television

Broadcasters, 1998, p. 4). In Japan too, an array of speculations and upbeat

pronouncements emerged as soon as the Ministry of Post and Telecommunications

(MPT)[11] announced that it would digitalize broadcasting in 1997.

However, the new narratives that celebrate its virtues in Japan are couched in

plain economic terms, lacking even of the old, familiar political romanticism given to

other technologies. As the phrase "catapulting television into the Internet broadband age"

---

[11] The Ministry of Post and Telecommunications has been integrated since January 2001 with the Ministry of Home Affairs and the Public Management agency to become the Ministry of Public Management, Home Affairs, Post and Telecommunications. With this reorganization, the former MPT's Communication Policy Bureau, Telecommunication Bureau, and Broadcasting Bureau have been combined to become two bureaus: the Information Communication Policy Bureau and Basic Bureau for Integrated Communications. Broadcasting services, including cable broadcasting, were placed under the control of the Information Communication Policy Bureau.

(The Telecommunication Council, 2000) suggests, the Japanese government treats digital television primarily as fortification of an Internet-based national technological infrastructure. Similarly, major newspapers and commercial media lionize the economic ramifications of digitalizing TV: "the new service, which enables large-volume data transmission, brings with it a range of new functions such as electronic commerce and home banking" (Nakamura, 2000, p. 1); "consumers will be able to receive services including e-mail, online shopping, banking, ticketing, and downloading music as well as store necessary data and TV programs" (Boyd, 2000, p. 1). Even the NHK, Japan's sole public broadcaster, is inclined to stress the benefits of digital television in terms of interactive services, such as TV shopping and data-casting, rather than projecting cultural and political visions (Nagaya, 2001, p. 3).

It seems that, as illustrated, the introduction of digital TV is reduced to a means to boost Japan's IT (information technology) industry and to precipitate a digital convergence ensuring universal interoperability among disparate technologies of broadcasting and telecommunications. These discourses concern not so much the mechanical attributes of digital television as the social objectives and values by which the technological properties of digital television are measured and defined. In other words, whether uttered in the form of technophilic tributes, policy guides or commercial hype, these discourses prioritize social objectives by highlighting/veiling and aggrandizing/downplaying particular capabilities and potentials of digital TV. In what social milieu, then, is the ascendancy of economic discourse privileged? In what ways is the digitalization of television seen as rescuing Japan's moribund economy? What networks of institutions, ideologies, and values are defining the potential uses of digital television? Finally, what are the social implications of this frenzied mobilization of digital TV?

Using the questions above as a guide, this chapter examines the Japanese state's discursive-policy endeavors to situate digital TV within the fast-changing configuration of info-capitalism. The first two sections of this chapter propose that the digitalization of TV should be viewed as a socio-economic endeavor with particular intentions and interests, not as a self-ruling evolution and proliferation of digital technology. The following two sections explore the intersection between the digitalization of TV and Japan's economic environment. With an emphasis on its national strategy to achieve premier status as a global IT powerhouse, I examine ways in which the digitalization of TV becomes the focal point of promoting Internet-based transactions. The last part of this chapter discusses the potential repercussion of the digitalization of TV (not digital TV as such) driven by economic purposes. In this section, I argue that the dominant discourses and practices regarding the digitalization of TV cluster disparate cultural technologies that in turn constitute new social subjectivities compatible with the requirement of the so-called "advanced information economy."

Although my analysis centers on political-economic interests held and practices used by the power cartel of policy bureaucrats and business elites, I do not wish to discount the formation of counter-hegemonic discourses. That is, the prevailing attempt to position digital TV as an alternative gateway to the Internet and the fulcrum of the so-called "anytime, anywhere information network" is by no means uncontested or final. On the contrary, it should be understood that the ways in which digital TV will be shaped and used have just entered, with the initiatives of state-corporate elites, the long process of social negotiation.

The War of Embedding

From a technical standpoint, digital television is nothing more than a new broadcast technology that transmits and receives radio waves in digital codes. Yet the prefix "digital" vis-à-vis "analog" destabilizes the conventional identity of TV by ushering in more channels, better picture quality, increased interactivity, and the storage/retrieval of information. Beyond the comprehensive restructuring of broadcast

54

television (programming, services, revenue sources, ownership structures, and outside partnerships), the most significant social implication is that it paves the way for the full integration of television with telecommunications technologies such as telephone, cable, computer, and satellites. The issue of digital compatibility between broadcasting and telecommunications, coupled with the multifunctional versatility intrinsic to digital television, presents a future that is highly complex and uncertain in terms of social uses and practices.

It is this initial stage of inserting technologies into social circuits that gives rise to a high-intensity "war of embedding." By "war of embedding," I mean a struggle among various social constituencies to finalize the meaning and uses of a new technology. Of course, the notion of a "war of embedding" is by no means original. Indeed, it is akin to what Paschal Preston and Aphra Kerr (2001) call "a process of appropriation" (p. 110), or what Arturo Escobar (2000) deems a "regime of technosociality," defined as a "broad process of sociocultural construction set into motion in the wake of the new technologies" (p. 57). I deploy the notion of a "war of embedding," however, with the intent, first, to refute a teleological view that mythologizes the transition from analog TV to digital TV as an inexorable process of technical evolution and, second, to accentuate the element of power struggle over the use of digital TV, most evident during the early phase of domestication.

A teleological view of digitalization would have us believe that the transition from analog to digital is an autonomous, natural process determined by the principle of survival of the electronic fittest (Kroker & Kroker, 2000, p. 96). Tony Feldman (1997), former director of the Macmillan group, portrays the move towards digital media as an "organic process of development: a logical, step-by-step progress into an extraordinary new future" (p. xiii). Here, the process of digitalization is depicted as a spontaneous evolution according to the predetermined trajectory encoded in the genes of technologies. This asocial account of digitalization is in close liaison with technological determinism.

55

Defining a technology as a physical apparatus, and a medium as a use to which a physical apparatus is put, Neil Postman (1985) maintains that "a technology becomes a medium as it employs a particular symbolic code, as it finds its place in a particular social setting, as it insinuates itself into economic and political contexts" (p. 84). He further argues that a "technology is merely a machine while a medium is the social and intellectual environment *a machine creates*" (emphasis added, p. 84). The notion that a machine itself creates the best-fitting social and intellectual environment is what the "war of embedding" diametrically opposes, for it hazardously dislodges human agency from the invention and subsequent use of technologies. Technology is, as Robert Hassan (2000) asserts, a "force emanating from a human agency steeped in the interactions of power, culture, politics and economics" (p. 19). Ian Miles (1988) also contends that technology does not "cause" particular social changes though it can change the parameters within which humans interact. In a nutshell, social forces and particular technologies reciprocal effects (Winner, 1985, p. 26).

Likewise, particular modes of using a technology are by no means an unavoidable, natural outcome. Nonetheless, much of the Japanese government documents, press releases, and newsletters tend to portray the speeding up of media convergence and E-commerce as an inevitable destiny of technological innovation. For example, the Telecommunications Council (2000) states, "the increasing sophistication of info-communications is . . . tending to bring about what is referred to as the convergence of telecommunications and broadcasting. The digitalization of broadcasting is destined to accelerate this trend" (p. 13). What this statement implicitly preaches is the mythology of the spontaneous trajectory of technological development, programmed outside of human controls and intentions. Similarly, the Study Group on Convergence and Developments in Telecommunications and Broadcasting depicts the diffusion of electronic commerce as an "inevitable result of convergence." The reality is quite the opposite. Recent innovations in IT, including digital TV, are occurring to a considerable degree according to the

56

template set by the information industry and policymakers. Media convergence and E-commerce are social artifices (Hassan, 2000, p. 21) that are consciously fostered within the mechanism of informational capitalism. Digitalization of TV also has a "premeditated" destiny at which research and development of new technologies are meticulously aimed. In this respect, the way digital TV is constructed as a device to stimulate IT economy cannot be deemed a natural unfolding of digital TV, uncoupled from socio-economic interests and intentions of particular groups. This understanding necessitates an appraisal of the Japanese state's involvement in the IT sector through the lens of the "war of embedding," upon which I will elaborate below.

State Hegemony in IT Policy

Preston and Kerr (2001) aptly argue that issues of media technology should be scrutinized in relation to policy initiatives and the associated discourses on information society, which have been relentlessly promoted by the "hegemonic industrial and policy elites in the 1990s" (p. 111). Needless to say, most development in information technology is steered by corporate giants who embody the contemporary enmeshment of political and commercial intentions. In addition, most policies for the IT industry are engineered by a coalition of established corporations and political bureaucracies. The unequivocal alliance between the state and the business sector has strikingly solidified in the alleged era of neo-liberalism. Herbert Schiller (1998) observes, for instance, that the U.S. Federal initiatives and massive financial support for new information technologies, over the last half-century, have scarcely diminished in the present digital age (p. 22). Rather, the growth of the information infrastructure has become a top government priority (Schiller, 1998, p. 22). Granted, Robert McChesney (2000) is not wide of the mark to dismiss claims that the government's function will be subordinated to market governance in the age of deregulation. The only discernable difference in the age of neo-liberal deregulation is, according to him, that "there is no pretense that the government should represent the public interest vis-à-vis commercial interests" (McChesney, 2000, p. 14).

The Japanese state has exercised unabated influence in shaping policies, discourses, and practices around the new technologies. But the degree to which the Japanese state favors profit-oriented sectors has strikingly heightened during the post-1991 economic downturn. Desmond Bell and David McNeill (1999), for instance, analyze Japan's "multimedia craze" during the early and mid-1990s as representing a drive by Japanese capital and the state to restore conditions for capital accumulation in the context of the post-bubble recession. They contend that the role of the Japanese state is "increasingly becoming one of facilitating an informationalization of Japanese society designed primarily to benefit the business sector" (Bell & McNeill, 1999, p. 759). This tendency has remained unaltered in the digitalization of TV. The MPT, in particular, has controlled the process of digitalizing broadcasting through various methods and has never relinquished its command.[12]

Upon close examination, however, one might recognize that the supremacy of the MPT has been largely mediated and bolstered by numerous para-state bodies, which consist of a considerable number of civilian, academic, and business delegates. For example, since 1995 the MPT has been running, and at the same time has been run by, a number of study groups (*benkyokai*), including the "Development of Digital Broadcasting Technologies for the Multimedia Age" and the "Vision for Advancement of Broadcasting." These study groups have conducted research and brought forth policy

---

[12] Furthermore, the MPT's control is not unique only to digital broadcast standard; it has influenced various broadcasting policies since the inception of the ministry. Virtually all the major changes of broadcasting technology and industrial systems, such as conversion to color TV and UHF, introduction of the multiplexing system, and the launch of Direct Broadcasting Satellite (DBS), were ordained by the MPT without consultation of the Diet members specializing in telecommunications and broadcasting.

proposals essential to the implementation of digital broadcasting.[13] Furthermore, the Promotion Committee on Digital Terrestrial Broadcasting Experiments was established under the auspice of the MPT in September 1999 to supervise and coordinate R&D on digital terrestrial broadcasting.[14] There are more reasons to cast doubt about the mythology of the unbridled power of the "government" (as opposed to the state, as an ensemble of various institutions and organizations affiliated with and involved in the process of national policy making).

In March 1997, the MPT announced that it would prepare the legislative and technical environment for the launch of digital terrestrial broadcasting before 2000. This "sudden and unusual"[15] announcement not only reversed the original plan[16] but was also made without due consultation with other institutional bodies and business sectors, including the NHK (Japanese Broadcasting Corporation) and major commercial broadcasters. The autarchic decision-making elicited criticisms and disputes among the leading Japanese broadcasters. For example, Seiichiro Ujiie (1998), President of National Association of Commercial Broadcasters in Japan (NABJ), charged the MPT with neglecting Japan's peculiar conditions in a rash emulation of the U.S and UK. Ujiie states,

> We are worried about this haste. Unlike the United States, Japan
> has a large number of relay stations per broadcaster, which means
> vast facility investment . . . . If this investment creates a financial

---

[13] For instance, the MPT is also subsidizing the Intelligent Television Forum (ITF), a private organization inaugurated in May 1995 to promote digital broadcasting.

[14] Ministry of Post and Telecommunications, Japan. (1999, November 1). *Press Release*. Tokyo: Ministry of Post and Telecommunications, Japan.

[15] According to Kanayama, the MPT's sudden decision came less than two weeks after a telecommunication ministry advisory panel said Japan should immediately go digital for its next generation of broadcast satellites.

[16] Originally, digitalization of terrestrial broadcasting was due between 2000 and 2005.

crisis for Japan's commercial broadcasters, making them unable to fulfill their fundamental roles, we cannot help wondering about the necessity of digitization in the first place (p. 3).

It is estimated that the digitalization of terrestrial TV will require roughly one trillion yen (approximately US $10 billion). Major commercial broadcasters boycotted the government plan and decided to concentrate on the digitalization of satellite broadcasting by 2000. Even the NHK, which has been a close partner of the MPT in forming Japanese broadcasting policies, was ill at ease with the drastic plan to digitalize terrestrial broadcasting immediately. Concerned about the astronomical financial burden of digitalizing broadcasting, Katsuji Ebisawa (1998), president of NHK, posited that the government needed "public approval before proceeding with this project" (p. 2). Although digital HDTV via satellite had already been inaugurated in December 2000, the strong protests of broadcasters pushed the MPT to reset the schedule for digital terrestrial broadcasting. According to the new schedule, finalized by the MPT in July 2001, three major regions in Japan (Tokyo, Osaka, and Nagoya) will see the launch of digital terrestrial broadcasting in December 2003, to be followed by other regions in 2006. The MPT also decided to discontinue current terrestrial analog TV broadcasting services as of July 24, 2011.

It needs to be explored precisely what initially propelled the MPT to implement the digitalization of TV over the loud protests of domestic broadcasters, and also why and how the major broadcasters finally endorsed the compromise plan to go digital. Analysts suggest there are two main interrelated reasons behind Japan's rush toward digital broadcasting. First, the MPT stepped up its digital plan to catch up with the U. K. and the U. S., whose digital terrestrial broadcasts were slated to start in 1998 (Ujiie, 1998; Kanayama, 1999). Shuji Kusuda (1999), the MPT's director general of the Broadcasting Bureau, allegedly admitted that Japan urgently needed to introduce digital broadcasts to keep up with the U.S. and major European nations. It would be a mistake, however, to characterize this as only a "catching up" scenario. What perturbed Japanese state officials is less the nation's delay in technologies for digital broadcasting than its lagging behind the global race towards digital convergence. Digital convergence, being the nucleus of the so-called "IT revolution," is believed to be the key contingency that determines the overall economic competitiveness of a nation in the epoch of informational capitalism. In turn, digital TV is the axis upon which digital convergence is built.

The second scenario casts the rush to digital broadcasting as an attempt to stimulate the nation's electronics and communication equipment industries. Kazuo Kaifu (1997), a senior researcher at NHK, argues that the significance of digitalization lies in its ability to open up "a completely new and extensive market for the manufacturers of audio-visual and telecommunications equipment" (p. 9). He further suggests that the digitalization of broadcasting and its technical standardization in other leading industrialized countries also be examined in this light (p. 9).

The implementation of digital broadcasting in Japan surely bestows enormous opportunities to Japanese electronics makers, just as the introduction of color television in the 1960s created a bonanza for the electronics industry. Roughly 20,000 digital TV sets per month have been sold since the kick-off of digital HDTV satellite broadcasting in December 2000. An estimated 8.21 million sets of digital equipment, according to the Japan Electronics and Information Technology Industries Association (JEITA), will have been shipped by the end of March 2004.[17] In addition, digital TV may also mean a boon for semiconductor manufacturers and makers of other home electronic appliances. The scale of the market for electronics manufacturers is truly colossal, and the anticipated chain reaction in the IT sector and other associated industries cannot be overstated. On the other hand, this account is confined within the industrial (manufacturing) framework, eliding the informational façade of digital TV. Moreover, such an approach fails to

---

[17] See Japan's TV Leaps High. (2001). *Broadcasting Culture & Research*, 15, p. 2.

appreciate the interstitial nature of digital TV, which facilitates digital convergence with other information technologies.

It needs to be stressed that the ultimate utility of digital television is determined not so much by its anticipated impact on the broadcasting industry itself as by its synergistic capacity to accelerate the all-embracing convergence of information technologies. This is why the rapid introduction of digital television in Japan calls for a contextual approach that sheds light on the nation's overarching strategy of IT convergence and development. On a global scale, it is a locus inexorably bound up with fast-changing configurations of info-capitalism. On a national scale, it becomes a vital means by which the rejuvenation of economic competitiveness is aggressively sought by Japanese state bureaucrats and corporate elites.

Japan's digitalization of TV, in this regard, can be examined as what Raymond Williams (1975) calls a "symptomatic technology." What this concept suggests is that technology can be a manifestation of both social change and also the ways in which power reacts to these changes (Mackay, 1995). Williams offers, for example, the emergence of various mass media as responses to political and social crises, such as augmented mobility, loss of social perspective, steep alteration of material environments, or loosening of familial bonds. In a similar vein, David Gunkel and Ann Gunkel (1997) view the unruly commercialization of the Internet as revealing a hegemonic vision of an advanced information society, which is nonetheless situated under the "conceptual domination of the old" since "one finds only what s/he wanted to find and discovers only what one, in advance, already desires to produce" (p. 124).

However, the notion of symptomatic technology differs sharply from a utilitarian view of technology that would endorse the old aphorism, "necessity is the mother of invention." What informs this functionalist perspective is the supposition that technology is an impartial reaction to human needs that exist uniformly across all social sectors. The fallacy of the utilitarian view consists in its segregation of technology from the larger

62

social/historical struggles among various social forces over the question of "whose necessity and for what end?" Williams, in contrast, sheds light on the architecture of social competition and the bargains struck in developing and defining media technologies. He sees, for instance, the emergence of broadcasting as a powerful apparatus intended for social integration and control with socially, commercially and politically manipulative uses. The rapid introduction of digital television in Japan can be viewed in the same light. It is at once a symptom, tightly linked with the extensive reorganization of capitalism, and a tool by which fanatical social campaigns to restore economic competitiveness and profitability have intensified. The next section discusses in detail of what social changes and crises Japan's digitization of TV is a symptom. This inquiry will be organized around the question: under what material and discursive climates is TV—a traditionally entertainment-oriented and passive medium—being reconstituted as an information portal, a major lever in building a digital information network?

Economic Crisis and IT Economy

Japan has been swamped by a decade-long economic recession since the burst of the bubble economy (*Baburu Keizai*) in 1990. Analysts tend to diagnose the prolonged slump as stemming from structural problems rather than something transitory. Japan's economy in the 1990s has been bogged down by both external and internal factors. Domestically, such challenges as the hollowing out of key industries, extraordinarily high living/business expenses, an aging population, near-depletion of natural resources, and declining birth rates were placing severe burdens on labor efficiency and productivity. The radical reshuffling of the international trade engendered by global info-capitalism called for a shift away from the nation's reliance on an export-oriented manufacturing system. Furthermore, the surge of NIEs (Newly Industrializing Economies) of East Asia during the 1980s and South Asia during the 1990s steadily eroded Japan's comparative advantage in industrial technologies and goods.

The high-tech niche used to be one in which Japan was miles ahead of its neighbors. The microchip and LCD industries were the centerpiece of Japan's global edge in television, personal computers, and many other information-related products. Five Japanese firms that in 1998 were among the top 10 chip-making producers in the world together accounted for 32 percent of the global market, following the 56 percent share claimed by U.S. firms. But Japan has seen its share of worldwide production decline drastically in those sectors. In 2000, its share of worldwide semiconductor shipments shrank to 22.9 percent from its 40.2 percent peak in 1988, according to World Semiconductor Trade Statistics published in 2001. Taiwan and South Korea pick up the slack, with their combined output in 2000 amounting to 25.1 percent of world shipments. Japan's production of telecommunications equipment like optical fibers, which form the basis of the Internet infrastructure, is also on the brink of being overtaken.

It was at this juncture that IT was invoked as the magical cure for the ailing economy and the sense of crisis pervading Japanese society. Accordingly, the government established an IT strategy council within the cabinet secretariat and proposed a bill that consolidates national strategies to assist the reorganization of the IT industry. Subsequently, the IT council members, as well as leading businessmen and state officials, called in unison for the construction of an "advanced information society."

An advanced Information Society is hazily defined as a "new socioeconomic system whereby people can realize free creation, circulation, and sharing of information and knowledge (the products of human intellectual activities) and harmonize daily life, culture, industry, economy, nature and the environment" (Advanced Information Telecommunications Society Promotion Headquarters, 1998, p. 2). As mentioned in the previous chapter, however, the notion of an advanced information society has been a much-favored mantra in many countries since the late-1970s. In Japan, it is an offshoot of

64

"information society theory" (*Johoshakai-ron*), a well-worn subject that has been consistently touted by Japanese scholars, technicians, bureaucrats, and businessmen since the late 1960s. It was, after all, Japan who pioneered the notion of an information society and set the tone for subsequent discussions.[18] Yet, the "advanced information society" craze in the 1990s is more than a repetition of an old tune.

With stronger doses of IT-fetishism and renewed fanaticism during the unprecedented economic crisis, the resurrection of the advanced information society discourse in the 1990s aimed specifically at a mass relocation of the economic and social activities of business and ordinary citizens toward information-intensive domains. Hence, Japan's aggressive journey towards achieving an advanced information society forsook the industrial paradigm as a "malfunctioning system," with which, paradoxically, Japan had accomplished dazzling growth until 1990. Its headlong plunge into an "advanced information society" on a vehicle called "digital convergence" goes invariably together with a mystification of IT as a "panacea" (Bell & McNeill, 1999, p. 766) for Japan's flagging economy and other social predicaments. For instance, the Advanced Information and Telecommunications Society Promotion Headquarters (1998) hails advanced information technologies as bearing the transformative power to "lower social costs, increase real income by correcting high-cost structures, reduce the occurrence of daily stress, and improve the convenience of daily life" (p. 3).

Following the lead of the Advanced Information Telecommunication Society Promotion Headquarters, numerous other para-state organizations carried out fanatical discursive campaigns to promote ICTs (Information-Communication Technologies). In a

---

[18] The notion of "Information Society" was first used by Tadao Umesao in 1963 and subsequently took off as a central rallying cry for reforming the Japanese industrial structure. A document titled "Tasks for *Johoka* (Informationalization): Report on the Development of Information Processing Industries" issued by the Information Industry Section of MITI's (Ministry of International Trade and Industry) Industrial Structure Council in 1967 epitomizes the Information Society. See Lyon (1995) and Castells (1998).

report entitled "Info-Communications Vision for the 21st Century: IT Japan for all,"
Telecommunications Council (2000) exalts ICTs and the advanced information society as
follows:

> The impact IT will have on our society is comparable to that of the
> agricultural revolution or the industrial revolution. The permeation
> of IT in our society and economy . . . will set up a stage
> encompassing the entire world where anyone can easily create,
> distribute and share information and where partners from around
> the world can participate in activities together. The ultimate result
> being that, with the contribution of partners from around the globe,
> greater success can be achieved than ever before . . . . [In an
> advanced information society], people will find true self-
> realization through the increased leisure time provided by
> teleworking and through broader intellectual activities resulting
> from remote education, and can anticipate healthier and safer
> lifestyles resulting from more sophisticated social systems through
> widespread adoption of remote medical treatment" (pp. 4-5).

Gripped with the exigent task of reinvigorating the economy, various para-state
institutions scrambled to publish a host of policy guidelines and instructional booklets.
The first of the kind was the project entitled "21st Century Visions for Info-
communication" drafted by the MPT, along with the Ministry of International Trade and
Industry (MITI) in June 1997. Following the project, a constellation of similar plans were
introduced: "Policy Planning for Implementing National Strategies on Information
technology," "Info-Communications Vision for the 21st Century: IT Japan for All"
complied by the Telecommunications Council in March 2000, and "Policy Package for
New Economic Development toward the Rebirth of Japan" in October 2000. Many of the
booklets include statements that border on propaganda. For example, the Advanced
Information and Telecommunications Society Promotion Headquarters (1998) presents
the paradigm shift from an industrial society to an information society as "a task which
the entire nation must tackle. Failure to devote sufficient energy to such efforts now will
result in Japan falling behind other nations such as the United States . . . . Such neglect
will inevitably weaken Japan's international competitiveness in the medium to long term"
(p. 2). Other government documents are also peppered with such flag-waving slogans as

"reinventing Japan," "rebirth of Japan," and "second nation-building," etc. A line from *Info-Communications Visions for the 21st Century: IT Japan for All* reads, "we must recognize that to reinvent Japan as an attractive country within the international community to live, visit, work and invest in, it is necessary to become a world leader in the application of IT to promote and accelerate socio-economic reform" (Telecommunication Council, 2000, p. 23).

This imperious and solemn campaign to replenish socio-economic vitality is echoed in a speech delivered by former Prime Minister Yoshiro Mori to the National Diet in September 2000.[19] In his address, Mori asserted that the most important pillar in the "rebirth of Japan" is IT strategy and vowed to build a so-called "E-Japan," which would make Japan a nation that stands at the forefront of information and communications. Mori instructed the Finance Ministry to set aside a special quota of 250 billion yen for information technology projects in the fiscal 2001 budget, and sought collateral investments from the private sector. The exorbitant financial endorsement was justified by the pseudo-scientific prediction that the economy was to boom as the information revolution made inroads into Japan. Wishful speculations proliferated in the guise of economic analyses, predicting that corporate productivity would see a dramatic increase, but only if more internet-based businesses were to debut and if major companies increase their information-related investment and shift to a new business model: "The size of the info-communications market will have risen from 29 trillion yen in 1995 to 125 trillion yen in 2010. It is predicted that a total of 2.44 million new jobs will be created, which is more than three times the number of jobs (0.77 million) in the automobile industry during 1995" (Telecommunication Council, 1997, p. 24).

---

[19] See full text of Prime Minister's speech to the Diet in *The Japan Times*, September, 22, 2000. http://www.japantimes.co.jp/cgi-bin/getarticle.p15?nn20000922a4.htm

Major policy documents issued by MITI and MPT harp on the significance of network business, citing the reports from the U.S. Department of Commerce that the United States achieved low inflation and double productivity through Internet-based businesses during the second half of the 1990s, and that 35 percent of the growth in the US GDP was made possible by the use of IT between 1995 and 1998. The mainstream media have been loyal teammates in this endeavor. They often refer to stock indexes as an infallible indicator of the irreversible economic restructuring. "Share prices in information-related industries are often quoted in five or six digits, while those in the construction, chemical, steel, paper-pulp, nonferrous metal and other traditional industries are mostly in three digits" (Iwao, 2000). Some of them even employ the narrative of doomology, effectively threatening the business sectors slow in their conversion to IT-religion: "companies adapting to the new business model will have abundant profit-making opportunities, while those failing to shake themselves free from the traditional business model will be phased out." Goldman Sachs, too, chipped in to the campaign, predicting that business-to-consumer e-commerce alone (business-to-business is not counted) could boost Japan's gross domestic product by 5.8 percent by 2010. As shown, the IT campaign was a concerted effort. The Japanese government, being the headquarters of the promotion, acts in tandem with other para-state apparatuses, research institutions, business organizations, and mainstream media to press the "digital revolution."

The ferocious drive has had some measurable repercussions among both businessmen and ordinary citizens. For example, in recent years investment in information and communications technology by the private sector has grown measurably. It reached 18.3 trillion yen in 1999, marking a 13.2 percent increase over the previous year and 1.5 times the 1995 level (the MPT, 2001, p. 47). According to MPT's White Paper 2001, Japan's information and communications industry in 1999 ranked as the largest industry, and its real gross domestic output totaled 108.9 trillion yen, which

68

accounted for 11.4 percent of total real domestic output by all industries (p. 46). When the nation achieved GDP growth of 0.5 percent in fiscal 1999, after suffering negative growth for three years in a row, many economists, including Kakashi Imai, the chairman of the Japan Federation of Economic Organizations (*Keidanren*), quickly ascribed the feat to the government's lavish spending on information technology.

While Japan expects to spur reform of its economic framework and bring greater efficiency to industry via digital economy, it has curiously lagged in the overall penetration rate of PCs and the use of the Internet. According to MPT's White Paper 1999, only 11 percent of households owned personal computers with Internet access as of 1998. Far worse, Internet usage by business management in Japan is only 15 percent, woefully low compared with countries like Canada, Spain, and the U.S. that boast over 60 percent usage.[20] Undoubtedly, Japan's lethargic Internet penetration has posed a major hurdle to the global economic competition where Internet-led commerce reigns with augmenting supremacy. It has become a token of faith amongst believers that global capitalism rests its performance heavily upon information technologies in general, and the Internet in particular. Since the late 1980s, worldwide stock and bond markets have been operating twenty-four hours a day on various information technologies. From the mid-1990s onwards, there has been a gradual and yet massive influx of capital and commodity flow into the domain of the Internet. Not only amongst financial institutions and multinational corporations, but also much of the ordinary commerce within and among industrial nations has been executed via the Internet. The U.S. government, correspondingly, supports E-business as the foundation of the nation's emerging digital economy (Ingersoll, 1998, p. A3) and forecasts it to expand as much as $ 300 billion by

---

[20] This data was obtained from the source released by Anderson Consulting (1999) entitled "Internet usage by management." See Telecommunication Council, Japan. (2000). *Info-communications Vision for the 21st Century: IT Japan for All.* Tokyo: Ministry of Post and Telecommunications, p. 31.

2002 (Hof, 1998, p. 31). It is estimated that about 200 million people worldwide were using the Internet as of 2000, and a report released by United Nations Conference on Trade and Development in 2001 predicted that by 2003 some 25 percent of global trade transactions will take place on the Internet.

Under this condition, the Japanese government and the business sector have spurred on Internet business since 1997. The government-stoked E-commerce fervor in Japan became so overwhelming that in 1999 the Tokyo Stock Exchange discontinued floor transactions, ending a more than one hundred-year-old tradition, in a rush towards network transactions. Moreover, major *Konbini* (convenience store) chains in Japan have set up delivery services for Internet-ordered goods in addition to telephone orders. Businessmen like Naoyuki Akikusa, Fujitsu's president, responded to the E-business craze by adopting a slogan of "Everything on the Internet" (Boyd, 2000, p. 1). As a result, network transactions in Japan have accelerated dizzyingly in both volume and velocity. As of 2000, according to Daiwa Institute of Research, there are 2.5 million online trading accounts, which are used to conduct over one fourth of all trading by individuals in Japan. Even the so-called "dot.bomb" in the U.S and other Internet-savvy Asian countries did little to curb Japan's enthusiasm toward the digital economy. A Telecommunication Council's report (2000) shows that electronic commerce in the case of the business to consumer transaction (Business to Customer) will see a dramatic expansion from a mere 65 billion yen in 1998 to 3.16 trillion yen by 2003—a fifty-fold increase (p. 17).

Although little doubt can be made on the vitality of information technology for economic growth, many harbor reservations about the blind rush to the mythical IT goldmine. Tetsushi Kajimoto (2000) argues that E-commerce inevitably prompts a large-scale restructuring of production and distribution system by eliminating multiple steps of intermediate transactions, which currently accounts for roughly 30 percent of Japan's GDP. As a result of corporate streamlining and changing job specifications, he estimates,

70

Japan will see 1.63 million job losses by 2005 (Kajimoto, 2000). The director at Sanwa Research Institute warned against the huge toll Japan has to pay to expand online transactions. Since the boom will not benefit everyone, socio-economic polarization could further accelerate, not only among existing classes but also among companies and industrial sectors. As media and information technology mergers increase, the concentration of wealth and power could become even more starkly unbalanced.

Glyn Ford (2000) dubbed Japan's IT drive the "dangerous ride" of a "high-tech juggernaut." The danger Ford alluded to soon became evident in many parts of the world. In the U.S, the growth rate of e-commerce has slowed down. Share prices of e-commerce companies have dropped 30-40 percent from their highs. Contrary to initial expectations, those companies have so far failed to produce high profits. By 2002 the stock price of the Amazon.com fell 40 percent from its high. Between 15 to 24 percent of the Internet venture companies have gone bankrupt in Taiwan, Hong-Kong and Korea. Obsessed with the miraculous promises of the IT industry, the Japanese state has neglected other pressing economic issues, including the unstable financial system, falling land values, unemployment, deterioration of the educational system, etc. In a way, Japan's IT drive is reminiscent of the Enclosure Movement. It hollows out "rustic" industries and funnels their resources into the digital conurbation. It represents a political prioritization made with a heavy dose of fatalism.

Even though Internet use in Japan is increasing at a remarkable pace, Japan was ranked only 14th in the number of Internet users as of 2000.[21] Anderson Consulting Company and the Electronic Commerce Promotion Council in Japan jointly predicted in

---

[21] The number of Internet users in Japan reached 47.08 million by the end of 2000. The MPT expects that the number of users may nearly double by 2005. See Ministry of Public Management, Home Affairs, Post and Telecommunications (2001). *White Paper: Information and Communications in Japan*. Tokyo: General Policy Division, Information and Communications Policy Bureau, p. 6.

2000 that a meager two percent of household consumption purchases would be made electronically by 2004 (as cited in Tetsushi Kajimoto, 2000). A major obstacle was the lack of domestic demand, which basically stemmed from the lack of enthusiasm toward the PC, Internet, and online transaction among the general public, let alone business. For instance, Japanese industrial robot makers remain competitive because there is a strong domestic market, mostly by automakers, for their products. Similarly, what nurtured the competitiveness of Japan's electronics industry was a constant stream of domestic demand. In contrast, online business is not the most beloved type of transaction, nor is the computer medium. For instance, there were only 15 million net users in Japan as of 1999 and only half of them had shopped online more than once. Reflecting on this quandary, strategists in the Japan government, in coordination with big corporations, threw in a "unique IT strategy" that would radically alter the situation. This process of adopting new technologies such as digital television and broadband cable is entirely subordinated to the "unique IT strategy". Put bluntly, the most significant reason that MPT bureaucrats hailed and hastened the digitalization of television was its compatibility with the Internet, the centerpiece of digital economy, with which Japan has been recently preoccupied. The following section explores how digital TV is tied into Japan's IT strategy. This unique strategy can be characterized as diversification/integration of information terminals by encouraging non-PC-based Internet use.

Japan's Unique IT Strategy

Castells (1996) notes, "while capitalism's restructuring and the diffusion of informationalism were inseparable processes on a global scale, societies did act/react differently to such processes, according to the specificity of their history, culture, and institutions" (p. 20). The same holds true for digital convergence. It is obvious that the global proliferation of a digital standard for TV and its uses are necessarily attended and transfigured by local/national contingencies. This process of vernacularization unfailingly takes place across the heterogeneous fields of adoption, adaptation, and appropriation of digital television, carried out by a variety of social constituents within a set of local peculiarities. These include the dynamics of policymaking, economic configurations, and cultural predispositions. In a country like the U.S, where the PC has been the driving force for the information networks of the Internet and E-commerce, the prevalent perspective towards digital broadcasting is couched in terms relative to PCs. As U.S. representative Fred Upton (the chair of the House Committee on Telecommunications and the Internet) puts it, the digitalization of TV is "another way of enabling television to talk the language of computers" (U.S. Subcommittee on Telecommunications and the Internet of the Committee on Energy and Commerce House of Representatives, 2001, p. 5). This secondary status of digital TV in the US is also mirrored by the fact that digital TV is getting a rather lukewarm reception from American broadcasters and audiences, who have otherwise embraced the "digital revolution." The proliferation of digital terrestrial broadcasting has remained slow since its beginning in 1998. According to National Association of Broadcasters (NAB), only 195 out of the 1600 (12 percent) broadcasting stations had equipment to transmit digital programs as of May 2001. Sales of digital TV receiving equipment haven't been brisk either, totaling only 1 million as of May 2001 (U.S. Subcommittee, 2001, p. 44).

In contrast, TV in Japan is undergoing a major metamorphosis that is transforming it into a "home-based information network," the centerpiece of the IT economy. This renewal of TV through digitalization is being carried out under Japan's overall IT strategy called "diversification of information terminals." The MPT's study group on the convergence of broadcasting and telecommunication submitted a report titled "Diversified Info-communications Developments" in May 1998, which emphasized convergence not as a process toward unification or homogenization but rather as the diversification of info-communications. The idea of diversifying info-communications is lucidly explained by Tadashi Okamura (Toshiba's CEO), who bestows on digital TV sets,

73

mobile terminals, and PCs the status of the "three sacred treasures"[22] of the information

technology era. Okamura states that the era when information technology was a synonym

for personal computers has yielded to the era of diversified information technologies,

whose interaction creates a value chain. He observes, "In offices, information technology

is based on PCs. When people are on the street, they use mobile terminals, mainly

cellular phones. At home, digital TV sets will be the center of IT."[23] Strategists in the

MPT and businessmen like Nobuyuki Idei (chairman and CEO of Sony Corp.) validate

the strategy as resonating with Japan's peculiar industrial structures and cultural

orientations, namely, its relative indifference to PCs and the sluggishness of the Internet-

based economy.

On a more practical level, however, the "diversification of information terminals"

boils down to appointing mobile phones and digital TVs as alternative information

portals networked with the Internet. For instance, the MPT (2001) designated 2001 as the

year for "qualitative change"[24] in Internet usage by promoting access through mobile

phones and digital TVs. In the same spirit, the chairman of the Japan Federation of

Economic Organizations (*Keidanren*), Kakashi Imai, urged the nation to expand mobile

phone-based and digital television-based Internet business.[25] Consequently, non-PC-

---

[22] This term originated in the 1960s when a TV set, a refrigerator, and a washing machine symbolized dazzling national economic growth as well as the affluence of Japanese households. See Sachiko Hirao. (2000, September 7). Quest for Three Sacred Gadgets: Toshiba Transforms for IT Revolution. *The Japan Times*. http://www.japantimes.co.jp/cgi-bin/getarticle.p15?nb20000907a2.htm

[23] Ibid.

[24] "Qualitative change" refers to a system that (1) permits the sending and receiving of any form of information quickly (2) with constant connection and (3) connection via means other than PCs, such as cell phones and digital television. See Ministry of Public Management, Home Affairs, Post and Telecommunications (2001). *White Paper: Information and Communications in Japan.* Tokyo: General Policy Division, Information and Communications Policy Bureau, p. 4.

[25] Takashi Imai (2000, July 21). Stimulus Policy Should Continue. *The Japan Times*, http://www.japantimes.co.jp/cgi-bin/getarticle.p15?nb20000721c1.htm

based Internet use in Japan is growing forcefully. The number of Internet users in Japan at the end of 2000 jumped to an estimated 47.08 million, marking a 74.0 percent increase over the year 1999. The dramatic surge in overall Internet use occurred as a result of the introduction of Internet-connected cellular phone service in February of 1999. Cellular telephones that allow viewing of websites and transmission of e-mail over the Internet have sprung up in a short time. During the year 2000, some 37.23 million users accessed the Internet via PC, while 23.64 million gained access via cellular phones. NTT (Nippon Telegraph and Telephone Corp.) predicted that its income from fixed telephone lines will drop from the current 50 percent to 20 percent of its total income, while that from mobile and Internet communications will increase from 50 percent to 70 percent by the end of fiscal 2004.

Even higher expectations are placed on digital TV to boost Internet use. The debut of digital TV in 2000 has given a great momentum to the long-standing ambition of Japan's media policymakers to place TV at the hub of a media convergence that absorbs PC functions. Takashi Yamada, Deputy Director-General of NHK, posits, "digital TV is actually a computer . . . equipped with a built-in CPU, RAM, ROM and modem. TV will develop as a medium that performs all the functions of a personal computer."[26] Whether TV will devour the PC, or the functions of TV will be annexed to the PC, has been a contentious issue (West, Dedrick, & Kraemer, 1996) and still remains uncertain. What seems obvious, however, is that Japanese state officials and business leaders concur that digital TV should be the driving force behind the so-called digital home network, integrating digital products such as cellular phones, video cameras, and other home electronic appliances. Thus, MPT officials and corporate managers have beefed up their

---

[26] This phrase was stated in a symposium titled "Digital broadcasting: creating 21st century broadcasting dreams." See Manabe, Tomohito. (2001). Digital Broadcasting. *Broadcasting Culture and Research*, 15, p. 5.

efforts to transform conventional TV into a "home-based information network." Along this line, a NHK administrator says that "it is inevitable that TV will evolve into a new basic information provider for the next generation, adding a different dimension beyond conventional TV through its high-speed, portable, interactive, personal and other qualities, with the functions of digitalcasting and TV commerce."[27]

The push to transfigure digital TV into the "home-based information portal" is further corroborated by the fact that in Japan Internet use in the home far surpasses that in the workplace. A nationwide survey conducted by Dentsu Company in January 2001 indicates that an estimated 24.14 million Japanese now use the Internet at home versus 17.58 million in the workplace. Hopeful that digital TV will expedite the triadic integration of the Internet, mobile phones, and television, Japanese electronics makers are concentrating their efforts on connecting digital television to the Internet. In October 2000, Hitachi, Matsushita, Sony, and Toshiba corporations announced a joint venture to create a so-called "e-platform," which will make digital televisions interoperable with the Internet via set-top boxes. The MPT has also cleared the way to team mobile phones with digital terrestrial broadcasting. For that purpose, NHK, NTT (Nippon Telegraph and Telephone Corp.), and Sony Corporation formed a consortium to develop technologies that make mobile phones capable of transmitting and receiving moving images of the same clarity as that of digital TV. The MPT has also prepared for legal consolidations and recently presented the National Diet with two bills regarding the integration of TV, the Internet, and mobile phones.[28]

---

[27] See Japan's TV Leaps High (2001). *Broadcasting Culture & Research*, 15, p. 3.

[28] A bill on Broadcasting Used for Telecommunications Services and a bill on Promoting the Convergence of Telecommunications and Broadcasting. The latter was passed on June 1, 2001 in the Diet.

As mentioned, digital TV is a development being cultivated and promoted under the national IT strategy called "diversifying information terminals." According to this strategy, the TV that the Japanese audience has known thus far could undergo euthanasia only to be resurrected as a "home-based information network." It should be emphasized that the proposed transformation of TV is guided by the grandiose goal of making Japan an "IT powerhouse" via the construction of a de facto universal information network. This ultra information infrastructure, named an "anytime, anywhere information network" is an embodiment of info-capitalism's drive to ensure the omnipresence and omnipotence of information, unobstructed by spatial and temporal barriers. In what follows, I will discuss both the economic impetus and the social implication of subordinating digital TV to the exigency of an "anytime, anywhere information network."

Anytime, Anywhere Information Network

It seems necessary to reaffirm the relevance of discussing digital TV through the "anytime, anywhere information network." In brief, the former is simultaneously a catalyst for and a microcosm of the latter. They are structurally isomorphic in their shared pursuit of universal compatibility among different electronic technologies. Moreover, both quest for a thorough penetration into, and expropriation of, virtually all social spaces and activities in the name of informationalization.

Creating a universal network that merges different info-technologies into a whole has been more than a two-decade old undertaking in Japan, as in other advanced industrial countries. Prior to the "anytime, anywhere information network," and its former variant "total digital networks,"[29] various projects had been launched to forge an

---

[29] This is a plan put forward in *Vision 21 for Info-communication* submitted by the Telecommunication Councils in 1997.

integrated digital information infrastructure. Its long history corresponds to and is anchored in the tenacious desire instigated by the new mode of capitalist production, which emerged around the 1970s. In 1982, for instance, Japan introduced an archetype information network called INS (Information Network System, the Japanese version of ISDN), which blends various telecommunication technologies with computers. According to Kitahara, former Executive Vice-president of NTT, INS is an "integrated information system which can economically and efficiently handle transmission, storage, conversion and processing of information through the marriage of telecommunications and computers. It is also expected to be the infrastructure of an advanced information society in the twenty-first century" (as cited in Tachikawa, 1983, p. 49). It enabled free exchanges of computerized data among various communication technologies, thereby suturing spatial and temporal disjunctures of its users. There can be little doubt that the INS was an immediate response, albeit not exclusive, to the then burgeoning information capitalism. Similarly, I suggest that Japan's present thrust towards the "anytime, anywhere information network" is a rejoinder to the radical economic changes structured around the Internet and other digital technologies. Sitting in the juncture between information technologies and capitalism, both the INS and the "anytime, anywhere information network" are socio-economic devices that systematically integrate quotidian communicative acts into electronically mediated economic spheres.

In contemporary informational capitalism, an instantaneous and ubiquitous flow of data through diverse space-shifting technologies is a top priority. However, the shift in the economic makeup and the concomitant advent of the ubiquitous information network present an assortment of unsettling issues, such as drastic innovations of socio-economic control over both public spaces and social activities. First, for example, it radicalizes the "space-binding" nature of communications media. A MPT document prepared by Study Group on Convergence and Developments in Telecommunications and Broadcasting (1998) reads, "existing constraints in distance and time will be totally removed and by

78

supplementing or substituting the activities of the actual society, new social and economic activities will be realized" (p. 3). In other words, the exploitation of information networks is aimed at overriding the divisions of human activities developed distinctively and conditionally in correspondence to the demarcations of space and media technologies. Consequently, the extant social boundaries of labor, play, education, and consumption are to either collapse or be overhauled within the hermetically sealed machinery of the "anytime, anywhere information network."

Its space-effacing function may also render Marshall McLuhan's much-cited maxim "the medium is the message" obsolete. It may do so, as a passage from "Vision for 21" reads, by "enabling" the users to "enjoy" a wide range of multimedia services "without being consciously aware of which medium they are using" (The Telecommunications Council, 1997, p. 8). As manifest here, this network is intended to assemble what were previously distinct actions attached to particular media (say, watching drama on TV, speaking on the phone, and chatting on the Internet) into new behavioral concoctions, such as banking via digital TV, checking weather on the street through cell phones, and watching movies via PCs. Hideki Maekawa, the Director of Tokyo Broadcasting System (TBS), sums up the importance of free information transfer among broadcasting, the Internet, and mobile telephone networks as creating a "chain system in which the 'value' of information accrues along with its mobility" (as cited in Manabe, 2001, p. 5). This remark stunningly resembles one of the fundamentals of financial capitalism: the value of capital derives from its constant motion. In addition, this reflects the conspicuous reification of information as meta-currency that both substitutes for financial values and displaces other social values. In this light, the ubiquitous information network exemplifies a socio-economic machinery that is engineered to transfigure the current mode of human activities into bits and bytes of advanced information capitalism. Seen from this perspective, the "anytime, anywhere information network" is a project deeply imbued with technological fetishism that displaces human practices associated with media—such as work, watching sports events, emailing, ordering goods, listening to music, or checking weather reports—into a totalized notion of information creation and consumption. In the end, it signifies a technological herding mechanism that drives human practices away from unwired, uninformational, and therefore un-value-added entities.

As a microcosm of the "anytime, anywhere information network," digitalization of TV is largely shaped by the impetus to transform TV into the primary means of production and the direct channel of consumption in the regime of informational capitalism. Even before the digitalization of TV was announced, the Telecommunication Council (1997) harbored the image of digital TVs as "shopping malls that are displayed in people's homes" (p. 69). In other words, digital TV is envisaged as an intersectional, hybridized medium where the audience buys and pays for goods and services, sends and receives bank statements, in addition to watching dramas and quiz shows. This vision is firmly grounded in the belief that "even in fields where markets do not exist, IT will create new markets and bring the buyer and seller closer together" (Telecommunication Council, 2000, p. 4). Japan's digitalization of TV, together with its network's larger project, is emblematic of the inexorable infiltration of informationalism into public and individual life, where virtually all human activities are recast by information technologies as value-producing activities. It is here that Tatsuro Hanada's (1999) reprimand on the policymakers' equation between the national audience and the national consumer (p. 17) should be heard with woe and awe.

Conclusion

I have so far discussed the ways in which digital TV is constructed by the Japanese policymakers and the business sector as a cardinal apparatus of informational capitalism with the euphemistic name of a "home-based information network." In so doing, I ran the risk of supposing too neat a correspondence between political-economic requirements of the hegemonic blocs in Japan and the advent and further unfolding of digital TV. It would be misleading, however, to assume that the aforementioned dominant discourses and practices would readily vanquish the deep-seated cultural practices and ideologies organized around conventional TV. Moreover, it falls outside my intention to have the reader believe that the hegemonic attempt to tap TV into Japan's information economy is a uniform, finalized move, sealed off from other possibilities of exploiting digital TV.

At this point, I should call attention to the emergence of critical discourses that defy the hegemonic framework of digital TV, even though they are not vigorous enough to offset the dominant voice. For example, Masao Iida (1999) censures the government for creating an imbalance between public services and commercial interests, while Hanada (1999) advocates the freeing of digital TV from corporate and state interventions. The president of NHK, Ebisawa (1998), has repeatedly vowed that NHK, as the sole public broadcaster in Japan, will remain dedicated to serving the public interest by exploiting digital TV. Indeed, NHK has launched innovative child education programs that permit new audience participation and multi-text learning through the combined use of TV with the Internet.

These are trace indications of uncertainty about whether the digital television will evolve according to the state-corporate power bloc dictates. David Noble (1984) once said, "close inspection of technology development reveals that technology leads a double life, one which conforms to the intentions of designers and interests of power and another which contradicts them—proceeding behind the backs of their architects to yield unintended consequences and unanticipated possibilities" (p. 325). The indeterminacy pertaining to the use of technologies holds true for digital TV in Japan, partly due to digital TV's intrinsic multi-functionality. Apart from the mechanical properties of digital TV, the uncertainty hinges on the collective social will and political initiatives in Japan. Whether digital TV would function as an enhanced visual delight, or integrative

81

information portal, or gateway to the Internet, or instrument for social education and intelligence is highly contingent upon the dynamics of heterogeneous social practices.

This is not to say that the future of the information technologies depends squarely on "what we call it" (Gunkel & Gunkel, 1997, p. 133). Rather I am suggesting that pinpointing the uses and meanings of new technologies is an inherently plural and unfinished practice. Although the interests of business sectors aligned with policy elites tend to prevail, the uses and meanings of new technologies remain up for grabs. Both the advent and the further unfolding of new technology is a social program comprised of a series of negotiations among different constituencies over various modes of use and practice. This "war of embedding" should be understood as a tentative and continuous procedure structured by the multilateral interplay among demand, production, acquisition, experiment, adaptation, and integration of technologies into the existing and changing socio-economic milieu. Hence, while being wary of the cursory romanticization of human agency, we should not haphazardly brush aside the clash of intentions and purposes around digital TV. Such a move would eliminate the possibility of re/dis-articulating digital TV with objectives other than the predatory motives of capitalists allied with state bureaucrats. "The new technology," argues Williams (1975), "is a product of a particular social system and will be developed as an apparently autonomous process of innovation only to the extent that we fail to identify and challenge its real agencies" (p. 135).

Chapter IV

HDTV, NHK, and The Spectacularization of

digital broadcasting

<u>Introduction</u>

On December 1, 2000, Japan unveiled digital Hi-Vision (Japan's own version of

High Definition Television) broadcast via digital Broadcast Satellite (BS henceforth).[30]

The synchronized launch of Hi-Vision and digital BS was calculated to boost both digital

broadcasting and HDTV sales. This strategic marriage was arranged for two reasons: (1)

digital BS is an optimal testing ground for Hi-Vision and (2) the visual appeal of Hi-

Vision would draw the nation's attention to digital BS.

The following chapter is a discussion of the meaning and place of HDTV as the

linchpin of the entire digital television enterprise. The first section of this essay is

devoted to unraveling how and why HDTV arose as a "knight in shining armor" that

rescued a hitherto-stalled digital BS rollout. The second part focuses on the way in which

the MPT "administered" the market dynamics of HDTV receivers so as to hasten the

growth of digital BS and digital terrestrial broadcasting. The third part traces the history

of HDTV development in Japan, bringing to light the juncture where the development of

HDTV technology meets with political discourses and economic maneuvers. The last

section addresses the paramount status of NHK as a national public institution that has

shaped the topography of Japan's and international HDTV cultures. I will argue that

NHK, a national public institution, represents an emergent form of the state proxy (not in

any conventional or derogatory sense), an interagent capable of bridging visual events

with political mobilizations, and administrative initiatives with corporate undertakings.

---

[30] Prior to digitalization, it was called DBS (Direct Broadcast Satellite).

Digital Broadcasting Satellite (BS) and Integrated Services Digital Broadcasting (ISDB)

Prior to December 2000, the commencement of digital BS was embroiled in some disputes. Broadcasters as well as policymakers at the MPT seemed at a loss as to how to weave digital BS into the intricate fabric of Japan's mediascape, especially in terms of content provision. Unlike digital CS (Communication Satellite) services, which provide a package of highly specialized programs on discrete channels, each BS channel airs an assortment of variegated programs running from sitcoms to news. This meant that Japan's digital BS channels were to function more or less like a replication, or an extension, of conventional terrestrial networks.

This redundant attribute of digital BS was acknowledged by some executives in commercial broadcasting before its inception in December 2000. Hideki Maekawa, Executive Division President of the Office of International Media Policy and Strategy at Tokyo Broadcasting System (TBS) admits, "It is not yet certain how different DBS[31] programming will be from today's general [terrestrial] programming. Successful DBS broadcasting calls for very strenuous efforts in programming" (Ohgami, 1998, p. 5). This uncertainty stemmed from the MPT's hasty decision to commence digital BS without having laid solid groundwork for a system that allows a steady provision of programs suited for the medium.

The MPT granted licenses to the five key commercial stations to kick-start multiple BS channels in a desperate effort to popularize digital television before the full-blown implementation of terrestrial digital services in 2003 (Tokyo, Osaka, and Nagoya area), 2006 (other major cities), and 2011 (the final nationwide switch to digital broadcasting). The five new channels that got off the ground—BS Nippon (Nippon TV

---

[31] DBS (Direct Broadcasting Satellite) is the ex-denomination for current digital BS. After the kick-off of digital BS in December 2000, however, the denomination ceased to be used.

network), BS Fuji (Fuji TV network), BS Asahi (TV Asahi network), BS Japan (TV Tokyo network), and BS-I (TBS network)—are solely committed to digital BS service, while NHK BS-1 & 2 and WOWOW soldier on with their digital and analog simulcast. Ill-equipped for the material best suited for the medium, commercial broadcasters adopted a tactic that massively recycles terrestrial programs. Takeo Mutai, Director General of the Media Planning and Corporate Development Department at Nippon Television Network Corporation (NTV), states, "We are thinking of using broadcasts produced for terrestrial transmission for DBS broadcasts with different screen effects— what we call 'multiple use of one software product'" (as cited in Ohgami, 1998, p. 5).

Many scholars and media critics expressed their concerns about commercial broadcasters' impetuous scramble to digital BS business. Koichi Kobayashi from the University of Tokyo contends that the BS market is already over-saturated by services provided by two NHK channels and that the mindset of commercial broadcasters— seeking extra returns from advertisers by duplicating existing terrestrial programs— would further chip away at the existing market. He reprimands commercial broadcasters, maintaining that the urgent task they should undertake is to improve basic services, "strengthening the public nature of broadcasting and the environment for universal access so as to benefit the millions of viewers" (as cited in Ohgami, 1998, p. 6). BS is, Kobayashi claims, "neither a basic medium like terrestrial broadcasting, nor does it offer special interest channels like CS broadcasting." Calling BS a hollow technological ornament at its best, Kobayashi asserts, "Its existence is undefined. It should be euthanized" (as cited in Ohgami, 1998, p. 6).

Kobayashi's qualms reverberate with reservations expressed by many others. Shunsuke Kitamura, Corporate Director & General Manger at TV Asahi's Satellite Broadcasting Development, points out that "DBS broadcasting can hardly become a medium to compete with existing terrestrial broadcasting" (as cited in Ohgami, 1998, p. 6). Underlying this skepticism is the apprehension about lackluster software production

85

that contrasts sharply with the channel outlets' sudden increase. Yoshiko Hashimoto, President of Documentary Japan, suggests that the development of new media does not guarantee the development and distribution of quality software, and the inadequate development of software will result in the deterioration of program quality and ultimately of audience interest in digital broadcasting. She concurs with Kobayashi that DBS is an dead weight. "Although new software and software for multiple uses must be developed," laments Hashimoto, "program producers now are too busy to think about such things" (as cited in Ohgami, 1998, p. 5).

As illustrated, the prospects for digital BS seemed vague and unstructured. It was at this juncture that the MPT and NHK's long-term plan to harness digital BS as a launching pad for the initiation of ISDB (Integrated Services Digital Broadcasting) came into play. ISDB is a comprehensive template developed by NHK for Japan's future broadcasting system. This template was to be implemented as a steppingstone for the completion of a nationwide digitalization of broadcasting. Under this ambitious plan, digital BS was redefined as a bridge for the inauguration of full-fledged ISDB. Hiroshi Shiina, Associate Director-General of NHK's Digital Broadcasting Development Bureau, states, "because NHK is aiming for ISDB (integrated services digital broadcasting), it is important to develop DBS broadcasting using the special properties of digital broadcasting" (as cited in Ohgami, 1998, p. 6). The president of NHK, Katsuji Ebisawa concurred, repeatedly vowed to prioritize the digital BS project before the nationwide digitalization of terrestrial broadcasts between 2006 and 2011.[32]

---

[32] Of course, this vision reflects NHK's own peculiar conditions. NHK holds its precedence over commercial counterparts in digital BS, because it has run DBS (Direct Broadcasting Satellite) since the late 1980s in the analog format and drawn over 12 million subscribers out of 36 million households nationwide. Other commercial broadcasters, however, could not but conform to the strategy laid out by NHK and endorsed by the MPT.

As such, a variety of advanced features integral to ISDB—such as datacasting, interactive functions, personal video recording (PVR) with a 30-GB hard drive built into the set-top box— have been piloted by digital BS. One of the most central services commenced through digital BS is called Mobile Terrestrial Reception (MTR), which enables the users of mobile phones and laptop computers to receive broadcast television signals. MTR is a program indispensable to the establishment of ISDB, because the MPT and the broadcast industry seek to promote digital television as a "home-based information portal" interlinked with ever-diversifying mobile information and communication technologies. A document published by NHK International Public Relations (2003) reads,

> Mobile reception is one of the major features of digital broadcasting. In the near future, digital terrestrial broadcasting will make it possible to send out programs to cellular phones, car navigation system, and other mobile devices using highly compressible technology (p. 1).

From the viewer's perspective, however, these amazing gifts of digital television could mean an overwhelming technological vertigo or a perplexing functional excess. Instead, the most tangible and inviting benefit digital television offers is audio-visual splendor. Hence, the audio-visual excellence of HDTV has come forward as the nucleus of publicity efforts, overshadowing all other innovative utilities presented by digital BS.

HDTV (High Definition Television) as
the Fulcrum of Digital BS

It is axiomatic that a gamut of magnificent functions that the digital broadcasting system provides—interactivity, personal video recording, datacasting, multi-channel services, Mobile Terrestrial Reception (MTR) and TV-based commerce (T-commerce), among others—cannot fully blossom without strong viewer/consumer demand. This was a lesson demonstrated by many other countries, such as England, America, Germany, France, and Sweden, who swung to digital broadcasting in the late 1990s but foundered due to the slow penetration of digital television sets (Ministry of Public Management, home Affairs, Post and Telecommunications, Japan, 2002, p. 25). The viewer/consumer was simply not enticed to purchase the high-priced gizmo for excessively futuristic functions with which they had not yet acquired intimacy. In the case of the U.S, the television networks, as well as cable and satellite distributors, remained hesitant to accelerate the costly production of digital programs because of the inadequate penetration of digital television receivers, which further curbed demand for the novel technology (Swann, 2000, pp .11-14). Japan learned that, in order to avoid the vicious cycle experienced by its European and American counterparts, a swift and wide spread of digital television sets at an early stage is key to the robust growth of digital broadcasting en bloc. It is in this context that the HDTV television set was summoned as the cognitive interface between TV users and digital broadcasting as a whole. As the gateway into digital broadcasting, HDTV sets induce the public's empirical/emotional connections with diverse aspects of digital broadcasting.

This explains the sudden rise of a ferocious publicity campaign on HDTV that has been waged by the MPT, NHK, and other para-state organizations since early 2000. A report made by the Advisory Committee on Pubic Interest Obligations of Digital Television Broadcasters (2000) accentuates the superb audio-visual qualities of HDTV. It reads,

> HDTV images have a 16-to-9 aspect ratio (the ratio of width to height), providing a wider image than the 4-to-3 ration that has characterized television since 1941. This higher resolution and different aspect ratio makes HDTV images substantially more vivid and engaging than the images produced by the existing television format, and that effect is enhanced by five discrete channels of CD-quality audio (p. 4).

The emphasis on the audio-visual clarity of HDTV has been most loudly trumpeted by NHK. Detailed descriptions of the technical specifications of Hi-Vision have been announced repeatedly in numerous press releases, one of which reads,

An HDTV image has five times more visual information than a conventional television picture, and 1,125 scanning lines in an HDTV system give pictures their detailed realism. Also, a wide-screen format with a 16:9 aspect ratio provides a powerful viewing experience. HDTV also provides CD-quality sound and 5.1 surround sound broadcasting, which is capable of reproducing sounds with a realistic feeling of depth that gives listeners a heightened sense of involvement by using six-channel speaker system. NHK has delivered spectacular images from the Space Shuttle, the ocean depths and Antarctica. Almost 90% of NHK's main channel (Digital General TV) is broadcast in HDTV (NHK International Public Relations, 2003, p. 1).

In his congratulatory address to NHK's Science and Technology Research Laboratories on the occasion of their 60th year commemoration ceremony, Ebisawa said,

NHK's Hi-Vision (HDTV) system, which is the core of digital BS broadcasting, has been adopted as an international standard for the HDTV format. Through this system, NHK's level of technical capability has become highly esteemed. Now, I see myself as a 'preacher of HDTV,' with the determination to diffuse the HDTV system globally. With confidence and pride, it is my hope to popularize and promote HDTV, one of the most significant inventions in the latter part of the 20th century. . . . I especially encouraged everyone to personally experience outstanding displays, such as the 4,000 scanning line ultrahigh-definition TV that can provide a sensation of reality higher than that of HDTV, and a flexible TV display that can be bent freely. (NHK Science and Technical Research Laboratories, 2002).

Then, why should the Advisory Committee on Pubic Interest Obligations of Digital Television Broadcasters ardently acclaim the visual wonder of HDTV, other than the aforementioned reason? What made NHK declare that "The core of the digital terrestrial broadcasting, as well as satellite digital broadcasting [digital BS] . . . is Hi-Vision (HDTV)" (NHK International Public Relations, 2003, p. 1), when it has consistently promoted digital television as a "total information gateway" (NHK International Public Relations, 2003, p. 1)? In other words, why has NHK, an unwavering champion of the informational purpose of television over the amusement value, become an ambassador of HDTV spectacle? What are the stakes involved in lauding HDTV sets, domestically and internationally, and culturally and economically?

The veneration of HDTV (or Hi-Vision in Japan's context) as the single source of spectacular televisual experience and as the epitome of digital television is a necessary mythology for the joint endeavor of the broadcasting industry, HDTV manufacturers, and the MPT to move digital broadcasting in Japan forward. HDTV is, by definition, a specific type of television receiver that provides higher resolution than the NTSC standard by way of compressing, storing, and delivering a greater amount of image and sound information than previous transmission systems. There are a number of competing HDTV standards, among which Japan's Hi-Vision is a prime archetype. Unlike common mis/conceptions, not all HD televisions are digital. Nor does the digital HDTV necessarily guarantee a better audio-visual fidelity than the analog HDTV. In fact, NHK's Hi-Vision had adopted an analog format until 1996 and yet could offer an equally astonishing audio and video resolution as a digital counterpart. Additionally, HDTV is not the sole foundation of the audio-visual grandeur of the digital television system.[33] Digital BS alone could enhance audio-visual quality to a considerable degree,[34] since it involves no mediation of transmission towers or ground cables, thereby decreasing the chance for the deterioration of broadcast signals.

Accurate or erroneous, the adoration of HDTV as the end-all and be-all of visual excellence would place the entire edifice of digital broadcasting in Japan on a pedestal. More specifically, it is expected to have a dramatic impact on the viewer's awareness of digital broadcasting, and consequently, adoption of more advanced, multifunctional digital TV sets. As the audience is exposed to the crisp, vivid images of HDTV (Hi-

---

[33] Technically, not all HDTV can assist or accommodate diverse functions (e.g., interactivity) that the digital broadcasting service would normally offer. Nor can all digital television receivers, likewise, convey as good a picture quality as a HDTV would proffer. As the digitalization of broadcasting became an irreversible national policy of Japan in 1996, electronics companies tended to blend the two technical specifications, manufacturing only digital HDTV sets. And as the digital HDTV becoming a norm in the industry, digital television and HDTV are often used interchangeably, regardless of their technical and conceptual differences.

[34] The heightened audio-visual quality of digital BS was made possible by two geo-synchronous broadcast satellites (BSAT-2a and BSAT-2b) managed by Japan's Broadcasting Satellite System Corporation (B-SAT).

Vision), they will see a compelling reason to switch to digital broadcasting. A wide and speedy diffusion of digital HDTV is a prerequisite for the energetic growth of digital broadcasting and a barometer to measure such growth. Second, digital HDTV sets are considered an axial item for the reinvigoration of Japan's economy led by the three engines: the AV equipment industry, electronics manufacturing, and online business. With over forty some years of rigorous R&D endeavors, Japan claims a lion's share of the global HDTV and associated A-V equipment market. HDTV is no longer a plain "household appliance" but a core IT technology, equipped with cutting-edge apparatuses, ranging from memory chips, mobile transmitters, and LCD, PLP monitors, to various paraphernalia that enable interoperability with other digital devices. Third, Japan's Hi-Vision technology forms the backbone of the nation's lead in the global digital TV program race. Japan's expertise in the production of HDTV programs is believed to be second to none in the world, which shores up its effort to have Hi-Vision adopted as the global HDTV standard. Because of the unique and central place that HDTV occupies in both broadcasting business and IT equipment industries, the MPT, para-state organizations, and NHK have given enormous stimuli to HDTV sales.

The MPT for HDTV Sales

The rapid dissemination of digital HDTV in Japan can be ascribed in part to the familiarity of Japanese viewers with analog HDTV. Prior to the introduction of digital HDTV, more than a million households owned analog HDTV, which became available in 1992 with a format named MUSE (Multiple Sub-Nyquist Sampling Encoding).[35] Along

---

[35] MUSE (Multiple Sub-Nyquist Sampling Encoding) was first developed by NHK Science and Technology Research Laboratories and is standardized for the Hi-Vision transmission system via broadcast satellite (BS) in Japan. MUSE adopts motion adaptive processing, which is an important technology in a TV signal processing. It is used in such devices as noise reducers and interlaces to progressive scan converters. It is required to detect motion and moving areas for motion adaptive processing by frame differential signals, etc.

with the public's acquaintance with HDTV, the publicity effort choreographed by the MPT hand in hand with major broadcasting and the electronics industries had substantial impacts on the expeditious proliferation of digital HDTV. To get digital broadcasting off to a better start than it did in the U.K and the U.S., the MPT has relentlessly executed creative and often unusual publicity campaigns.

For instance, the MPT coordinated the public exhibition of HDTV in post offices and other civic spaces. This public display of HDTV was carried out in accord with the private sector, which implemented their own exhibition plans of digital HDTV sets at numerous home electronics showrooms and 10,000 retail stores nation-wide. The public exposure to digital HDTV (Hi-Vision) started with the Sydney Olympics in 2000 and the Okinawa G-8 Summit in the same year. The Okinawa G-8 Summit, in particular, can be characterized as a marketing circus for Japan's digital Hi-Vision. The official summit schedule included a demonstration of Japan's digital Hi-Vision, wherein former U.S. President Bill Clinton and other leaders of the G-8 attended a detailed presentation of Hi-Vision by NHK's president Ebisawa, who calls himself a "missionary of Hi-Vision." Concurrently, the specifics of the G-8 Summit were aired in the digital Hi-Vision format to the general public on a trial basis. The Japanese audience was prodded to pay attention to the crystal-clear image of Hi-Vision—and to the captivating body of the HDTV set itself—as displayed in shopping malls, post offices, railway stations, street corners, etc.

The state involvement was most pronounced in the course of HDTV sales promotion. The marketing effort rallied around the ambitious goal of selling "10 million sets within the first 1,000 Days." This drive was steered by the Association for Promotion of Satellite Broadcasting (BPSA), an ad-hoc committee convened by the MPT and composed of electronics manufacturers, NHK, and commercial broadcasters (Asahi Newspaper, 5/10, 2001). The broadcasters and electronics manufacturers have showed great confidence in achieving the goal. According to the Association for Promotion of Satellite Broadcasting, roughly 203,000 digital HDTV receivers and 402,000 tuners had

92

appeared on the market within four months of the campaign's inception in December 2000. As of April 2001, a total of 1.8 million households were viewing digital HDTV, including approximately 1.2 million households receiving digital HDTV through cable services. A survey conducted by the NHK Broadcasting Culture Research Institute (2001) found more than 78 percent of viewers who had bought digital receivers were satisfied with their purchase, and 90 percent of viewers were pleased with the picture quality of the digital HDTV broadcasts via digital BS (p. 1). The Electronic Industries Association of Japan estimates that demand for digital HDTV sets will grow to 5.1 million units in fiscal 2005.

The level of state intervention escalated in the following years, since the propitious diffusion of digital television receivers was integral to the implementation of terrestrial digital broadcasting services slated for December 2003 in Tokyo, Nagoya, and Osaka metropolitan areas. Hence, the MPT nudged electronics manufacturers to keep the price for HDTV receivers under 500,000 yen (US $5,000) and to produce set-top boxes that convert analog signal into digital format for an appealing 20,000 yen (US $200). The electronics manufacturers complied with the MPT's arbitration on the price ceiling, because the imperative of popularizing digital HDTV was deemed beneficial to all the parties involved, i.e., the broadcasting industry, electronics manufacturing, viewers/customer, and above all, the national economy.

The MPT's intervention into the HDTV receiver market in the form of promotion and price adjustment can be evaluated from many different angles. One of the key premises validating its participation in market affairs is the belief, as we have seen in chapter 2, that the extensive penetration of digital HDTV is equivalent to the establishment of an essential and rather peculiar type of national information infrastructure. Strictly speaking, digital HDTV sets won't fall into the conventional definition of infrastructure, construed as the physical facilities that move people, goods, commodities, water, waste, energy, and information. While highways are a form of infrastructure, automobiles are not; broadband cables are a type of information infrastructure, but computers are not. By the same token, the digital HDTV television set per se is not a "public utility," which means that the universal diffusion/installation of digital HDTV television sets is ultimately a matter of the user/consumer's choice, where the public authority has little power to meddle.

Nevertheless, individually purchased and operated information terminals—such as telephones, television sets, and computers—are increasingly accepted as a vital component of what might be called a "greater information infrastructure sphere." These terminals cease to be mere reception devices of already processed informational materials but operate as networked intermediate outposts that transmit, create, refine, and modify informational ingredients. As a matter of fact, Japan's new economy stimulus packages announced in the early 1990s specifically classified supercomputers in universities, personal computers in schools, and optical fiber networks to the home as a "New Social Infrastructure" ("Building Japan's Information," 1993). In the context of Japan, therefore, it would not be invalid to regard digital television sets as a "New Social Infrastructure" or a quasi-infrastructure at least, given the fact that they are engineered to be a "home-based information hub." This unusual nature of HDTV in Japan's distinct domestic conditions facilitated, and validated, the active involvement of para-state bodies and non-business organizations for the nationwide penetration of HDTV.

However, the use of digital BS in tandem with HDTV is causing a sharp division among the national audience. As of October 2002, the total number of households receiving digital Hi-Vision programs represents less than 5 percent (at the most liberal estimation) of the TV audience in Japan. Moreover, this figure does not reflect the number of households owning digital HDTV sets. To access the digital BS channels, one should purchase either a digital TV set with a built-in tuner or a set-top box that converts analog signals into digital. Only 882, 000 units of digital TV with built-in tuners and 730,000 units of set-top boxes are sold as of October 2002 (Ministry of Public

Management, Home Affairs, Post and Telecommunications, Japan, 2002, p. 6). This means that many households receive an unauthorized transmission of BS programs via their cable providers at no extra cost, to avoid the heavy expenditure of purchasing digital equipment and subscription fees.[36] This illegal reception of digital BS program is indicative of growing gaps among national televisual denizens.

Because of the public reluctance to incur additional spending on the yet-to-be-proven worth of digital BS, five commercial broadcasters are currently offering digital BS programs free of charge but poised to introduce various fee-charging systems at any time. NHK, on the other hand, levies 945 yen (roughly US $ 9) per month for those subscribing to BS (both analog and digital) television, in addition to 1,345 yen (roughly US $12) for terrestrial services. Having practically monopolized the market since the outset of analog BS in 1987, NHK continues to enjoy a relatively huge number of subscribers (roughly 12 million, analog and digital BS combined). However, many of them prefer not to bother with expansive digital reception equipment and therefore remain subscribed to only analog BS services. This schism, determined by both the subscription-based access-ability to digital BS program and the ownership of digital HDTV sets, contradicts the MPT and NHK's long-standing commitment to universal broadcasting.

This contradiction is derived from the manifold functions ascribed to HDTV within the overall strategy of digital broadcasting in Japan: HDTV as a visual delight, corridor to advanced digital technology, expedient for digital terrestrial broadcasting, and leverage for economic recovery. The multifarious attribute of HDTV is embedded in the decades-long drama of Hi-Vision development in Japan. The following section recounts

---

[36] Although the number of households subscribing to NHK's BS-1 and BS-2 (broadcast both in analog and digital formats) reaches 12 million, only a small portion of the subscribers equipped with set-top boxes or TV with built-in tuners can access digital BS.

how Japan's endeavor to promote Hi-Vision as *the* global HDTV standard has been ineluctably coupled with and fashioned by larger political discourses and economic aspirations of the time.

<u>Techno-Nationalism and Hi-Vision in the 1980s</u>

The effort to promote Hi-Vision as the global HDTV standard dates back to 1964, when engineers of NHK began to envision the "most desirable media for humans to watch": a future-oriented, large-screen, high definition television set (NHK, 2002, p. 16). The research gained momentum during the early 1970s, when the MITI (Ministry of International Trades and Industries) and the MPT stepped into the scene with extravagant research subsidies. Before long, Japan's electronics heavyweights like Matsushita and Sony joined the project, launching a series of joint R&D programs for HDTV. The united front formed by the MPT, NHK, and the electronics industry bore fruit in 1983 with the birth of the MUSE (Multiple Sub-Nyquist Encoding) system and other related equipment by technicians in NHK's Science and Technical Research Laboratories. Using primarily analog technology to save on data processing time, MUSE was adopted as a band compression method for NHK's own analog high definition television introduced in 1985, i.e., Hi-Vision.

Japan's Hi-Vision was clearly seen as a potential threat to the U.S. electronics business, when it was presented to international broadcasters convened at the U.S. NAB (National Association of Broadcasters) conference in 1984. One of the leaders of the U.S electronic industries expressed his shock by stating that Japan's HDTV "would engulf the American computer, microchip, appliance, telephone, film and industrial-equipment technologies and markets" (as cited in Gilder, 1992, p. 13). This techno-scare, which was also felt by the CEOs of Intel, Zenith, and IMB, wasn't the first to be expressed publicly. Earlier, Sony and Matsushita, together with NHK, bombarded international technological delegates with their state-of-the-art media technologies at an annual gathering of the

96

Society of Motion Picture and Television Engineers (SMPTE) held in San Francisco in 1981. Brandishing Japan's cutting-edge media equipment became a frequent event in the years that followed. During Tsukuba Expo'85, the Japanese government proudly installed a huge pavilion, where the futuristic Hi-Vision and a multi-purpose video system using HDTV technology were exhibited to the enchanted gazes of international business circles (Kobayashi, 1985, pp. 14-15).

But the shockwaves created among US and international media dignitaries weren't merely about the sleek three-by-five-foot flat panel screen hung on the wall and the lifelike images it presented. Rather, it was about the seemingly infinite extent to which Hi-Vision could be applied and modified, and the concomitant industrial and economic repercussions of that adaptability. As George Gilder (1992) reports it,

> The new television, full of microchips and other advanced electronics, would function like a state-of-the-art video computer that would not only present pictures but reshape and manipulate them as well. With appropriate peripherals, such as color printers and editing systems, HDTV would transform an array of related industries, from still photography and movies to medical diagnostics and missile defense (p. 12).

As widely known, Japan–U.S. relations during the 1980s were brimming with bitter trade disputes. Until the 1970s, the trade feud between the two countries pivoted around "purely" economic matters: e.g. the surging exports of Japanese products such as color televisions, automobiles, and steel to the U.S. But the intensity of friction escalated into a qualitatively different stage during the 1980s. The U.S. government and mass media discharged a barrage of denunciations toward Japan's allegedly "foxy" business practices, barring foreign—and especially U.S.—products from entering Japan's industrial and consumer markets (Suzuki, 1999). The economic discord began to gather an increasingly political charge, when Japan's then Prime Minister Nakasone Yasujiro in 1986 fired an inflammatory remark against the U.S., stating that America's technological capacity could not approach that of Japan, because the average American intellect is lower than that of the Japanese.

America's paranoia with the formidable growth of Japan's power in technology and economy was further fueled by comments made by Japanese politicians like Shintaro Ishihara, who declaimed a new Japan that could rise up against U.S. hegemony. Ishihara's infamous pamphlet, *The Japan that Can Say No*, was a sensational wake-up call to politicians, academicians, and civilians in the U.S. and Europe. He jeers at the incompetence of the US science, technology, and educational systems throughout his manifesto-like prose, wherein the US's reliance on Japan is highlighted in a repugnantly sardonic manner.

> American imports from Japan are mostly products which require a high tech capacity to produce. Many of these products fall into the area of military procurement, but it is true that even the private sector is buying Japanese products which are technologically indispensable. Even some of the inexpensive home electrical appliances may be obtained from Japanese manufacturers within a short time frame if they require high technological skills in the production process. America has left the production responsibility with Japan, resulting in a heavy dependency upon Japan. American politicians only talk about the results of this situation, blaming Japan for the trade deficit to get votes. Yet it seems that these same politicians don't even know specifically what it is that America buys from Japan. If they took the time and the effort to seriously investigate the matter, they could not condemn Japan so out of hand (Ishihara, 1991, p. 84).

Although many of Ishihara's claims were overblown, the nightmarish permeation of Japan's media equipment and other high-tech products was indeed perceived as foreshadowing America's declining economic and cultural sovereignty. The general public had to undergo an overwhelming ego-shock, which was most palpably sensed among industrial experts in media and telecommunications. Gilder (1992) states,

> U.S. telephone and computer executives, who speak of the year 2010 or even 2030 as the target for completing an American network, are kidding themselves. If the U.S. does not act sooner, the network will be built by Japan and made of Japanese fiber and optoelectronics and possibly Japanese computers. Much of the system used by the U.S. might even be located in Japan. As Jack McDonald, executive vice-president of Contel Corporation, has warned, a Japanese edge in switching efficiency might well mean that calls between San Francisco and Los Angeles will be switched in Tokyo (p. 108).

98

Many American compatriots would also soon warn that the political denouement of a group of strategic technologies, from HDTV to IC chips, might give Japan a type of supremacy akin to what Britain had two centuries ago with steam and steel. One journalist pithily caricatures the American anguish over its media/communication environment being besieged by the Japanese media-electronics cabal:

> Now Sony can control the whole chain. Its broadcast equipment division manufactures the studio cameras and the film on which movies are produced; in Columbia it owns a studio that makes them and crucially, determines the formats on which they are distributed. That means it can have movies made on high definition televisions, and videoed with Sony VCRs. It can re-shoot Columbia's 2700-film library on 8 mm film, for playing on its video Walkmans (as cited in Morley and Robbins, 1995, p. 150).

Herbert Schiller also made nervously sinuous comments on what then was described as the "reverse-cultural imperialism" of Japan.

> The buyout of MCA/Universal—one of the Hollywood 'majors'— by the Japanese super electronics corporation Matsushita has already had one beneficial effect. It has caused the American news media, along with the government foreign-policy makers, to recognize a problem whose existence they have steadfastly denied for the past twenty-five years—cultural domination by an external power (as cited in Morley & Robbins, 1995, p. 150).

The U.S. Strikes Back: Digital Shock in the 1990s

As manifest, Japan was many steps ahead of the US and other countries in the race for HDTV broadcasting during the 1980s and well into the early 1990s. Long before the introduction of digital broadcasting, Japanese audiences had enjoyed higher resolution pictures. Analog Hi-Vision broadcasting was implemented in 1991 on an experimental basis using broadcast satellite BS-3, which was launched in 1990. As Hi-vision broadcasting became available for the general audience in 1995, more than 500,000 sets of analog HDTV were sold prior to December 1997. By contrast, the U.S. Federal Communication Commissions (FCC) issued its first notice of inquiry on advanced television service in as late as July 1987, and the first congressional hearing on HDTV was held in October 1987. Until June 1990, Japan's Hi-Vision standard—based

99

on an analog system—was the front-runner among 23 different technical concepts under consideration, its unrivalled image/sound quality comparable to that of 35mm film.

A major turning point occurred when an American company, General Instruments, demonstrated the feasibility of a digital television signal. The FCC finally settled with the digital format, citing the disadvantages of Japan's analog Hi-Vision based on the MUSE system: sensitivity to atmospheric interference, poor compressibility and difficulty of manipulation and storage. According to Tsutomu Kanayama, however, the FCC's adoption digital TV standard wasn't simply drawn from the identification of the technical drawbacks of Japan's analog HDTV system. It was rather, argues Kanayama (1999), based on "consideration of the strong U.S. economic base in the computer industry" and "prediction that a digital standard will facilitate the already immanent convergence between personal computers and television" (p. 1). The FCC's decision carried a considerable international ramification. To make the matter worse, world-class satellite broadcasters favored America's digital solution, for they sought compatibility between television and computers and additional channel capacity (Johnson, 1982).

The consequences of this decision were devastating to Japan. Not only did it make "the undisputed leader in developing a future television standard [into] the follower" (Kanayama, 1999, p. 11), but also struck a fatal blow to Japan's domestic broadcasting and other allied manufacturing industries. As mentioned earlier, the stake that Japan had held in the effort to promote analog Hi-Vision as a world standard of HDTV was extremely high. In association with domestic electronics companies and NHK, the MPT has long jockeyed to dominate the global TV manufacturing industry by researching next-generation TV. For that purpose, Japan poured tremendous energy and money over three decades into the development of the first and foremost analog HDTV in the world. Since the early 1980s onward, Japan's terrestrial TV broadcasters, and electronics and manufacturing industries as a group, had marched forward to the drumbeat of a unified analog-based standard. A host of investment projects and experimentations by electronics

100

manufacturing, direct broadcast satellites, cable, and telecommunications had to be abandoned, when the MPT eventually proclaimed in 1997 that Japan would give in to the digital standard.

Because of the high stakes, Japan's broadcasters at first refused to surrender to the digital imperative. Yet, on balance, Japan's electronics industry showed relative flexibility. Electronics makers such as Matsushita and Mitsubishi hailed the decision and attempted to persuade the Japanese National Association of Broadcasters (J-NAB) into embracing the digital karma. In the wake of strong protests against the abrupt conversion to digital, the MPT conceded to underwrite the digitalization of Japan's terrestrial broadcasting. The J-NAB continued to hector the MPT for additional financial support to milk it of more than an initial $ 780 million earmarked to broadcasters for the acquisition of digital equipment and other facilities. The negotiation between the government and the broadcasters made for strident discord. But the fact that the government assumed the indemnity for the investment of the private sector, and remunerated the commercial broadcasters for the future entrepreneurial endeavors, testifies to their continuing long-term partnership in plotting the future trajectory of television industry. Soon, they reunited under the solemn mission of catching up with the U.S. and European competitors in the second round of the HDTV battle that began in the late 1990s.

NHK was quick to adapt to the new digital environment. It has reconfigured Hi-Vision protocols to suit the digital broadcasting system and allocated approximately 18.1 billion yen (US $180 million)[37] annually to Hi-Vision operations since 1998. As the major opinion-forming institution and only national public broadcaster, NHK undertakes a variety of publicity events to stimulate public interest in digital broadcasting in general, and HDTV in particular. NHK Culture and Research Institute, a research hub of NHK,

---

[37] This amounts to nearly 3.1 percent of NHK's annual budget.

has proven itself to be an outstanding resource in the Hi-Vision promotion drive. Virtually all volumes of the institute's quarterly newsletter detailed up-to-date news and information crucial to the progress of Hi-Vision. A number of editions have repeatedly sounded determined messages that NHK will make a full commitment to digital Hi-Vision, since it is "at the heart of the broadcasts of the future" and will "play a leading role in the digital age" (Ebisawa, as cited in Nagaya, 1998, p. 1). The institute has faithfully performed the task of evangelizing the value of Hi-Vision and organized a number of symposiums, seminars, and events.

As a result of the dogged struggle of MPT, NHK, and electronics manufacturers, Japan's Hi-Vision resurfaced to be a chief digital HDTV paradigm and was adopted as the international studio standard by the International Telecommunication Union (ITU) in 2000. Moreover, it was shown off on other notable occasions including the United Nations Millennium Summit, the U.S. presidential election in 2000, and the U.S. space shuttle, from which an astonishingly crystal image of the planet was taken and released to the world.

Japan's astounding rebound in such a short period of time is buttressed by the strong domestic supply and demand in HDTV receivers and programs. According to the Japan Electronics and Information Technology Association (JEITA), the domestic shipment of digital television receivers continues to rise. As of March 2003, 3.5 million households nationwide are estimated to own digital HDTV sets (Magnetic Media Information Services, 2003). For the month of December 2003, when digital terrestrial broadcasting commenced, 435,000 digital television sets were sold. Additionally, Cable TV companies have expanded their relay and retransmission services, offering digital HDTV programs to both those not subscribing to digital BS and to areas where digital terrestrial television broadcasting (DTTB) is not available.

Commensurate with the brisk sales of digital television receivers and HDTV sets is the augmentation of HDTV programs. In contrast to U.S., where digital BS providers offer only two channels of high definition television programming (supplied by cable networks), Japan's HDTV features a 24 hour, seven-channel service consisting of NHK, five major Tokyo-based commercial broadcasters, and WOWOW (Japan's first commercial fee-charging broadcaster). The range of programs is also extensive, covering news, documentaries, sports, drama, music and entertainment shows. The subscription-based digital HDTV service commenced with digital BS in December 2000 has gained a greater momentum with the inauguration of digital terrestrial services from December 2003. In digital terrestrial broadcasting, nearly 50 percent of prime time programs on the chief commercial broadcasters (Asahi, Nippon, TBS, Fuji, and TV Tokyo) are aired in the HDTV format. Also, over 90 percent of all programs provided by NHK digital terrestrial channels in the Tokyo, Nagoya, and Osaka metropolitan areas are available in the HDTV format (Maruyama & Takahashi, 2004, p. 20).

Digital HDTV penetration is reaching new heights across North America, Europe, East Asia, and Australia, while countries with massive potential growth like China and India are next in line. Some Japanese HDTV makers like Matsushita have already landed on China's digital broadcasting market, which boasts over 100 million cable TV subscribers, launching HDTV cable broadcasts on a trial basis in preparation for selling compatible digital TVs. Despite South Korea's formidable challenge, Japan maintains its lead in the global race for HDTV, as Japanese electronics—Sony, Hitachi, Sanyo/Epson, Toshiba, and Pioneer—continues to dominate the digital HDTV market.

Japan's unparalleled primacy in digital HDTV cannot be recounted without the presence of NHK. Throughout the history of Japan's HDTV development, NHK has stayed at the hub of all epic developments, ranging from R&D, public exhibition, and sales campaign to international marketing, program innovation, and product engineering. NHK's omnificence should be illuminated in light of the plastic and composite nature of Japan's national-public institutions as a self-governing state proxy. The following section examines the role played by NHK in advancing Japan's digital HDTV enterprise since 2000, inquiring into the status and identity of national-public institutions in Japan.

<u>NHK and the Spectacularization of HDTV</u>

The most notable achievement that NHK has made is the development of arguably the world's best HDTV format, Hi-Vision. Beyond the invention of Hi-Vision, NHK has tirelessly brought its leadership to bear on the formation of HDTV culture, both domestically and internationally. Its contribution can be grouped into three major areas: technological, industrial, and organizational. These three fields interact and intersect with one another, for they are guided by and committed to one overarching charge: the spectacularization of Hi-Vision, digital broadcasting, and eventually Japan's technological preeminence.

Over the last few years, NHK has generated a wide array of programs that make the best use of the Hi-Vision's outstanding qualities. Hence, NHK and other digital BS providers put out the catch phrase of "*Migotaesugi*" (television that is exceptionally worth viewing), to play up the enhanced ocular and acoustic sensations that the combined use of High-Definition TV and DBS could offer. NHK went as far as to say "The easy-to-use functions, together with the high-quality, wide screen images that turns TV into a home theater, will bring the family in front of the TV" (NHK International Public Relations, 2001). The sheer emphasis on spectacle was, of course, out of tune with NHK's commitment to remaking television as the hub of information networks. Nevertheless, it was conceived as a charming doorway through which the public can be ushered into the cosmos of digital terrestrial broadcasting with a minimum cultural and technological allergy.

In December 2000, it presented special programs such as *Digital Dream Live* (live music concerts with nationally celebrated guest performers) and *NHK Cup Figure Skating* to hype the launch of digital broadcasting. Between December 2000 and

104

December 2001 alone, NHK aired over 190 special programs of the two-hour prime time "HDTV Special" that took full advantage of the excellent sound and image quality of Japan's Hi-Vision. The parade of sight and sound spectacles to satiate the audience's quest for visual splendor has continued.

Along with six other digital BS providers, NHK held a promotion, showcasing 100 special HDTV and other digital programs from November through December 2003. The endeavor was meticulously planned to jibe with the December 2003 launch of digital terrestrial broadcasting in Tokyo, Nagoya, and Osaka. The programs during the month-long campaign were shown in the High-Definition mode (Hi-Vision), including a MLB game live-cast from New York Yankee Stadium. They also offered interactive quiz programs and song contests, where viewers could participate as contestants and jurors from their own living rooms. Not only did the promotion trumpet at full volume the audio-visual marvels of HDTV, but also placed enormous emphasis on the ingenuity of digital BS and digital broadcasting in the hope that the public's fascination with them would smooth the passage to the onset of digital terrestrial broadcasting. In other words, the campaigns put together "spectacular" programs to "spectacularize" digital broadcasting and HDTV itself. The strategy of appealing to the audience with the audio-visual excellence turned out successfully. Programs such as sports, documentaries, movies, and epic dramas enjoyed a demand windfall and the number of households subscribing to digital BS neared 1.5 million as of March 2001. The number grew rapidly and reached 1.9 million in August 2001 and 5 million by the end of 2003 (Nihei & Suzuki, 2004, p. 11).

The extravagant array of Hi-Vision programs weren't limited to domestic broadcasting. NHK has also successfully placed their Hi-Vision programs on the international broadcasting arena. NHK conducted the first global broadcasting of a high definition live broadcast by covering the U.S. Republican and Democrat conventions during the summer of 2000 and offered its digital feat to many foreign broadcasters at no cost. During the Salt Lake Winter Olympics in 2002, NHK offered a total of 260 hours of coverage in HDTV format. NHK teamed up with International Sports Broadcasting (ISB), the host broadcasting organization of the Olympics, to produce HDTV programs of ceremonies, speed skating, figure skating, and ice hockey. Since 2001 NHK has produced a host of programs including *Fosse*, *Kurosawa*, *Space Millennium*, *Over Alaska*, and various classical music performance programs in HDTV format together with PBS of the U.S. and the BBC of the U.K. In December 2003, NHK captured the first total eclipse over Antarctica, live-casting it in a Hi-Vision form from three locations in Japan, Canada, and the U.S. The program later was sold to China's CCTV and Korea's KBC.

The rage of spectacle wasn't contained within HDTV screens. Numerous public exhibits organized by NHK fueled the spectacularization of Japan's digital industry as a whole. From October to December 2001, NHK organized a nationwide campaign to demonstrate the excellence of Hi-Vision at over 8,000 sites around the country. It is reported that approximately 20 million people have experienced the "unsurpassed superiority" of Japan's HDTV during the exhibit jointly organized with manufacturers and electrical appliance outlets. During this exhibit NHK unabashedly vocalized that it hosted HDTV exhibition campaigns to "boost sales of HDTV receivers" (NHK International Public Relations, 2001b). It continues to communicate a patently industrial/commercial perspective in evaluating the growth of digital broadcasting: "The launch of Japan's digital terrestrial TV broadcasting in December 2003 boosted the popularity of digital TV sets which have grown to become a flagship that leads the consumer-electronics industry" (NHK International Public Relations, 2004).

NHK has independently hosted an annual BS Digital Fair at its Shibuya headquarters in since 2001. In 2001, the fair attracted 130,000 visitors in a four day exhibition of Hi-Vision and data broadcasting. The 2002 Fair was unambiguously evocative of a HDTV business exposition.[38] The event showcased a variety of plasma display panels (PDPs), Japan's chief export item in the IT industry. The PDPs were installed in model living rooms and Japanese *tatami* rooms, offering visitors a virtual HDTV home theater experience as they watched the NHK Hi-Vision special programs unfolding in front of their eyes. The event, which attracted more than 100,000 visitors in four days, not including the audiences who watched the show on TV, displayed an array of state-of-the-art A-V products developed by Japan's key electronics makers.

This public display of HDTV and digital broadcasting apparatuses is mainly organized by NHK's Science and Technology Research Laboratories (STRL), Japan's most fertile technological breeding ground that nurtures Japan's broadcasting equipment, A-V electronics, and applied optical equipment. During the 56th annual open house of the NHK STRL in May 2002, it introduced to the general public the advanced Integrated Services Digital Broadcasting (ISDB), the template for Japan's television broadcasting system to be set in motion by 2011. It also displayed an overwhelming 320 inch Ultrahigh-Definition Wide-screen with 4,000 scanning lines, which offers a four times better resolution than regular Hi-Vision. It plans to present a 600-inch giant screen Super Hi-Vision that presents 16 times more visual information than current HDTV (with 4000 scanning lines) at the 2005 World Exposition to be held in Aichi, Japan.

The Lab works closely with industrial organizations and other businesses. In 2002, it announced a new PAL-HDTV standard converter, making it possible for Japanese audiences to receive European HDTV programs encoded in the PAL system. Numerous devices of digital broadcasting, including HDTV mobile reception technology and a digital HDTV wireless camera system, have been invented. With the cooperation of NHK STRL Fuji Photo Optical Co., developed the "Precision Focus Assistance System

---

[38] The author toured the 2001 fair but watched the 2002 fair only on TV.

HDTV Zoom Lens Device," which can automatically modulate the focus in capturing moving objects. Recently it developed, in collaboration with Analog Devices Inc., the real-time encoder/decoder PC board for Hi-Vision applications, using the JPEG2000 standard. It could transfer picture images from the Internet, digital cameras, mobile terminals, as well as SDTV (Standard Television) and HDTV.

Not only has the Lab cooperated with the industry but also spearheaded direct marketing of its own brainchild, the Hi-Vision system, to foreign broadcast corporations. For example, the NHK STRL has published numerous Hi-Vision manuals and guidebooks in English and other languages, proselytizing foreign broadcasters into the adoption of its ultra-modern equipment. A book titled *High Definition Television: Hi-Vision Technology*, for instance, tactfully details how Hi-Vision satisfies the need of the broadcasting industry in America.

> [Hi-Vision's] new capacity known as multicasting or multiplexing is expected to allow broadcasters to compete with other multichannel media such as cable and direct broadcast satellite systems. Another capability is to provide new kinds of video and data services, such as subscription television programming, computer software distribution, data transmissions, teletext, interactive services, and audio signals, among others, referred to as 'ancillary and supplementary services' under the Telecommunication Act of 1996. These services include such potentially revenue-producing innovations as providing stock prices and sports scores, classified advertising, paging services, 'zoned' news reports, advertising targeted to specific televisions sets, 'time-shifted' video programming, and closed-circuit television services (NHK STRL, 1993, p. xii).

Conclusion

Odd it may sound, Japan's development of HDTV is infused with what might be called "techno-nationalism" that has intensified throughout its competition with the U.S. for economic and technological supremacy. The four-decade long endeavor of promoting Hi-Vision (both in analog and digital forms) as the global HDTV standard has been at once a medium and a theater of the techno-economic contest between the two techno-egos. Hi-Vision is, after all, as much a political game as a business matter; as culturally intense a project as a technology-intensive battle.

No other organization in Japan could have shouldered the complex and taxing project more effectively than NHK has. The source of NHK's competence is its fluidity and omnimorphousness, guaranteed by the nebulous identity as a public (non-governmental and non-profit) institution. NHK is more than a domestic public broadcaster. It is one of the most powerful national institutions of Japan, a "national" institution in the sense that it exists and works for the interests of Japan, be they economic, cultural, or political. As a national "public" institution, it freely liaises with business organizations and the state. It is not, strictly speaking, a part of the government but does participate in governmental affairs; it is not a business organization but it does business. As instantiated by the HDTV case, its duty is truly omni-directional, stretching from technological inventions and program production to organization of various events and sales business. It internalizes, therefore, the raison d'être of the state as an organizational hub that interlinks commerce and policy, civil and political spheres, business and government. The national-public institution can be seen as a specialized, mini state and, more accurately, a state in extension.

CHAPTER V

RENATIONALIZING DIGITAL SKY: MURDOCH AND

JAPAN'S COMMUNICATION SATELLITE (CS)

Introduction

On August 29, 2003, Rupert Murdoch's News Corporation Inc. made a startling announcement. The company decided to relinquish its entire stake in SkyPerfecTV, the leading Communication Satellite television platform (CS henceforth) in Japan, to which Murdoch himself gave life. Murdoch's decision to pull away from the worlds' second largest media market was, of course, a discomforting loss for the transnational media titan who has wielded an enormous sway over the global media market. At the same time, however, it is a stimulating instance that problematizes the accepted view of media globalization as an unstoppable juggernaut steered by transnational media conglomerates. Murdoch's withdrawal forces scholars of global media to reexamine the fabled demise of cultural sovereignty of the local/national in the era of planetary media integration.

In the wake of Murdoch's departure from SkyPerfecTV, this chapter explores the institutional and cultural milieu that compelled Murdoch's withdrawal from the most lucrative and fast-growing niche in Japan's media business. The focal point of this chapter is to look into the intersection where the trajectories of Murdoch's Sky television in Japan encounter with a set of deregulatory measures the country has implemented. I submit that Japan's deregulatory measures that allow the entry of foreign capital should not be understood as an unequivocal U-turn from its formerly secluded national media spheres. Although initiated to lure foreign capital into its burgeoning digital CS television market, Japan's deregulatory policies have enacted subtler forms of control guided by the ethos of re-nationalization. At the same time, Japan's media industry and policy agents have leveraged the arrival of transnational media corporations, siphoning off their capital, business leadership, and technological know-how, as exemplified by Murdoch's case. I will argue that Japan's deregulation in digital CS exemplifies a ventriloquist voice and a hypochondriac mindset.

On a more theoretical front, this essay counters the chimerical omnipotence of global media titans on the one hand and critiques the valorization of the local/national media as a heroic underdog on the other. Scholarship in the study of media globalization tends to polarize—those focusing on the relentless expansion of multinational media Goliaths (Ginneken, 1998; Sklair, 1997; Boyd-Barrett, 1997) and those focusing on the clever jockeying of local/national media guerrillas (Featherstone 1996; Straubhaar 1997; Wang, 2000). However, the two polarized camps commonly subscribe to a transparent antithesis between local/national media and transnational media. Preoccupied with the adversarial *collision* of the local/national and the global media, both groups remain inattentive to voluntary and compulsory *collusions* between the two allegedly conflicting forces.

Rather than adhering to the academic inertia, this paper contravenes the categorical clarity between multinational media corporations as domineering predator and local/national media as the beleaguered prey. Their resemblance in orientation and praxis, it seems to me, outstrips their dissimilarity in size and geo-cultural habitation. Also, tactics and strategies the local/national media employ are analogous with and equally problematic as those harnessed by the transnational titans. I will illustrate in what follows that the sudden withdrawal of News Corporation from the frontier of Japanese media is an event that blows the whistle on the alarming rise of local, petty media tyrants, who duplicate and proliferate the domineering practices of transnational media behemoths.

This chapter interrogates a range of interlaced instances—economic, legal, cultural, historical, ideological, etc.—around the rise and fall of Murdoch's Sky television in Japan. This incident transcends what classical political-economic or institutional approaches encompass. It is hoped that this approach could refine our grasp of the multifarious trajectories of media globalization in a vexing time of de/re-regulation.

Controlled *Glasnost*

Roughly speaking, broadcasting via digital Communication Satellite (CS) is an enterprise that bundles many channels together and wholesales the package. Of all present forms of broadcast television (terrestrial, cable, and satellite), digital CS is the one that is most critical to the establishment of a multichannel environment in Japan. Currently, there are more than 300 CS channels (249 for television and 52 for data-casting) run by approximately 125 broadcasters (content providers and distributors) nationwide.[39] But the super-abundance of Japan's CS was made possible largely by transnational media corporations. Being a central conduit through which transnational media conglomerates entered Japan's media market, digital CS has been a major battlefield between Japan-based media companies and foreign capital.

Japan's first CS broadcasting began in 1992 with the conventional analog system. Four years later, digital CS broadcasting got off the ground when PerfecTV opened business by taking over Japan's first analog CS service, Skyport. PerfecTV was then run by Japan Digital Broadcasting Service, a company funded by twenty-eight Japanese trading and financial corporations: Itochu, Nissho Iwai, Sumitomo, Mitsui & Co, etc. Contrary to expectation, PerfecTV drew but meager attention by scholars, policymakers, and even broadcasting entrepreneurs. It was at this time when the officials in the Ministry of Post and Telecommunications (MPT)[40] were timidly dwelling on the gains and losses

---

[39] See Ministry of Public Management, Home Affairs, Post and Telecommunications, Japan. (2002). *Major Aspects of Japan's Broadcasting Policy*. Tokyo, Japan: Ministry of Public Management, Home Affairs, Post and Telecommunications, 3-4.

[40] MPT was the department that oversaw Japan's media industry in general. It was integrated in January 2001 with the Ministry of Home Affairs and the Public Management agency to become the Ministry of Public Management, Home Affairs, Post and Telecommunications. With this

of introducing a full-scale digital plan. Because of the indecisiveness of policymakers, the potential subscribers stood back uninterested and few Japanese broadcasting corporations dared to embark on digital CS.

Amid this vacuum, a host of corporations that hadn't previously engaged in the media industry crossed the threshold of the hitherto well-sheltered enclave. Toyota Motor Corporation, for instance, bid for a niche in CS digital broadcasting for businesses to cover automobile navigation and transportation-related communication tools. Another notable contender was Sony, who had long geared up to provide a variety of next generation digital content, ranging from movies and television programs to interactive data transmission and Internet-based e-commerce services. The Japanese government, in the meantime, responded to the entrepreneurial enthusiasm with favorable legislative packages. A set of bylaws was adopted by the Diet, lowering the admission bar for the broadcasting industry by alleviating aspirants from the burden of committing enormous sums of money to satellite equipment. In the same spirit, a new licensing policy was introduced in June 2001, substituting an inspection-based approval process for a simplified registration system.

Japanese businessmen weren't the only ones enthused by the legal arrangement, however. Foreign media conglomerates, who had long sought to penetrate Japan's media fortress, were also elated, since the revision of Broadcast Law in 2001 further relaxed regulations on foreign media capital from 1989's initial benchmark. The effect of this second legal reorganization loomed most tangibly in digital CS broadcasting. However, opening the door to digital CS broadcasting didn't mean an unrestrained liberalization of Japan's domestic television market. Rather, it has been a *glasnost* tightly controlled with

---

reorganization, the former MPT's Communication Policy Bureau, Telecommunication Bureau, and Broadcasting Bureau have been combined to become two bureaus: the Information Communication Policy Bureau and Basic Bureau for Integrated Communications.

two main purposes: complying with the hegemonic doctrines of international free trade on one hand and capitalizing on massive financial and program inputs from transnational media firms on the other.

Needless to say, attempts to make headway into Japan's broadcasting arena by multinational media corporations preceded the recent wave deregulating foreign media capital. Since the early 1980s the liberalization of Japan's telecommunication and broadcasting markets has been a perennial issue pushed by U.S. and EU delegates in major conventions like G8, APEC, WTO, and other trade-relevant assemblies. One of the most contentious issues during the 1990s was the high interconnection rate that Japan's NTT (National Telegraph and Telephone Co.) charged for international telecommunications carriers who wished to enter Japanese market.[41] But the opening of Japan's media industry was by no means a reluctant and imposed move. Apart from the external pressure, a wide consensus was being forged among Japanese officials, especially those in the Ministry of International Trades and Industries (MITI). Well-cognizant of Japan's lag in digital broadcasting vis-à-vis the U.S and Western European counterparts, the MITI elites put forth plans to entice multinational media companies into bankrolling Japan's burgeoning media technologies such as satellite, cable broadcasting, and other digital telecommunications. The confluence of domestic ambition and foreign pressure expedited the flow of foreign capital into Japan's media industry, a tendency that has become increasingly pronounced in the domain of CS broadcasting since the mid 1990s.

Participation by foreign media capital occurred first in the telecommunication sector. Microsoft and Tele-communications International (now Liberty Media) were the initial pioneers to set foot in Japan in January 1995. They partially funded the venture of

---

[41] This became a crucial agenda during the summit between former U.S. President Clinton and former Japanese Prime Minister Yoshiro Mori in April 2000.

two multiple system operators (MSOs) named Jupiter Telecom (better known as J-Com) and TITUS.[42] A few months later, the MPT approved the operation of overseas satellite programs received in Japan by subjecting them to the directives of Japan's Broadcast Law. Since then, foreign satellite broadcasters operating in Japan have grown at a breathtaking pace. In about two years since the initial authorization, eleven overseas broadcasters with twenty-two satellite channels were brought into play in 1997. The rising number of foreign broadcasters caused little angst among Japan's policymakers and media entrepreneurs, since most of them were stationed outside Japan and didn't muddle the ownership structure of the Japanese media industry. The advent of Murdoch's JSkyB, however, triggered a sequence of shockwaves.

Perry's Black Ships and Murdoch's Sky

Before News Corporation's foray into Japan's CS broadcasting, there was another foreign company hovering over Japan's CS broadcasting: DirecTV, which inaugurated a CS platform in October 1997. While PerfecTV was fully subsidized by Japan-based corporations, DirecTV was a mélange in its financial and management composition. Major sponsors of DirecTV were Hughes Electric (owned by General Electric), representing American capital (35 percent), and Matsushita and Mitsubishi, representing Japanese capital (65 percent). The two early settlers of Japan's digital CS broadcasting were soon joined by Murdoch's JSkyB in 1998.

Shortly after the successful launch of BSkyB in Britain, Rupert Murdoch held a press conference in Tokyo on June 12, 1996, unveiling his plan to embark on a satellite

---

[42] J-COM was founded in 1995 as a joint venture between Japan's Sumitomo and cable provider Tele-Communications International (now Liberty Media). The company's major stakeholders include Sumitomo (36 percent), Liberty Media (35 percent), and Microsoft (15 percent). In contrast, TITUS used to be a subsidiary of US software giant Microsoft and was later purchased by Jupiter Telecom in September 2000. They both offered integrated serviced for cable, telephony, and the Internet.

Sky television platform in Japan, namely, JSkyB. In order to kick-start his proposed mammoth CS platform with over 100 channels, Murdoch needed a grip on a domestic broadcasting network which would furnish JSkyB with ample content favored by Japanese viewers. It was TV Asahi that came into Murdoch's line of sight. In an attempt to milk TV Asahi of its rich media software, Murdoch acquired 21.4 percent of Asahi National Broadcasting stock, an event that badly wounded the nation's pride in its advanced broadcasting system and immaculate self-governance. Since the opening of television broadcasting in 1953, Japan had remained "unsoiled" by foreign media capital, preserving an astounding level of self-sufficiency across the fields of production, distribution, management, and ownership.[43]

Hence, some Japanese newspapers went as far as to analogize Murdoch's landing to the arrival of Black Ships (*kurofune*) led by General Commodore Matthew Perry in 1853. As is widely known, the arrival of Black Ships in Kanagawa Prefecture near Tokyo, marks one of the most critical moments in the modern history of Japan. It heralded the onset of the turbulent modernization in Japan, bringing to an end the nation's insularity that had lasted over several centuries. The incident is remembered with profound ambivalence: both as the marker of feeble nationhood that caused the opening of the country to alien forces and as the watershed from which the backward-looking legacies of the feudal regime were shelved. Murdoch's entrance to Japan re-invoked the jumbled emotion of apprehension and anticipation that Japanese people had two centuries ago. Newspaper headlines such as "Sudden Arrival of Black Ship" in *Sankei Shinbun* and

---

[43] This, according to Iwabuchi Koichi, has been a consistent tendency except during the 1960s when programs imported from the U.S. flooded the Japanese broadcasting market. Iwabuchi also notes that more than 95 percent of programs on Japanese TV have been produced domestically since the early 1970s. See Iwabuchi Koichi. (2000). To Globalize, Regionalize, or Localize Us, That Is the Questions: Japan's Response to Media Globalization. In Georgette Want, Jan Servaes, & Anura Goonasekera (Eds.). *The New Communication Landscape: Demystifying Media Globalization*, p. 142-145.

"Breaking the Isolationism of Japanese Broadcasters" in *Asahi Shinbun*[44] poignantly illustrate the mixed feelings toward the arrival of Murdoch. Yet, the main note in the "Black Ship" allegory was self-traumatization and victimization. As Iwabuchi Koichi (2000) notes, "The threat posed by Murdoch to Japan was" perceived as "the possibility of control of the Japanese media industry by foreign capital" (pp. 143-144).

The discourse of self-victimization before the "incursion" of foreign capital is a narrative neither unprecedented nor solely unique to Japan's broadcasting industry. Japanese business elites and policy bureaucrats routinely rekindled it during the 1990s to such a degree that alarms about the arrival of foreign capital can now be deemed a hollow ritual. The state officials in America, too, would vocalize the hyperbolized threat posed by alien enterprises. It was only two decades earlier that the specter of "Japan Inc." loomed menacingly over the US. Overwhelmed by Japan's then-advanced telecommunication and television technologies, US business leaders and politicians rang a jingoistic bell, dubbing Japan an "economic fox" and "trade predator."[45] The outcome of the witch-hunt campaign was, according to a Harris Survey, that the American people saw Japan as a greater threat than the U.S.S.R. with its nuclear arsenal.[46] On both sides of the Pacific, the level of jeopardy presented by foreign media capital has been consistently overstated during the economic Cold War between Japan and the U.S.

Although the shrill greeting of Murdoch's entry into Japan was a ritualized complaint from previous decades, it nevertheless augured the tough challenge that Murdoch had to face to make headway into Japan's digital CS business. Murdoch, of

---

[44] See Kaifu Kazuo. (1998). Digitization of Japan's Satellite Broadcasting. *Broadcasting Culture & Research*, 3, 7-9.

[45] George Gilder (1992). *Life After Television*, p. 11.

[46] David Morley and Kevin Robbins (1995). *Spaces of Identity: Global Media, Electronic Landscapes and Cultural Boundaries*, p. 148.

course, was well aware of the potential cultural resistance to his entry into Japan. That he was cautious and meticulous enough in hacking into Japan's CS world is exemplified by his decision to form a strategic partnership with Softbank Corp., a Japan-based major computer software company that commands a sterling public reputation to date. Murdoch's alliance with Softbank had two main purposes. First, it was intended to circumvent the restriction on foreign investment in Japan's media industry, as stipulated in the Japanese Radio Law. The Law limits the percentage of foreign capital in a Japan-based broadcasting company to 20 percent or lower, while leaving a huge loophole for indirect possession through a joint venture, as in Murdoch's case. The other rationale behind the joint acquisition was to use Softbank as a buffer zone lest the acquisition of Asahi's stock inflame the nationalist sentiment of the Japanese people and media industry.[47]

Although Sky's landing engendered major public unease, Japanese broadcasting wasn't as vulnerable or fragile as it was narrated to be. Time and again, Japanese companies outperformed, stymied, or drained off the assets of the media mogul. For example, Murdoch's plan to leverage a vast range of media archives owned by TV Asahi was far from trouble-free. Asahi Shinbun, a major stakeholder of TV Asahi, responded defiantly to Murdoch's scheme to exploit the company's program properties. With his takeover attempt thwarted, Murdoch had to pull back his stock ownership on TV Asahi in 1997. Frustrated, Murdoch made another attempt to launch JSkyB in 1998. This time, he vied with only nine channels composed mostly of News Corporation's own stations, including Fox News, Sky Sports, Star movies, etc. The second endeavor was called off, since the proposed line-ups were unappealing to Japanese audiences deeply habituated to

---

[47] This preemptive move is, of course, an involuntary one. Many countries including Britain, India, China, Korea, keep stock ownership of foreign investors under 50 percent.

programs congruent with national cultural sensibilities and specific to local social climates.

After two previous failures, Murdoch finally entered Japan's CS arena successfully by launching JskyB in 1999. The emergence of JSkyB is often regarded as the upshot of Murdoch's successful incorporation of Sony and Fuji TV. But it is hard to determine who incorporated whom, given that the shareholdership was equally distributed among the three participants. Similarly, the popular representation (by mainstream media and scholars alike) of the birth of SkyPerfecTV as being indebted to Murdoch's absorption of Japan-indigenous PerfecTV lacks justification. In effect, the merger between Murdoch's JSkyB and PerfecTV should be viewed in a different light.

When the deal between JSkyB and PerfecTV was struck in April 1998, PerfecTV had already grown to 100 channels with nearly half a million loyal subscribers. At that time PerfecTV was experiencing a minor slowdown in gaining more market share, partly because its rival DirecTV has siphoned off some prospective subscribers. PerfecTV, hence, invited in JSkyB via the mediation of Sony and Fuji TV, offering Murdoch an opportunity to take part in Japan's CS business. Things happened as planed, and a gargantuan empire of digital CS broadcasting was born: namely, SkyPerfecTV. Yet the power distribution among the four main players wasn't quite evenhanded. Murdoch assumed only 8.1 percent of common stock, whereas Sony, Fuji TV, and Itochu seized 9.9 percent respectively. Given the uneven allotment of stock, it wouldn't be sensible to claim that Murdoch was the one who held the upper hand in the formation and subsequent structuring of the conglomerate station. In other words, the merger embodied the fusion of competition and cooperation between local and transnational media, a dangerous wedlock in which the tension between the two parties continued to build up.

In any case, the post-merger state of affairs evolved in a fashion where Japan's Itochu, Sony and Fuji all blew their nose without getting their hands wet. As an amalgamation of Murdoch-led JSkyB and Itochu-led PerfecTV, Sky PerfecTV came to control a total of 300 channels (television and radio combined) as of May 1998. After the merger followed a barrage of advertisements aimed not only to boost public interest in SkyPerfecTV but also to oust its rival, DirecTV Japan. Although DirecTV was a veteran player in global digital CS broadcasting,[48] its branch in Japan could not weather the belligerent strategies of SkyPerfecTV, and went out of business in 2000. Absorbing 322,000 viewers from the now-defunct DirecTV Japan, the total households subscribing to SkyPerfecTV added up to 2.4 million as of October 2000. In hindsight one can reasonably argue that Japanese media enterprise dexterously exploited the transnational media Goliath for ousting DirecTV and quickening the development of Japan's digital CS enterprise, which had lagged significantly behind its European and North American counterparts. The way in which Sony, Fuji TV, Itochu, and other leading media companies engaged with Murdoch's JSkyB is akin to the vampires' blood-feeding techniques in many ways. While complying with the imperative of media transnationalization, Japan's media industry further solidified its toehold by devouring foreign media capitals and programs.

Hypochondriac Mentality

Why, then, did Japan's media industry respond to the arrival of Murdoch's Sky channel so hysterically? Did the advent of Murdoch's JSkyB in 1998 actually set off a disorder in Japan's broadcasting industry? Yes, perhaps. The arrival of foreign satellite broadcasters sparked intense rivalries and fleeting alliances between Japanese media capital and foreign media behemoths. The encounter between the two forces in the arena of Japan's digital CS has clearly unsettled such sensitive issues as ownership structure, management, and content production/distribution. In light of the turbulent reorganization in broadcasting, Kaifu Kazuo (1997), an executive researcher at NHK, states that

---

[48] As of July 2003, Direct TV had over 12 million subscribers in the US market alone.

120

internationalization and deregulation have introduced market principles and will force a shift in Japan's public broadcasting-oriented systems (p. 9). In a similar vein, both Iida Masao (1999) and Hanada Tetsuro (1999) argue that advances in digital technology coupled with global media consolidation are testing the raison d'être of Japan's broadcasting.[49] They caution that indiscriminate liberalization policies would wreak havoc on what otherwise was an orderly landscape of Japan's broadcasting province.

Nevertheless, the frenzied competition and mergers were the price that Japan was willing and prepared to pay in exchange for making a leap forward in the long-awaited multichannel broadcasting system. Perfect TV showcased over seventy channels, immediately attracting some 300,000 subscribers in one year since October 1996. To catch up with Perfect TV, Direct TV Japan introduced a new CS platform with a staggering 100 channels. With additional 120 channels added by JskyB shortly, Japan's broadcasting industry suddenly found itself on a plateau of channel super-abundance less than three years since the outset of digital CS. Aside from the exponential multiplication of channels, the unprecedented competition has transformed Japan's CS topography in a rewarding fashion, as far as the diversification of program and the introduction of new services are concerned. Some even point out that the liberalization of Japan's broadcasting allowed an opportunity to promote Japan's media products to international markets. Iwabuchi asserts, "what is at stake seems less a foreign invasion of Japan than Japanese advance into global media markets and the enhancement of the competitiveness of Japanese TV software" (p. 145).

There are more reasons to cast doubt on the view that portrays Japan's broadcasting en bloc as a victim of multinational media globalization and market

---

[49] See Iida Masao. (1999). The Digital Broadcasting Debate: How to Harmonize Public and Commercial Services. *Studies of Broadcasting*, 34, 81-103; and Hanada Tetsuro. (1999). Digital Broadcasting and the Future of the Public Sphere. *Studies of Broadcasting*, 34, 9-40.

liberalization. It should be noted that it was Japan (more precisely, the coordination between Japanese state and its media industry) that methodically encouraged the wedlock between market-thirsty multinational media firms and momentum-hungry Japanese broadcasters. The self-victimization rhetoric deployed on the eve of Murdoch's landing, in this respect, can be interpreted as a hyperbolic defense mechanism of the vulnerable— either imagined or actual—whose melodramaic self-perception paradoxically manifests the will to keep its national media environment intact. Here, the notion of "hypochondriac" comes in quite handy.

Roughly speaking, the hypochondriac is characterized by an excessive attention to the microscopic symptoms of one's body in fear of illness. Hypochondriacs are, according to Freud, helplessly narcissistic in their obsession with physical functions and security. Caged in a fantasy of infection, these health maniacs administer medical cares beyond necessity. On the other hand, one cannot overlook a paradox intrinsic to the mindset of the hypochondriac. Always alarmed and busy taking heed to the workings of body, hypochondriacs are usually healthy, except for the habit of simulating the image of an ailing self. That is, hypochondria is a pseudo-disease which can be therapeutically advantageous. This irony applies to the overall architecture of the hyperbolism Japan's media industry has shown. The excessive caution that the Japanese media circle exercised in response to Murdoch's foray into the CS business is indeed a form of hypochondriac obsession, a remedial sacrament that keeps its media habitat "sterilized." In a sense, the (collective) hypochondriac mentality is a survival technique for Japan, as well as other local/national media, who are under constant anxiety of being eradicated, ravaged, bought-off by transnational "vultures."

Ventriloquism in Liberalization

This duality consistently surfaces in the legislative endeavors designed to stimulate the digital CS industry by hosting foreign investment. Deregulatory legislation often bifurcates, summoning up a series of counter-maneuvers even before the influx of foreign capital looked ominous to the integrity of Japan's broadcasting. The divestment of Murdoch from SkyPerfecTV epitomizes how legislative efforts to liberalize Japan's broadcasting industry have been offset by a strong undercurrent angled toward the re-nationalization of the domain. This duality, bifurcation, and schism within the same entity, I shall call a ventriloquist plot. It is a scheme that transmits multiple voices (or signals) by discrete subjects or the same subject in different tones. Not only does Japan's ventriloquism utter multiple voices in heterogeneous tones, it also overlays plural articulations to the bewilderment of foreign media corporations. On the one hand, Japan encourages the internationalization and liberation of domestic media; on the one hand, it actively seeks re-nationalization and re-regulation.

For instance, a number of Japan's major broadcasters hailed some amendments to Japan's Broadcast Law made to lure foreign satellite broadcasters.[50] NHK has been quite vocal in championing the internationalization of TV programs, and Fuji TV, Itochu, Matsushita, and Sumitomo have taken active postures toward foreign media players in Japan.[51] Notwithstanding legal relaxation and the creation of favorable environments for foreign investment, Japan's Broadcast Law (the master law that governs other sub-categorical mandates) continues to police the traffic of foreign capital and foreign procurement of Japan's broadcasting title. The Broadcast Law article 5 (paragraph 1, from number 1 to number 3), for instance, clearly spells out the ban against over 20 percent aggregate ownership of a Japan-based broadcasting company by foreigners (persons and corporations combined). When exceeded, the Broadcast Law decrees, the

---

[50] The amendment promulgated in 1989, for instance, differentiated broadcasters into facility-supplying and program-supplying categories, hastening the participation of foreign content providers in Japan's broadcasting market.

[51] See Yasuma Sosuke, Kodaira Sachiko, and Hara Yumiko. (1993). A Study on the Internationalization of TV Programs. *Study of Broadcasting*, 29, 125-50.

license of the company can be canceled by the MPT. Furthermore, Article 52-8, Paragraph 1 of the Broadcast Law requires a public announcement to be made when the cumulative ownership (entailing voting right) of foreigners surpasses 15 percent of a Japan-based broadcasting company.

Using this restriction, SkyPerfecTV has profitably kept the stock ownership by foreigners (the largest shareholder *was* of course Rupert Murdoch's News Corp.) below 20 percent and placed forewarnings that would deter further stock purchases by or registration of foreign investors. In February 28, 2003, for instance, the share (inclusive of voting rights) of SkyPerfecTV held by foreigners reached 19.7 percent of its total stock outstanding. In observance with the Broadcast Law, SkyPerfecTV had to post a notification in the morning edition of *Nihon Keizai Shimbun* on 12 March 2003 that deterred further acquisition of its stock by foreigners. Coupled with the defensive statute are subtler forms of barricade: cultural and psychological resistance, which would bring multinational media titans to a helpless shipwreck. Owing to the austere legal control supported by the mainstream media, the overall stockholding of foreigners has been on a decline lately. The percentage of stock held by foreigners in Sky PerfecTV has ebbed away from 19.7 percent in February 28, 2003 to 15.61 percent in October 22, 2003.[52] As of March 31, 2003, Murdoch's News Corporation possessed only 8.13 percent of common stock outstanding,[53] and the only other foreign company with a comparatively high stake in SkyPerfecTV was State Street Bank and Trust Company (4.84 percent.), a U.S-based multinational financial corporation. Even though Murdoch was one of the chief architects of SkyPerfecTV, his foothold in the company has steadily weakened to

---

[52] See *Nihon Keizai Shinbun*, October 22, 2003, Morning edition.

[53] SkyPerfect Communication. (2003, August 29). *Press Releases: Notice Regarding Change in Major Stockholders and the Ratio of Foreigners' Stockholding.* Available online: http://www.skyperfectv.co.jp/skycom/e/press/02-02/20030829_2e.html.

the point where he finally forsook his share in SkyPerfecTV completely. In the end, the new legal mandates promising foreign capital an easy access to Japan's CS market have been constantly impaired by the countermeasures that stifle foreign capital.

Schizophrenic as it may seem, the shifting balance between the reception of and the resistance to multinational media capital forms an exquisite division of labor. Rather than being sheer incoherence, the contrary orientations take on a rapport of supplement: coinciding, corresponding, and sometimes complementing each other. This is, however, not to suggest that the incoherence and disorientation produced by the ventriloquism were impeccably orchestrated by the Japanese state. Nor should this be taken as if the Japanese media industry in its entirety is a living organism with identical interests and a unitary goal. Quite the contrary, the very messiness, lack of coordination, and un-orchestrated cacophony are the sources that torment and baffle the multimedia troops. The ventriloquism in Japan's CS broadcasting is expressive of the overall contradiction inherent in the liberalization of Japan's media industry, which has generated (a) the shrinkage of the gateway that was initially designed to usher in foreign capital and broadcasters and (b) further tightening of jurisdiction over its national media landscape.

The Paean of Re-Nationalization: Semiotic Thievery

On August 29, 2003, News Corporation announced that it had transferred its 8.13 percent shareholding in SkyPerfecTV to the three major Japanese stakeholders, Sony Broadcast Media, Itochu Corporation, and Fuji Television Network. With 181,998 shares surrendered out of 182,000, News Corporation now holds only two symbolic shares in SkyPerfecTV, expressive of Murdoch's bitterness about the adverse business climate in Japan on the one hand and his determination to come back to Japan on the other. James Murdoch, a son of Rupert Murdoch and the executive vice president of News Corporation, commented that "We have enjoyed a close and profitable relationship with our partners, and together we have built a platform and a multi-channel market in Japan.

News Corporation remains fully committed to this market, and we will continue to take part in this business as a content provider . . . . I am certain of SKY PerfecTV's future success and plan to continue to work closely with it."[54] The part where he says, "*together we have built* a platform and a multi-channel market in Japan," is subtly coded. It elicits the resentment and frustration of the global media kingpin by reiterating the contributions that JSkyB has made to Japan's broadcasting industry.

In response to James Murdoch, Shigemura Hajime, President of SKY PerfecTV, said, "We are grateful for News Corporation's support in the establishment and consolidation of the pay television industry in Japan. . . . We will continue to consider ourselves a partner with News Corporation's global group of satellite platforms, and are planning to further enhance our relationship. We look forward to the continued exchange of information and programming cooperation."[55] The response by the president of SKY PerfecTV is, on the surface, a commendation for what News Corp has achieved in Japan's CS industry. Beneath the façade, however, the farewell speech was something of a golden handshake, somewhat apologetic and yet long-planned, to cheer up an ill-fated retiree.

The implications that the vanguard force of News Corporation retreated from the second largest media market in the world are enormous. At the most transparent level, Murdoch's News Corporation is bereaved of the gem of the crown. Unlike individual broadcast channels that News Corporation owns in Japan, SkyPerfecTV is Japan's foremost CS broadcasting platform and holds the key to the multichannel floodgate: it

---

[54] SkyPerfect Communication. (2003, August 29). *Press Releases: Notice Regarding Change in Major Stockholders and the Ratio of Foreigners' Stockholding.* Available online: http://www.skyperfectv.co.jp/skycom/e/press/02-02/20030829_2e.html.

[55] SkyPerfect Communication. (2003, August 29). *Press Releases: Notice Regarding Change in Major Stockholders and the Ratio of Foreigners' Stockholding.* Available online: http://www.skyperfectv.co.jp/skycom/e/press/02-02/20030829_2e.html.

commands more than three hundred channels, transmits a giant collection of popular programs to over three million households in Japan, and interconnects simultaneously with numerous other essential media outlets, including digital BS, cable, and Internet broadband service providers. Of course, News Corporation still retains a number of assets in Japan's media industry: 14.3 percent of J SKY sports, 17.8 percent of Star Channel, 15.0 percent of Nihon Eiga, and 10.0 percent of Space Shower Network, in addition its own Fox Channel, FOX News, and National Geographic Channel operating in Japan. Yet, even the combined value of all these is no match for SkyPerfecTV.

From the standpoint of Japan's CS broadcasting, SkyPerfecTV has finally restored self-determination and "national purity" in ownership and management. The shares News Corporation released were transferred to the hands of Japanese media victors, Sony, Fuji TV, and Itochu Corp., each of which now represents 12.65 percent stockholding (283,058 shares) in SkyPerfecTV. The top ten investors in SkyPerfecTV, with an exception of State Street Bank and Trust Company, are all Japan-rooted firms: JSAT, NTV, TBS, Mitsui & Co., Matsushita Electric Industrial Co., etc. Moreover, none of the board of directors is a foreign national or affiliated with multinational corporations: delegates from the Japanese shareholding firms completely occupy the chief posts, from two Chairmen through executive vice president and two managing directors to six non-executive directors and even the five standing auditors.

Aside from the re-nationalization in financial and managerial terms, SkyPerfecTV also broke free from its tainted history as a crossbreed of Murdoch's JSkyB and Japan's PerfecTV. What seems noteworthy here is that the prefix "Sky," a name bestowed by Murdoch's News Corporation, no longer evokes News Corp's foray into Japan's digital CS broadcasting; rather, it turned into a landmark "booty" that Japanese media firms seized from the hitherto indomitable multinational media giant. As a result, the "Sky" title has come into a semiotic aporia on a global scale: while "Sky" in other countries (BskyB in Britain, IskyB in Italy, etc.) remains the signatory banner of Murdoch's planetary satellite empire, "Sky" in Japan embodies the dethronement of the proprietor who gave life to it. The two divergent denotations undermine the transparency of the signifier "Sky" and, accordingly, suspend the mythical triumph of transnational media corporations. Consequently, the fractured ownership of the "Sky" trademark conjures up the fundamental ambivalence inherent in media globalization: the alterity or alternate-ability of the dominant and the dominated, the aggressor and the defender.

Another example along this line is found in the emergence of Star Channel in Japan. Star Channel, not Star TV, is a company owned and run by Itochu, one of the principal shareowners of SkyPerfecTV. Itochu's Star Channel was named after Rupert Murdoch's Star TV. Just like Murdoch's Star TV, Itochu's Star Channel specializes in the provision of foreign movies to Japanese audiences via diverse broadcasting venues of digital CS, BS (Broadcasting Satellite), and cable televisions. In fact, Japan's Star Channel was an outcome of a bizarre negotiation between Itochu and News Corporation. Itochu asked for the right to expropriate the trademark and contents of Star TV owned by News Corporation. News Corporation demanded in return a substantial amount of share from the local imitator, Star Channel. Through the tradeoff, Itochu came to possess copious content from News Corporation's Star TV, while News Corporation grabbed a measly 17.8 percent share of Star Channel, a "counterfeit" of Murdoch's own "genuine" Star TV. Arguably, one can say that Star Channel in Japan lawfully purloined the identity, prestige, as well as the content of Star TV, without subordinating to Murdoch's media empire.

Beware the Local Predator!

I have expressed above my suspicion toward the account that renders local/national media innocent prey to be devoured by transnational media carnivores. Beyond this suspicion, one has to be attentive to the similitude between the local and transnational media companies. Some local/national media copy predatory acts of

128

transnational media to the degree that a label of "performative proxy" of multinational media seems appropriate. The predispositions of local/national media, at least in Japan but possible more, are gradually turning into the clones of global media tyrants.

SkyPerfecTV, for example, has been no less belligerent and gluttonous than any other transnational firm. It has monopolized Japan's digital CS television market after driving GE-backed DirecTV away from Japan in 2000. Since then, the company has exercised an unobstructed reign by clinching telecommunication markets, hoarding stock ownership of other neighboring businesses, and frustrating the emergence of new competitors. In effect, the latest steps SkyPerfecTV has taken are reminiscent of the large-scale M&As occurring around the globe. The formation of the world's largest media titan through the merger between Time Warner and Vivendi Universal runs almost parallel to SkyPerfecTV's advance into the realm of cable TV/telecommunications via a joint venture with communications satellite operator JSAT[56] and telecommunication giant NTT[57]. Now that the cable industry is within a stone's throw, SkyPerfecTV is latching onto Internet services through a tie-up with Jupiter Telecommunications (J-COM Broadband), the largest broadband and cable service provider in Japan in terms of the number of customers served. This deal enabled SkyPerfecTV to absorb customers within reach of J-COM Broadband[58] not yet incorporated to its digital CS broadcasting. The outrageous expansion of SkyPerfecTV did not stop there, however. Allegations that it

---

56 JSAT is the nation's first private-sector satellite communications operator instituted after the enactment of Japan's Telecommunications Business Law in 1985. Owning and operating a total of nine satellites, JSAT is a leading satellite operator in the Asia-Pacific region.

57 NTT is Japan's premier telecommunications company.

58 J-COM Broadband is geared up for the commencement of its own digital CS broadcasting platform with approximately sixty channels by the end of June 2004.

attempted to obstruct the growth of other competitors abound, as demonstrated in the launch of Plat-One,[59] a new digital CS platform set in motion in March 2002.

Plat-One initially drew much attention for its potential to give pause to the monopolistic practice of SkyPerfecTV in the digital CS market. Financed by a group of established Japanese media and other corporations—NTV(Nippon Television), Mitsubishi, and WOWOW, among others—Plat-One was powerfully outfitted with a range of diversified programs: three free-of-charge network channels, four pay-per-view WOWOW channels, seven NTV CS programs, twelve data network channels, and two radio channels. It even premiered innovative services called "ep," a service that allows downloading, storing, and retrieval of satellite television/radio programs. Nevertheless, its growth hasn't been as impressive as expected. Although analysts attribute the holdup to the lack of satisfactory publicity, institutional backing, and originality in programming strategies, there lies another factor that accounts for the sluggishness, namely, the commencement of SkyPerfecTV2. No sooner than Plat-One inaugurated its service on 1 March 2002 did SkyPerfecTV open its second CS platform in July 2002.[60] What appears curious about Sky Perfect 2 is that it has scarcely presented novel programs but, instead, duplicated a number of popular channels from SkyPerfecTV1.[61] Due to the blatant recycling of programs from its parent station, the market standing of SkyPerfecTV2 remains pitiable. Then, one might ask, has Sky Perfect group dashed off the inauguration

---

[59] Plat-One is often called CS 110° because it is controlled by satellite N-SAT-110°, which is located at 110 degrees East. Another CS channel using this new satellite is SkyPerfecTV2. Those subscribing to digital CS 110° platforms can access both CS and BS channels via a single receiver with an antenna looking at 110 degrees.

[60] The two new digital CS platforms (a.k.a. CS 110°) share the same satellite: N-SAT-110°.

[61] There are of course some exceptions. The channel called Takarazuka Sky Stage and some data network channels are newly placed in. For more details, see SARJAM Communications Ltd. (n.d.). From Analog to Digital . . . Satellite TV Progresses. *Satellite Magazine Japan*. Available online http://www.sarjam.com/sate1.html.

of its second platform without conducting thorough market surveys and proper groundwork for program supply?

It is important to note here that the digital CS market in Japan has been overgrazed in a short span of time, and the audience's demand is approaching a temporary standstill. Despite CS's dazzling growth, the Japanese audiences' disinclination to swing to digital satellite remained strong, since analog broadcasting will continue until 2011 when the nationwide conversion from analog to digital broadcasting concludes. Additionally, the imminent start of digital terrestrial broadcasting slated for December 2003 casts a heavy shadow on the impending standstill of digital CS. However, these are facts known even to laypersons in Japan, thanks to repetitive publicity by mainstream newspapers, who are also major shareholders of terrestrial broadcasting companies and therefore troubled by the formidable expansion the digital CS over the last few years. It is highly improbable, therefore, that SkyPerfecTV embarked on another massive CS platform without conducting sufficient market analyses. One can infer, instead, that the chief aim behind the impetuous embarkation of SkyPerfecTV2 wasn't so much that of absorbing floating audiences; it was born as a straw-man to hamper the smooth landing of its potential adversary, Plat-One.

Apart from the fact that it replicates a good deal of programs from its parent platform, SkyPerfecTV2 is appallingly understaffed, underfinanced, and ill-defined. Moreover, it has shown little enthusiasm in soliciting new audiences, immediately after March 2002 when its contender Plat One got off the ground. Total subscribers attracted during the fourteen months since its birth sits around a humble 56,000 as of October 2003. This miniscule figure indeed stands in a sharp contrast with the staggering 3.46 million subscribers held by SKY PerfecTV1 as of September 2003.[62] Yet, the meager

---

[62] See for more details, Sky Perfect Communications Ltd. (2003). *Annual Report 2003*. Available online: http://www.c-direct.ne.jp/english/divide/10104795/ar2003/ ar2003e.pdf.

figure of 56,000 becomes substantial enough, when it is used to stymie and slash the market that could otherwise have been clutched by Plat-One. In this respect, the 56,000 subscribing households for SkyPerfecTV2 is in this respect as good as a group of detainees to curb the potential growth of Plat-One into a challenge to the dominance of SkyPerfect. After all, SkyPerfecTV2 is a scarecrow imbued with the spirit of monopoly.

Conclusion

Discussions on globalization have gradually shifted away from the fixed conception of the global as an almighty, universal force, and the local either a noncompliant challenger to or helpless victim of the global.[63] However, political economic approaches to media globalization have remained rather impervious to the paradigmatic shift, largely because media globalization has unfolded in a fashion that corroborates the binarism of the omnipotent, predatory global and the frail, besieged local. New charters and mandates adopted by G8, APEC, WTO, WB, and other international summits have undeniably shattered and overawed national/local media across the fields of ownership, management, and content production. Empowered by the new templates, transnational media corporations such as News Corp., Time Warner, Bertelsmann, Disney, and Viacom have torn down local/national barriers, making a frenzied sprint toward global media oligopoly. However, local/national media groups are forging flexible affiliations with various civil and state organizations, far ahed of the theories propounded by academics.

---

[63] Instead, the notion of *Glocalization*, a popular term first coined by the chairman of Sony and subsequently endorsed by many academicians has enjoyed wide currency. The notion of *Glocalization* rightfully attends the inevitability of negotiation and enmeshment between the analytically split units of the global and the local. As reciprocal corollaries, the global actively incorporates and adapts to local vernaculars, while the local becomes a site that always and already embodies the global idioms.

Japan is not the only country that implemented controlled *glasnost* and ventriloquist tactics. Similarly, hypochondriac reactions and the rise of local tyrants are relevant to other nations too. Like Japan, South Korea has witnessed the spread of hypochondriac attitudes, as well as the generation of incongruous ventriloquist speeches. In Korea, it was initially the Ministry of Culture and Tourism who called on News Corporation to invest in the country's CS market. When News Corp. finally decided to take part in the digital satellite industry in 2000, an official from the Ministry of Culture and Tourism commented that "We have nothing to be afraid of in Murdoch's entry. . . . The business [digital CS] requires hefty capital investment. So we hope domestic and foreign firms form a harmonious consortium."[64] Murdoch's entry to the country seemed auspicious and fail-safe, given the enthusiasm a number of domestic corporations had shown in developing a consortium with Sky TV. Yet, Murdoch's venture into Korea's CS market encountered a major obstacle when a national coalition made up of fifty separate civic groups initiated a boycott against News Corp. The leader of the coalition stated "we welcome foreign capital into our country but not from Murdoch. . . . . We also suspect Murdoch's investment here is aimed at securing a bridgehead for his attempt to move into China."[65] In effect, the latitude allowed for Murdoch's Sky channel in Korea was rather tight from the very onset. Korea's Radio Laws, like that of Japan, forbid foreign nationals from possessing over 33 percent shares of local broadcasting businesses. Additionally, the Radio Law keeps foreign media firms under close monitoring as to transmission of either "contentious or culturally unbecoming" contents, the elusiveness of which tightens the wriggle room for foreign content suppliers.

---

[64] See C.W. Lim. (2000, April 26). *Seoul (AFP)*. http://www.spacedaily.com/news/murdoch-00d.html.

[65] Ibid.

Compounding economic issues with cultural/political ones is not unusual in other countries. For example, the Indian government has adamantly demanded that News Corp should, in order to warrant its business in India, sell out 51 percent of Star TV India's equity to an Indian partner. This undue request was made amidst raging civilian protests against Star TV India for airing culturally offensive content. To the exasperation of Murdoch, the Indian government skillfully roped a cultural issue into an ownership deal by mobilizing Indian citizens' animosity towards Star TV India. There are many other countries employing similar strategies to cope with multinational media giants. Governments of these countries, hand in hand with their civic groups or media entrepreneurs, are flying in the face of global media leviathans, outfoxing and sometimes outlawing the latter's maneuvers.

It is still hard to forecast if Murdoch's departure from Japan will be followed by similar incidents. Almost concurrently with the divestment from Japan, News Corporation took a series of comparable actions, releasing its stake in the New Zealand newspaper business and selling off LA Dodgers baseball team. Yet these withdrawals could have been based on a sheer managerial judgment. Nor does Murdoch's desertion of SkyPerfecTV deliver a decisive blow to his ambition to build a global satellite empire. News Corporation's recent launch of Sky Italia and persistent attempt to procure DirecTV in the U.S. attests to the contrary. The scattered footprints that the global media mammoth has recently left are dizzyingly incongruous and make it too risky to prognosticate the company's next move. The hazy outlook for News Corporation and other multimedia giants is quite revealing of current state of affairs. It hints at the unfeasibility of adhering to a monolithic, static, and comforting interpretation of media globalization that has already outlived its own lifespan.

I have critiqued two prevalent modes of storytelling about media globalization. First one grieves over the dismantling of the local/national media by the wicked multinational media. I reject this melodramatic lamentation not because it has a hue of self-defeatism, but because it unjustly denies the agency of the local/national media, while exaggerating the power of multinational giants. The other paradigm exalts the potency of national/local agents in coping with the assault from multinational intruders. I also reject this view, since it is blind to the ever-growing resemblance between the two entities, thereby leaving unproblematized the disquieting practices of local/national media.

The case of SkyPerfecTV palpably testifies to the fact that the outright binary opposition between the covetous, omnipotent multinational giants and the innocent, emasculated local media should be abandoned; the resemblance between the two antithetically imagined forces increasingly outgrows the erroneously supposed polarity. It is profoundly risky and untenable to pity or lionize local/national media, simply because they are financial, organizational, and political underdogs.

CHAPTER VI

DIGITAL BROADCASTING AND THE IDEA OF

PUBLIC SERVICE BROADCASTING

Digital Technology, Deregulation, and Globalization

Marc Raboy (1997) once depicted the digital era as "a new communications

environment which has upset conventional ideas about the public obligations of

broadcasting" (p. 13). He mentions a number of factors that endanger the social existence

of PSB:

> Technically, the digital age is characterized by the convergence of
> communication technologies such as broadcasting, telephone,
> computer and satellite; structurally, this convergence has resulted
> in the emergence of a multichannel environment; politically, it
> coincides with the widespread globalization of issues and
> phenomena, of which broadcasting is an important one;
> economically, it is not favorable to . . . considerable involvement
> of the states, that is to say, it is deregulationist; socioculturally, it is
> marked by changing needs and increasingly demanding
> expectations of audiences and the individuals who compose them
> (Raboy, 1997, p. 13).

Indeed, the digital age brings to an end the key premise on which the institution of

public service broadcasting is validated, that is, the scarcity of the electronic spectrum.

Using an ever-decreasing sliver of the radio band, digital technologies challenge the

rationale of setting aside some electronic frequencies for purposes other than profit-

making, such as enhancing the level of social intellect, fostering democratic citizenship,

cultivating national culture, and fulfilling the information and journalism functions of

broadcasting.

The end of the era predicated upon spectrum scarcity is concomitant with the

dramatic increase in broadcasting channels, which in turn stimulates the diversification

and specialization of programs, and spawns services tailored to target groups with

particular interests. In Japan, a plethora of channels specializing on such themes as

sciences, documentaries, cooking, public affairs, and international sports have cropped up

136

via communication satellites or broadband cable services, robbing NHK, Japan's sole public and the largest terrestrial broadcaster, of its time-honored turf. The digitalization of broadcasting, thus, gives rise to a number of questions that unsettle the legitimacy of public service broadcasting (PSB henceforth): what is the justification for honoring the totalized notion of the public, when in fact the audience is segmented into myriad cultural pockets and served by a gamut of diversified channels? Should viewers continue to pay license fees, and should the government continue to subsidize PSB, even though the prime method of obtaining televised contents for the viewer is rapidly shifting to subscription or individual purchases? Finally, shouldn't the functions conventionally played by the PSB be left to market mechanisms consistent with the operatives of the viewer's demand and cultural trends?

Responses to the demanding questions posed by digitalization of broadcasting run a wide range. Some observers are disconcerted by the increasing obsolescence of PSB in the wake of digitalization, some espouse the digital crisis passionately as an opportunity to overhaul PSB, and others cautiously grope for a middle ground. The varied reactions stem from the multi-dimensionality of digital technology that could either undercut or boost the values upheld by PSB, as well as the complex situations that PSB is facing internally and externally.

Robert Ottenhoff, executive vice president of PBS in the U.S., for example, is elated by the introduction of digital technologies. He says digital television is "tailor-made for public broadcasters . . . [and] will allow PBS to break free of analog television's spectrum straitjacket and enable us to deliver multiple education services" (Ottenhoff, 1997, p. 7). He suggests that the digital revolution will enable PSB to displace the era characterized by all-in-one channel and move toward a new epoch when "a channel for preschoolers, another for elementary and secondary school students, and yet another for college and adult learners" (Ottenhoff, 1997, p. 7) may well be available. Ottenhoff's upbeat anticipation is not without reason. During the Clinton administration, Al Gore

137

promised to distribute more channel capacity to the PBS in the U.S.: "digital technology will greatly enhance the opportunity available to broadcasters to utilize multiple channels. The public interest obligations should be commensurate with these new opportunities" (as cited in Raboy, 1997, p. 13). Regrettably, the exact opposite happened in the U.S. during the Clinton administration, and America's PBS underwent severe congressional budget cuts, a downsizing in crews, and an increase in corporate sponsorship. No extra channel was allotted to PBS, while hundreds of commercial channels mushroomed.

Aware of the dire situation, Robert Phillis, BBC deputy director-general and chief executive of BBC worldwide, communicates a more prudent view. The spread of digital technology, he points out, could either undermine or bolster the values upheld by PSB, and, therefore, PSB must adapt to new circumstances without feeling threatened by them. "The enduring values which we seek to embody," states Phillis (1997), "will be no less important in a multichannel, multimedia universe that they are now" (p. 4). Phillis' idea is congruent with a mission statement on the BBC's role entitled "extending choice in the digital age" published in 1994, which states that public service broadcasting must be preserved as technology transforms the environment in which it operates. As a matter of fact, BBC has grappled with digital technologies to grant its audiences "digital dividends," such as a new twenty-four hour news channel on digital systems, an increase in the number of programs in wide screen format, an enhancement of educational offerings through the use of interactivity, and a reduction in production cost, which may finally lead to the corresponding reduction in license fees.

Pessimists, on the other hand, cast a jaundiced eye on the promise of greater abundance in the digital age. Instead, they forecast that the surge of digital technologies would take commercialism in broadcasting to new heights, eroding the doctrine of universality and equality enshrined by PSB, and eventually precipitating audience fragmentation and discrimination according to ability to pay for individuated services. Peter Dahlgren warns that, although the prophesies of the demise of public service broadcasting are quite exaggerated, the increasing wealth of commercial channels could considerably damage PSB's roles. Despite the continuing relevance and a respectable share of the viewing audience, posits Dahlgren (1997), PSB ought to redefine "what the actual mission of public service broadcasting is in the new situation" (p. 17) before digitalization destabilizes its already insecure foundation irreparably.

Of principal concern to Dahlgren and other like-minded critics is the fact that digital technologies are governed by the large-scale institutional and ideological changes that configured the order of global mediascape since the early 1990s. In other words, the present crisis of public broadcasting is caused not simply by the spread of digital technology but more importantly by the macro design of globalization, which dictates the use of digital technologies. Newton Minow (1993) posits,

> The globalization of media is . . . creating serious public service problems in most countries. There are questions of cultural sovereignty, the role of national production, the extent to which local markets will be open to foreign programs, and the degree to which national broadcasting will be subsidized to achieve cultural ends. These questions recur in almost every country, and predictably, public service broadcasting is at the center of this debate (p. xii).

The present form of globalization is molded largely by tripartite neo-liberalist initiatives: deregulation, privatization, and marketization. It is no exaggeration that the rapid deterioration of PSB's financial condition during the last two decades is essentially the consequence brought about by the ensemble of deregulation, privatization, and marketization. Since the late 1970s and the early 1980s, many industrialized countries experienced a drastic downturn in the cultural authority and economic viability of the PSB. This was the time when the Keynesian model of economy was losing its precedence to Hayek's laissez faire model, which overtook U.S. and U.K. public affairs since the Reagan and Thatcher administrations, later overflowing into most of the industrialized world. The doctrines of neo-liberalism continue to prevail, as the direction of globalization steered by U.S. and U.K gains an ever-increasing momentum. As a result,

139

PSB was confronted with an escalation in ideological and political attacks, which Willard

Rowland and Michael Tracey (1990) aptly caricature as follows: "The New Right was

questioning the very idea of public culture, and the New Left was calling the national

broadcasters elitist, statist, unaccountable, divisive, and exclusive" (p. 8).

The neo-liberalist crusade has been spearheaded by the principle of privatization,

which represents the subordination of politics to economics, whereby the governance of

the market keeps at bay the social requirements outside the sphere of financial gain.

Robert Avery (1993) observes,

> The move toward a global economy and the deregulation of
> communication industries as a precursor to the international trade
> of products and services had awakened a private sector previously
> blocked from market entry. With the shift away from state-
> imposed regulatory mechanisms came a change in political
> posturing that brought into question the utility of such concepts as
> the "public trust" in favor of more firmly based economic
> directives derived from consumer preferences and performance.
> The wisdom of this market-based model was supported by a
> growing awareness of ever-increasing program production and
> distribution costs at the precise moment when the public funds
> available to finance noncommercial broadcasting were at best
> stagnant and at worst facing continued erosion (p. xiv).

Under the command of privatization canon, the political intervention of the state

or other public authorities is denigrated as gratuitous meddling rather than a legitimate

treatment of public affairs and socio-cultural issues neglected by the hand of the

marketplace. As the intolerance toward the state's intervention permeates all sectors of a

society, the legitimacy of public institutions sees a dramatic decline. Severe budget cuts

for public organizations in the U.S., Australia, and Canada, for example, have driven PBS

(Public Broadcasting Service), ABC (Australian Broadcasting Corporation) and CBC

(Canadian Broadcasting Corporation) to the financial brink. According to Jay Blumler

(1993), the BBC, an international stronghold of public service broadcasting, has also

suffered multifaceted predicaments from the mid-1980s onwards, including the fractured

societal consensus over public broadcasting standards and arrangements, the dwindling

support for the purposes of the BBC by the government and the general public.

140

The omnidirectional crisis of PSB, including both rising costs and shrinking revenues, is situated within a pervasive climate of deregulation and ideological attacks on the political leadership of the state, which tend to fuel stronger challenges from commercial competitors, domestic and transnational. As the neo-liberalist wave has imposed the panoply of deregulatory burdens on the already flagging shoulders of PSB, Minow (1993) argues, "most countries face increasingly competitive commercial markets, with demands placed on public service broadcasters to support themselves and to make a new and better case for public funds" (p. xii).

The ferocious drive of commercialization, Minow believes, endangers the main principles of traditional public service broadcasting, consistent with the charter adopted by the UK's broadcasting research unit in 1988 and supported by the international round table of UNESCO in July 1995: universal accessibility (geographic), universal appeal (general tastes and interests), particular attention to minorities, contribution to the sense of national identity and community, distance from vested interests, direct funding and universality of payment, competition in good programming rather than for numbers, and guidelines that liberate rather than restrict program makers.

Digital Disparity:
Segmentation of the National-Public Audience

Apprehension about the coupling of digital technology and commercialization is most stridently voiced by NHK, Japan's sole public broadcaster. Notably, NHK has energetically sought ways to enliven and enrich the lofty purpose it holds by mobilizing digital technologies. In a symposium titled " Where is TV going?" held in Tokyo, 1998, the NHK president, Katsuji Ebisawa, stated that the multichannel capacity of digital television could be efficiently used for the enrichment of the public forums and lifetime education. Ebisawa (1998) emphasizes,

> Only NHK has educational programs in the terrestrial service, and
> NHK will possibly enlarge its service . . . introducing mutichannel

educational broadcasting, which includes a children's channel, elementary, junior high and senior high school channels, a life-long education channel, a language study channel, and so forth (p. 2).

While serving as the driving engine of Japan's digital broadcasting, NHK has been acutely watchful of negative fallouts of the digital crusade driven by the spirit of commercialism. NHK's unease with these consequences arises from the fact that it is Japan's sole public broadcaster and at the same time a major terrestrial station, two institutional positions generally considered to be most vulnerable to the sway of digitalization. When the MPT announced its plan in 1997 to digitalize Japan's broadcasting, NHK was instantly gripped by the fear that digitalization would facilitate the influx of commercialism. At that point, NHK officials regarded the digitalization of broadcasting as catalyzing an unruly expansion of profit-seeking channels to the detriment of the nation's long-standing commitment to the public nature of broadcasting. A few weeks after the MPT proclaimed the plan, Ebisawa (1998) cautioned against the latent hazard of digitalization thusly:

> The digital age has brought an escalation of commercialism in the media. The skyrocketing of broadcasting rights fees for sports events is posing an especially serious problem. This is particularly true with the broadcasting rights fees for the 2000 Sydney Olympics and the 2002 World Cup Soccer games. While appreciating the advantages of digitalization, we also have to admit the emergence of such problems as monopoly over coverage of international sports events (p. 2).

Tatsuhito Nagaya, NHK's executive researcher and unswerving advocate of public service broadcasting also warns that digital technology can be venomous to the mores of public broadcasting when left unrestrained by social and institutional checks. His central concern is that the multiplication of channels, steered by the united force of digital-deregulation, will necessarily partition the national-public audience into incommunicable segments. "The dispersal and integration of digital technology" maintains Nagaya (1998a), "will change the nature of broadcasting in the direction of fragmentation and differentiation as more specific services and the needs of individuals

142

and small groups of society are met" (p. 8). Commenting on the formidable leap of pay-per-view services in Japan, Nagaya (1998a) expresses grave concern that "universal appeal of general tastes and interests are divided into specific services, as strategic software triggers trends of segmentation and differentiation of . . . users, communities, and national cultures" (p. 9).

Here, he speaks of audience fragmentation in terms not only of cultural disunity but also of informational inequity, an issue that underlines NHK's profound mistrust of the market's governance in maintaining the egalitarian code that Japan's broadcasting has hitherto cultivated. Nagaya proposes that the information disparity in a multichannel environment derives from uneven growth between the number of channels and the volume of content provision. Prior to digitalization, broadcasting in Japan was a sector of limited competition, due largely to spectrum scarcity and the strict regulation of broadcasting licenses by the government. Paradoxically, the endowment of digitalization, i.e., the endowments of the spectrum with a copious supply of distribution channels, causes a relative poverty in the domain of content provision. The disproportion between the exponential increase of outlets and the comparative shrinkage in content input galvanizes fierce competition among distributors, who seek quality software that might attract the attention of the maximum audience. The elevation in competition for killer-software in due course will raise the price for such content, backfiring on the audience with heavily controlled access and higher expenditure for program reception. Nagaya (1998a) states,

> A limited amount of money-making software is considered as indispensable 'strategic software' for making a business a success. This is software that can win higher ratings and maintain a stable, paying audience. Demand concentrates on such software from around the world. The loss of broadcasting rights for a key software item, such as the right to broadcast soccer on a sports station, can mean bankruptcy or a merger. Keen competition over the broadcasting rights of Hollywood movies or major sports events is built into this structure of competition (p. 8).

Under this circumstance, the all-inclusive impulse of terrestrial broadcasting will be measurably impaired when scores or even hundreds of channels are vying for some content, and when the audience, method of delivery, and software are classed into different clusters with different price tags attached. Soon, what was readily available in terrestrial broadcasting for general audiences would become off limits, unless paid for at extra charge. This structuring of disparity in Nagaya's estimation revolves around two interconnected methods: time-space differential and subscription-based services. The former, exemplified by Hollywood's window strategy, refers to a pecking order in software distribution to different media outlets at different time slots. The latter, interlaced with the former, is an a-la-carte style of content distribution, best illustrated by on-demand and pay-per-view services, which grant select audiences an exclusive access to particular programs that are paid for. The two frameworks of audience segmentation are operated through meticulous control of three different coordinates: differentiation of media, time, and charging fee or payment methods (reception fees, viewing fees, income from advertising). For instance, a Hollywood movie that is recently produced won't be shown in different media at the same time. And the charging methods and fees would vary, conditional to whether it is on, say, a pay per view service or network television.

Nagaya rails against the condition under which only a select audience has exclusive access to highly commodified information, not simply because it impinges upon the ideal that public broadcasting observes but also because it causes profound informational disparities among viewers. Of the multiple factors and formats, Nagaya identifies the division of time as the most crucial means of audience segmentation. He posits, "stratification of the media by time slots is the basic strategy of software in the multi-media, multi-channel era. Making the best use of differences of space and time and specifying audiences at exclusive times of the software may be the essential components of fee-charging broadcasting" (Nagaya, 1998a, p. 8). Program providers are willing to pay a staggering premium to secure coveted programs ahead of other distributors, since

144

the extravagant expenditure to procure the right for early or exclusive airing is to be compensated by viewing fees from the audiences who can afford individual viewing at a preferred time. Segmentation of time, alongside the vertical differentiation of distribution methods, and payment scales, challenge the central tenet by which NHK stands firm: the synchronized reception of programming by the national-public audience. Time and access differentiation, he argues, "will inevitably expand monopolization and classification not only in services and software, but also in users and society" (Nagaya, 1998a, p. 9).

But the argument that channel multiplication, followed by the diversification and differentiation of distribution time and methods, will lead to the fragmentation of the audience and society is a questionable one. There are several reasons to be suspicious of the hypothesis of a direct causality between channel multiplication and audience segmentation. The multiplication of channel outlets could certainly give rise to the differentiation (specialization) of each channel, for broadcasters seek to steer clear of mutually damaging competition for limited sources. It is important, however, to note that the specialization takes place predominantly among different channels of a same media type, a phenomenon that can be dubbed a horizontal specialization. The outcome of horizontal specialization is often offset by other factors and doesn't necessarily conclude with the demise of a televisual commons. Since the purpose of horizontal specialization is to avoid head-on collisions among competing broadcasters, different channels of the same medium often broadcast identical contents at different time slots. An observation of different channels over a long span of time would reveal striking redundancies and affinities among various channels.

Secondly, horizontal specialization is further counteracted by its reverse phenomenon, vertical homogenization. Vertical homogenization refers to the incestuous sharing and borrowing of contents among different types of media with time variations. It can be understood as a window strategy translated from the perspective of receiver. A movie being released on theaters now will be made available on DVD and Video formats within two or three months, or sent to PPV services simultaneously or slightly later. Network broadcasters will be able to air the same movie in about one or two years from the original release of the move, which will then be passed along to syndication and then to independent stations. The long journey of the movie meanders through different media outlets at different timeframes and will eventually result in a maximum number of viewers, as well as maximum profit. Despite the gap in time, the majority of TV audiences, who are also viewers and users of other media, would hardly be expected to bypass major software, be they soccer games, news, or celebrity gossip.

Moreover, the asymmetrical growth between channel outlets and near-stagnant input inevitably encourages a massive recycling technique of the same software, curbing the sudden outburst of audience fragmentation. Time and access differentiation is, in this respect, a means of stratifying audiences and yet, at the same time, a device for uniting them within a dispersed and protracted time span of media use. Grasping the zero sum game between horizontal specialization and vertical homogenization, and between channel growth and content stagnation, would ballast the overblown apprehensions of Nagaya and his NHK cohorts over audience fragmentation.

What seems undisputable is that in a multichannel era, targeting will be shifted from the general public to specified groups of people, accentuating and further cultivating the different cultural preferences of audiences. The increase in the number of channels prompts the de-generalization of programs and de-homogenization of viewing patterns. Also predictable is that the proliferation of channels and programs tailored to smaller number of specified audiences would trigger shifts in the methods of obtaining revenue for content providers. One should question, however, whether it is the society that has already fallen apart into infinite demographic factions, or it is marketing discourses and commercial maneuvers that promote illusionary social divisions as a token of growth in individuality and the range of choice to express individual uniqueness. Equally dubious is

146

the extent to which media software and customized channels affect the alleged social fissures. Even if audience segmentation would occur, as a result of a channel increase, it is debatable whether the fragmented viewership will lead to the disintegration of national-public culture. Diversification and dehomogenization of cultural tastes have surely sped up, but they correspond to the decentralizing movements in socio-organizational and political economic spheres, a cumulative effect of which leads to a society of complex, flexible, and shifting networks of associations, not exactly atrophy in sociality as such.

The discourse of audience segmentation is anything but new in Japan. It can be situated within the theoretical lineage of the information society and the advanced information society, which took form in the late 1960s. It also closely confers with the theory of "segmented society" (*Bunshu Shakai Ron*), a cluster of ideas that Japan has evolved into a "segmented society" from a mass society, as a result of extensive use of then new communication technologies (Youichi Ito, 1991). There are a number of issues that set Nagaya's approach to digital-segmentation apart from the precursors, however. First of all, Nagaya and his cohorts seldom make reference to the factors outside the broadcasting media in considering audience and social segmentation, thereby conflating audience segmentation with cultural and social segmentation. In contrast, Y. Ito, who conceptualized *Bunshu Shakai Ron* (the theory of segmented society), does not attribute the compartmentalization of society exclusively to the spread of specialized information through diversified media uses and channels. Rather, Y. Ito relates the nuclearization of once unified mass audience to the centrifugal movements in ideologies, values and lifestyles, social and labor organizations, occupational and consuming patterns, etc. In addition, Nagaya views audience segmentation in a plainly negative light, whereas various editions of information society theory regard the decentralized production, distribution, and utilization of information as the driving force of societal, economic, and political progress. As was conceived by the proponents of information society, the audience segmentation, if any, could stand for a democratic reorganization of cultural

147

affiliations in broadcast culture, rather than being an unambiguous sign of decay in shared consciousness and equality. Just as the value of supporting the cultural integrity of national-public broadcast sphere cannot be overemphasized, the liberating value of extending individual preferences and loosening up too tightly regulated national-public culture should not be underestimated.

In Search of the Public

Apart from external factors, the institutional rigidity of Public Service Broadcasting in various dimensions is also responsible for its current crisis. PSB has deepened its alienation from the viewers it claims to serve by insisting upon an elitist interpretation of culture and overlooking the political import of popular cultures. Having overlooked the value of mass appeal, its dogmatic assertion of "excellence" and "quality" in program became hollow. Claims of serving "marginalized" groups have rang hollow as well, often bypassing actual media minorities such as senior citizens, linguistically marginalized groups, vision/hearing-impaired viewers, etc. Some claim that PSB's repeated failure to garner a respectable share of the audience was foreseeable from the very onset, due to its obscure identity and compromised mission.

More than three decades ago, Les Brown (1971) discussed the conundrum of PSB, calling it "a name without a concept" (p. 319). Brown's judgment echoed with the standpoint of Steve Millard (1976), who diagnosed PSB with a "chronic inability to name its own mission" (p. 185). For instance, the U.S.'s Carnegie Commission report (1967), from which the Public Broadcasting Act of 1967 was derived, spoke extensively of the grand mission of public television only in remarkably ill-defined terms:

> [Public televisions] provide a voice for groups in the community that may otherwise be unheard, help us see America whole, in all its diversity, increase our understanding of the world, open a wide door to greater expression and cultural richness for creative individuals and important audiences, seek out able people whose talents might otherwise not be known and shared, explore new dimensions of artistic performance not ordinarily available to our

148

nation's audiences, carry the best of knowledge and wisdom directly into the home (pp. 52-53).

The Carnegie report and the Public Broadcasting Act of 1967 was intended to provide an alternative programming service to what was readily available on commercial channels. But, as Anne W. Branscomb (1976) posits, the "language of the act remained less than helpful in defining the proper content of public broadcasting" (p. 11).

There is one structural reason why public broadcasting cannot spell out its mission lucidly: the murky notion of the "public" is its backbone. The notion of the public cannot but be abstract. At times, it represents an idealized mature citizenry responsible for the sound growth of democracy, or a valorized image of intelligent electorates cherished by philosophical and political luminaries. At other times, it is construed an imagined aggregate of diverse groups and individuals with heterogeneous concerns and interests, constructed through prescribed surveys and measurements such as voting system, polls, or ratings. The idea of the public embodied by PSB has undergone a pendulum swing between two poles of the quantitative and the symbolic: a sum total of flesh-and-blood individuals/groups and a formative map of social topographies crafted by political draughtsmen.

Many, including Anthony Smith (1973), have rejected the fictional and formative value of the public entrenched in public service broadcasting and instead stressed the denotative value of the public. Rather than being used as an institutional and political invention to which actual populace and viewing audiences are persuaded to adapt, the public in his opinion should correspond to actual breathing audiences. Hence, Smith rebukes the estrangement of public broadcasting from the public (in this case "audiences") that it claims to serve. "Public television in the United States," he claims, "has failed for the most part because it has never really gained any important relationship with the bulk of the American audience or even with any really important segment of it" (A. Smith, 1973, p. 282). Smith's admonition suggests that the public quality of PSB cannot be achieved unless it lays hands on a measurable volume of the actual viewing

149

public. On the contrary, critics like Willard Rowland chastised PSB for having been captivated by the image of undifferentiated mass society measured by a numerical gross. With the pressure for the "quantity-proper," Rowland charges, PSB has been involuntarily infatuated with the number and size of audience, landing itself in another dilemma. That is, if the size of the groups that PSB serves were not sufficiently hefty, then the tag of "public" is simply void; on the other hand, an outright pursuit of quantifiable success runs diagonally with "quality" broadcasting, an essential raison d'être of PSB. The simultaneous search for quality and quantity proved to be a paralyzing double bind rather than a vitalizing stimulus for PSB. In addition, the burden of making the public comparable with the major audience volume placed PSB in a severe competition with commercial broadcasters. PSB had to irresolutely wander between two farthest points: the public as a quantitative, economic, and concrete majority; and the public as a qualitative, political, abstract archetype.

During the 1970 and 1980s, PBS in the U.S. plotted its course with the paradigm that acknowledged the plurality of publics, instead of the uniformity of *the* public. The multiplicity of publics, of course, wasn't an entirely new narrative but was presciently told by John Dewey (1954) in 1927.

> It is not that there is no public, no large body of persons having a common interest in the consequences of social transactions. There is too much public, a public too diffused and scattered and too intricate in composition. And there are too many publics, for conjoint actions which have indirect, serious and enduring consequences are multitudinous beyond comparison and each one of them crosses the others and generates its own group of persons especially affected with little to hold these different publics together in an integrated whole (p. 137).

For Dewey, publics are too amorphous and unarticulated to be spoken of in entirety, while for PSB workers, to constellate publics as interconnected clusters was a practical necessity. As Millard (1976) puts it, PBS is "trying to serve a series of specialized audiences, with the programming that each needs most and loves best, and trying to reach all of the people—some of the time" (p. 187). A similar idea was put

150

forward by Minow who promoted "a program philosophy which seeks to serve many different audiences instead of a single mass audience" (as cited in Millard, 1976, p. 189) by presenting materials aimed at subgroups of the population that share special interests. Millard's and Minow's ideas dovetail neatly with then burgeoning principles of multiculturalism in the U.S., a shift in analogies from a melting pot metaphor to a salad bowl, and later a rainbow, in envisaging the nation. The significance of the new direction articulated by PSB in tune with multi-cultural politics is that it reconciles diversity with universality, and heterogeneity with connectivity. Embracing differences as a requirement for cultivating communal solidarity and solidity is a stance moved forward into the 1990s. Michael Tracey (1998), for example, advises PSB to eschew "the goal of amassing large audiences at every given moment" and to opt instead for "reaching a variety of smaller, special-interest audiences, thereby hoping over time to build up a large cumulative following" (pp. 111-112). Likewise, Dahlgren (1997) urges PSB workers to take into account "the growing diversification of viewers, the growing specialization of tastes and interests with populations" (p. 18), without jettisoning the idea of the publics as such. "If the 'general public' is partly a fiction, he emphasizes, "then 'plural publics' may be more accurate" (Dahlgren, 1997, p. 18).

The rediscovery of publics as an assemblage of varied groups affected PSB's programming strategies considerably. Nevertheless, it is a moot question whether generating large audience collectivities by creating a collage of diversified programs is a proper cure to the weak relationship between public broadcasters and their audiences. Admonitions of various sorts have been uttered as to PSB's strategy of pursuing pocket audiences and their respective interests. Firstly, the fragility of "publics," when slipped into a mathematical sum total of atomized groups with no palpable sense of commonality, could drift away from the foundational mission of public service broadcasting as a cultural glue within the polity of the nation-state. Secondly, as James Day (1995) points out, there are some incongruities between social minorities and broadcasting minorities.

151

Day cautions that the concept of minority audiences could be quite misleading, because the least served broadcasting minority would be "the better educated sector of the population, which expresses dissatisfaction but watches what everyone else watches" (p. 138) due to the lack of choice and diversification. Thirdly, how to envision the publics distinct from those visualized by commercial counterparts, whose sights are invariably set on a maximum number of audiences watching a program at the same time, remains an unsettled issue. The very idea of "specialized groups" is isomorphic with the demographic strategy of market segmentation employed by commercial broadcasters. In fact, particular group interests were being attended better by specialized cable and satellite channels than the centralized arrangement of public broadcasting. Satisfying immensely diverse and often conflicting interests of heterogeneous public groups by PSB alone is next to impossible and therefore requires collaboration or coordination with commercial counterparts, a phenomenon that has become increasingly salient from the mid 1980s onward. Under this circumstance, the PSB is pressed to rearticulate its own identity by redefining its relationship with commercial broadcasting.

Competition and Cooperation with
Commercial Broadcasting

Nicholas Garnham (2000) observes, "Contemporary societies and polities are increasingly riven by a shifting range of border disputes between the private and the public and by deep normative confusion about them" (p. 43). In the past, PSB has derided commercial broadcasters on various grounds such as lumping together distinct groups into a huge mass, disregarding the unique needs of diverse groups, pandering to the viewer's lowest common denominator, etc. The diametrical opposition between PSB and commercial cohorts has abounded far and wide: "whereas commercial broadcasting aspires to give the public what it wants, public broadcasting will give the publics what they need"; "to go out and shame the commercial networks with courageous and intelligent programming in such well-accepted 'categories' as public affairs and drama" (Millard, 1976, p. 188); "the lofty ideals of public service broadcasting have existed as a persuasive counterstatement to the crass and mercenary tenets of commercial free enterprise" (Avery, 1993, p. xiii).

However, the self-identification of PSB either as the antipode of or as an antidote to commercial broadcasting has reached a dead end, since PSB has been integrated into the system of competition with commercial broadcasters. The mantra of market competition is gaining wide currency, and political campaigns of deregulation are catapulting public organizations into a ruthless race with private corporations. The arrival of the multichannel environment, for instance, ignites a tougher competition between PSB and commercial broadcasters, further diluting their previous differences and intensifying the struggle for ratings and revenues. The competition takes place not only between national-public service and commercial ones, but also between the national public vs. international-commercial media mavens. The intrusion of transnational media companies transforms the national mediascapes, toughening the race for ever-denationalizing and pluralizing cultural loyalties of the audience. Competition by definition is a race for a common goal, and being in a competition means that PSB have to speak the same language as their competitors do. The establishment of the competition ethos as the name of the game draws PSB and commercial broadcasters ever closer and more identical than before. What this means is that a sheer dichotomy between commercial and public broadcasting is no longer tenable.

Blumler (1993) takes a step further and argues, "competition, commercialism, and markets [are] no longer pejorative terms . . . to be rejected or closely controlled but instead [are] criteria to be embraced and pursued more wholeheartedly" (p. 19). It is noteworthy that the demonology of market that depicts it as a sinister, amoral entity boomed during the acme of state-controlled economy, and other variants such as welfare states, developmental states, and state socialism. To ease the fabricated horror toward

153

market, Garnham (2000) informs that the market does not represent an antithesis of public interests, and "Adam Smith's primary founding argument was in favor of the market as a public institution and sphere of public behavior and it was made on moral grounds" (p. 56).

Along this approach, the Peacock Committee (1986) in the U.K. once recommended that BBC's main income source should be replaced by subscriptions, instead of license fee. BBC was thrown into an outrageous competition with Rupert Murdoch's BskyB, for example, as a result of the Peacock Committee's advocacy of an open and competitive programming market as the best way to enhance program quality and satisfy consumer's demand. Many have worried that the deep structure of competition between commercial and public services stands at variance with quality programming, for it necessarily precipitates an unrestrained contest to offer whichever programs most likely to win audiences. It has been also predicted that diversity and quality are likely to evaporate amidst the rat race for high ratings. Minow (1993) posits, "The pressure to maximize audiences may easily overcome the need to serve minority tastes and may adversely affect the ability of public broadcasters to take risks and experiment" (p. xii).

Although competition is the sine-qua-non tenet of the market, PSB's competition with commercial broadcasting does not amount to the abandonment of non-commercial codes. Raboy adds that although the prevalent characteristic of broadcasting today is hybridization, in which a distinction between the conventional categories of public and private broadcasting gets hazy, it does not necessarily mean a deterioration of the standard to which PSB has clung. He urges public service broadcasters to "program to local needs and interests; target audience as citizens, desiring to participate more fully in the public life of their society; be sensitive to expression for social demand, as well as the more obvious economic and political imperatives" (Raboy, 1997, p. 13). Other zealots of PSB have also rejected the view that depicts hybridization of broadcasting as an

154

inescapable lot whereby public broadcasting has to join the tide of mercantile communication. Instead, they argue, a sense of obligation and stewardship to serve the public should stretch to commercial broadcasters (Ottenhoff, 1997, p. 7).

Japan's broadcasting system offers an interesting model as to the ever-complicating relationship between commercial and public service broadcastings. Since the Broadcast Law and the Wireless Telegraphy Law were established in 1950, Japan's broadcasting industry has maintained a "two-pronged broadcasting system" wherein NHK (*Nihon Hoso Kyokai*, Japanese Broadcasting Corporation), the only public broadcaster, and commercial broadcasters operate hand in hand. The two-pronged structure, often characterized as an amalgamation of European and American broadcasting systems, binds the two heterogeneous entities in ways that a framework of cooperative competition or competitive cooperation is nurtured. The purpose of enforcing the dual system is, according to Masami Ito (1978), "to control broadcasting so as to meet the public welfare and to strive for the sound development thereof" (p. 25).

The two-pronged system is, as a matter of fact, not completely unique to Japan. In a sense, the U.S. broadcasting system too was conceived with an outlook akin to Japan. However, the orientation of PBS in the U.S. was formulated to be an apologetic compensation to commercial programming, more of an accessory than of a contra-balance to the domineering edifice of commercial broadcasting. Britain also implemented a twin-track policy in the late 1980s, preserving public service capabilities while adjusting the framework to admit new services and forces. "The stated aim is," as Raymond Snoddy has it, "to reconcile the traditions of British broadcasting with increased competition and choice" (as cited in Blumler, 1993, p. 21). It is designed to break the duopoly system maintained by BBC and to introduce a structure of innovative program provision that suits the changing needs and wants of the audience. A Peacock committee report (1986) reads,

155

> [The] public are best served if able to buy the amount of the service required from suppliers who compete for custom through price and quality. In addition, the stimulus of competition provides further benefits to the public through the incentive given to offer new and improved services . . . . The fundamental aim of broadcasting policy should be to increase both the freedom of choice of the consumer and the opportunities available to program-makers to offer alternative wares to the public (as cited in Blumler, 1993, pp. 18-19).

As illustrated, the rationale for implementing a two-pronged system in the U.K. differs slightly from that of Japan. The underpinning principle of the two-pronged system in Japan is the harmonization of NHK and commercial broadcasting to ensure diversity and balance, whereas the U.K. underscores the efficiency of market competition. For Japan's broadcasting system, cooperation is valued on par with competition. The longevity of the two-pronged broadcasting system in the postwar Japan is made possible, as Kazuo Kaifu (1997) explains it, by (a) rigorous enforcement of Broadcast Law that has effectively safeguarded the primacy of NHK by endowing it with an array of financial, technological, and organizational prerogatives; (b) effective intervention of the Ministry of Post and Telecommunications (MPT) in deterring excessive competition and monopoly by judiciously administering the broadcasting license system to control new participation; and (c) equitable labor division between NHK that emphasizes news, information, and educational programs and the commercial broadcasters that concentrate on entertainment and popular culture, which ensures a balanced supply of programs in terms of quality, quantity, and variety (pp. 5-9).

However, it is important to note that NHK has steadily maneuvered to embrace seemingly incompatible intonations in broadcasting —information vs. entertainment, national culture vs. local/ minority interests, etc. In other words, NHK has quietly interpolated and internalized the missions prescribed to commercial televisions. The absorption of what is normally considered commercial broadcasting's "expertise" into NHK's operative radius is, it seems to me, not so much of submission to commercialization as an adaptation to changing needs of diversifying audiences. The bi-

156

directional management of NHK is also assured in the Broadcast Law: "To broadcast excellent programs in the field of news, education, culture and entertainment, so as to meet a large variety of people's wishes, and thereby contribute to the elevation of the nation's cultural level" (as cited in Masami Ito, 1978, pp. 52-53). Also, a clause in Basic Services of Public Broadcasting encumbers NHK with the dual task to satisfy education and entertainment requirements simultaneously, and to foster traditional values and contemporary standards at once. It reads,

> NHK is *obliged* to provide well-balanced programming, ranging from cultural programs that satisfy intellectual interests to entertainment/performing arts programs that are recreational and emotionally satisfying, as part of efforts to transmit Japan's cultural heritage and contribute to the creation of new culture (NHK Broadcasting Culture Research Institute, 1998, pp. 10-11).

In fact, NHK has strived to chase the two rabbits (information and entertainment) by running a bifurcated system, wherein General TV 1 specializes in information-oriented programs (news, documentaries, reports, etc.) and General TV 2 focuses on entertainment-oriented programs (dramas, movies, sports, etc.), a structure extended to NHK's digital BS 1 and BS 2 recently. When put side by side, programs intended for education and information in G 1 and BS 1 are rubbing shoulders with trendy entertainment lineups in G2 and BS 2, including plenty of foreign programs like *Fuyu no Sonata* (from Korea), *Bay Watch, Friends,* NBA basketball, PGA reruns, etc. Beyond its espousal of entertainment, NHK's bifurcated programming strategy and organizational structure manifests its willingness to embrace the most sought after genres and programs, as well as to fill the gaps not covered by commercial broadcasters. It represents NHK's willingness to renegotiate a highest common denominator in terms of a maximum number of viewers.

This illustrates that NHK has leaned toward plural and eclectic interpretations of the public or the people, stitching together the public as an embodiment of ideal citizenry and the public as the shorthand for actual audiences. That is, not only does NHK suppose

157

multiple publics but also employs various diacritics in envisaging publics. The polyphony of the public is embedded in the socio-linguistics of Japanese too. The concept of "public" can be replaced with a number of different words, since, in Japanese, public (*koshu*), populace (*minshu*), mass (*taishu*), and the national citizen (*kokumin*) are often used interchangeably. The type of universalism NHK latches onto is populist in nature, for it interprets the public as anyone and everyone at the same time, the highest common denominator and a maximum number of viewers. "Public broadcasting (*Kokyo Hoso*) is," a publication from NHK reads, "not targeted at a limited audience but aims to play the role of a public forum open to anyone, and thus to contribute to the formation of a society where people can widely share common knowledge and experiences, deepen mutual understanding and reach consensus." (NHK Broadcasting Culture Research Institute, 1998, p. 11). Its dyadic approach (populist and idealist) to the public, its biaxial character that comprises entertainment and information evenly, and its insistence upon pliable universalism as to both the issue of access and the question of content orientation are accountable for the undiminished vitality of NHK as the nation's public service broadcasting.

NHK has been well sheltered from the crises experienced by PSB in many other countries: financial cutbacks, ideological delegitimation, shrinkage of viewership, etc. Its bifocal, adaptable universalism has been the fuel of its success and healthy growth, not the barrier. However, scholars like Garnham, skeptical of the compatibility of quality and quantity, popularity and excellence, suggests that a stress on universal access both in content and transmission can easily lead to lowering of cultural standards and to the defense of demagogic populism, a rhetoric that is often mobilized by Murdoch in justifying Sky TV's penetration into global local markets. Moreover, the very indiscriminating, all-inclusive breadth of NHK's universalism is being contested by digital multichannel conditions, which bring to the fore the imperative of channel specialization in place of holism and integrationist leaning that NHK and other terrestrial broadcasters have. Moreover, there appear to be some limitations as to NHK's capability to keep abreast of the infinitesimal fission of social interests, rapid-changing needs and lifestyles of a complex society like Japan. It is in this context that the universalized idea of public interest articulated by public service broadcasting is brought into question and subject to revision or, at the worst, renunciation.

The Right to Define the Public Interest

Defining "the common good" and "the public interest" is as difficult a mission as defining "excellence" and "diversity." Like the notion of the public, public interest is a slippery construct. It goes without saying that "public interests" articulated by disparate subjects and institutions vary and do not (and cannot) correspond with actual interests of each and every viewer or citizen as they are. It is essentially an epistemological issue, where the legitimacy of defining public interest rests upon the legitimacy of the subject and method of articulation.

But what PSB calls "public interests," an interpretation of what is deemed desirable for the common welfare of citizens in a national polity, could diverge from "audience preferences," which refers to the overall predilections of individual viewers. The former assumes the altruistic stewardship of broadcasters, while the latter claims to the authenticity of the audience's request. The former is reminiscent of Walter Lippmann's (1997) idea of the public interest as what an intelligent citizen, at the most rational and generous, would want for his community and even for mankind, now and for future generations, whilst the latter espouses an economic account of supply and demand coordinates, an objectification of what the viewing public is interested in at any given moment. Notwithstanding the difference in emphasis, both approaches furnish elements indispensable for a healthy feedback loop linking the producer and the viewer in a broadcast form of social communication.

Nonetheless, the gulf between public interests and audience preferences cannot be easily bridged, as much as the political and economic priorities pronounced by the respective concepts of the public and the audience vastly differ. The idea of public interests, essentially as a political judgment on societal matters, may well be at odds with the audience preferences. The former is comparatively stable, albeit ideologically malleable, whereas the latter is typically volatile, subject also to the fast agenda set by culture industries. Over the past few decades, however, we have witnessed a steady delegitimization of public interests enunciated by subjects other than publics themselves. Under these conditions PSB is increasingly compelled to unleash its grip on the prerogative to define public interests. This push gets stronger with the gradual phasing out of the era when the state's and state-sponsored organizations' self-appointment as the protégé of public interests was taken for granted. As a result, PSB is confronting a set of questions that unsettle its institutional validity: in what capacity can PSB assume the authority to identify the public interests? In what ways can the correspondence between the supposed public interest and the programs provided by PSB be substantiated? Should PSB prioritize public interests over audience preferences?

Concerned critics and scholars have wrestled with the questions to break PSB free from its daunting impasse. One of the common responses to the deadlock is to democratize the institutional, organization, and ideological makeup of PSB. Rowland (1976) suggests "an opening of programming policy-making to broader, more effective public input" (p. 113). He advises PSB to abdicate their vested prerogative to interpret "public interests," since common good and public interest hypothesized by the commissioners and producers of PSB often carry benevolent and yet helplessly elitist attitudes towards culture, community, and democracy. As Garnham (2000) persuasively states, PSB have harbored,

> [A] privileging of certain genres of media, especially to an assumption that news and overt political coverage are 'serious' and thus to an evaluation of its absence as a sign of 'dumbing down' or

160

'te-feudalization,' at the expense of entertainment and its role in the formation of public and as a site for the development of an understanding of issues of public importance or, a la Bakhtin, the carnivalesque subversion of imposed norms and hierarchies of significance (p. 45).

However culturally enriching and politically empowering a program that PSB provides might be, its interpretational monopoly over what the public interest is operates within the regime of discursive control that shields a paternalist, envoy democracy. The lack of democratic process cannot be substituted or exonerated by the supply of content aimed for democracy. Thus, the political validity of PSB to speak *for* the public can no longer sustain, unless a constant interplay between the audience and the producer is ascertained with widely accepted methods of mutual adjustment. Otherwise, "speaking *for*" the public translates to "silencing" the public, and its stately calling to warrant public interests can plummet to an autocratic task to undermine the public.

Recently, Japan has witnessed a powerful movement to decentralize and redistribute the authority of defining what public interest (*koeki*) means. Tadashi Yamamoto (1999) reports that the debate on the meaning of public interest in civil society has been particularly intense in the past several years, which shook "the basic premise of the public-equals-official schema under which the bureaucracy was seen as the exclusive arbiter of the pubic interest" (p. 8). Since the *Meiji* Restoration, a deeper connotation of the public interest has been, as Yoshida Shin'ichi discloses, whichever decisions made by the authority of government. With the sole authority given to the government in determining what the public interest is, according to Yoshida (1999), the public and private pair (*ko-shi*) in Japan normally emits "the nuance of a ruler-subject relationship" (p. 24). In the field of business too, the state authority, including the power of defining public interest, is largely delegated to numerous "public-interest corporations," because the government is still not free from the "suspicion that anything 'private' . . . will sooner or later violate the public-interest" (Yoshida, 1999, p. 47).

As a sole public-interest corporation in the field of broadcasting, NHK enjoys enormous privileges, financial, technical, and administrative, conferred by Japan's Broadcast Law. Under the auspices of the Broadcast Law, NHK has reigned as the only nation-wide broadcaster unrivalled in size and scale for fifty some years. It operates two channels of General TV and Educational TV channels on terrestrial waves (with over 35 million subscribing households), two digital broadcasting satellite channels, and one Hi-Vision channel. The commercial stations, on the other hand, are basically confined to services for regional audiences in each prefecture. Although five key Tokyo-based commercial stations have gradually developed cross-regional networks, their services cannot cover the entire nation as NHK's does.

The power asymmetry in what Japan calls a two-pronged system has been acrobatically well managed until recently, but the pot is ready to boil over, as Japan's terrestrial broadcasting faces challenges of the multichannel environment. An article in the Broadcast Law mandates NHK to "co-operate with commercial broadcasters in supplying broadcast programs and in the provision of technical assistance, in order to contribute to the advancement of the broadcasting world as a whole" (Kato, 1978, p. 53), which often places NHK in a position to exercise the upper hand over commercial broadcasters. A recent illustration of this is the fact NHK assumed 70 percent of all program production in running the digital Hi-Vision satellite channel, which is jointly operated by NHK and five major commercial stations. Left with a meager 30 percent to be divided into five slices, the key commercial broadcasters fiercely defied the unfair decision made by the MPT and refused to cooperate.

As a public-interest-corporation, NHK depends for its income on the reception fees paid by viewers (see table 1 below). This financial independence of NHK is quintessential to its identity as a public-interest-corporation. As Kato obverses, NHK's financial independence is designed to guarantee its freedom from both government and business. "The Broadcast Law has been very carefully formulated," says Kato (1978), "so as to ensure the autonomy and independence of the management of NHK, and to have the wishes of the people fully reflected in its operation" (p. 52). NHK's double negation (non-governmental and non-profit features that grant immunity from political influences and pecuniary concerns) forms a solid cornerstone on which a host of liberties and liabilities given to the public-interest corporation rest. Put differently, the insulation from business and politics permits NHK to operate as a "people's broadcasting," as portrayed by Kato (1978, p. 31).

Table 1: Reception Fees (tax included) for NHK Television Services

Type of contract	Form of payment	Monthly Amount	12-month Advance Payment
Terrestrial Television	Door-to-door collection	1,395 Yen	15,490 Yen
	Bank transfer	1,345 Yen	14,910 Yen
Satellite Television	Door-to-door collection	2,340 Yen	26,100 Yen
	Bank transfer	2,290 Yen	25,520 Yen

In reality, nevertheless, NHK is far from impervious to politics. The organizing structure of the NHK mandated by the Broadcast Law reveals a close connection with political authorities. Yoshida (1999) argues,

> The concept of 'public-interest corporation' exists in Japan in the texts of the Civil Code and other laws, but confirmation of an organization's public-interest orientation by the central government authorities is the condition for authorization of its legal status. Even after incorporation, such organizations are under the guidance and supervision of the ministries. There are 26,000 such public-interest corporations today, and many of them . . . help to buttress the public-equals-official structure (p. 47).

For example, the Board of Governors, the highest decision-making body within NHK, are appointed by the Prime Minister with the consent of both Houses of the Diet, and its annual budget is subject to Diet audit. Furthermore, non-profit guidance of NHK has been repeatedly violated. It has been involved in various profit-making activities

163

through numerous subsidies to the extent that it earned the nickname of "public conglomerate." There is a loophole in the Broadcast law, which prohibits NHK from engaging in any activities *primarily intended* for profit-making (Articles 9, 9-2, p. 39), but doesn't forbid profit-making as such.

Support for the public broadcasting among audiences used to be impressively robust. According to a survey conducted in 1997 by NHK Broadcasting Culture and Research Institute, 90 percent of respondents considered public broadcasting necessary, and only 22 percent of the respondents found the same for commercial broadcasters. As to the reliability of information, NHK topped the position with 79. 2 percent of respondents judging NHK to be reliable, followed by newspapers of 72 percent, the courts 66 percent, commercial broadcasters 38 percent, national assembly 18 percent, and government 16 percent (NHK Broadcasting Culture & Research Institute, 1998, p. 4). But the audience's support is dramatically dwindling, as NHK continues to abuse its quasi-monopolistic status. Recently, the level of anger and discontent is rising among fee-paying viewers, as corruption cases and financial embezzlements accrue within NHK and as political pressures are deeply internalized in every important decision-making process concerning programming, financial management, and other operational plans. As a result, a growing number of viewers are refusing to pay reception fees, leading to the resignation of former president Ebisawa in January 2005.

The public interest (*koeki*) NHK identifies is the creation and preservation of sound national cultural environments, in which the values, cultures, and mores of the nation are cultivated, critically examined, and amended. The very public-ness of public broadcasting draws from the fact that it institutionally crystallizes the political will of concerned citizens to preserve certain venues and resources intended for the cultivation of intelligent citizenship, elevation of culture, and enhancement of educational environment, causes that justify the allocation of state funding and other forms of public underwriting. But as the overall concerns and interests of the citizen shift over time, as societies move

164

into new material and technological directions, the content of the public interest should undergo corresponding adjustments.

One cannot afford to suppose a uniform, timeless and space-extraneous public interest, as Dewey (1954) exhorted us some seventy years ago: "the public cannot for any length of time identify and hold itself" (p. 137). PSB's monotonous and rather anachronistic translation of the public and public interests that have weathered several decades could hardly resonate with present audiences' rapidly shifting and multiplying cultural proclivities. Nor can it rival the elasticity entrenched in the notion of audience/consumer choice. Commercial broadcasters are busy at work to capture and probe the erratic movements of viewing patterns by employing an army of delicate measurements including ratings, surveys, and interviews with a minute-by-minute precision. Apart from their objectives, the mode of communication by which commercial broadcasters come into contact with viewers can be judiciously adopted and adapted by PSB to supplant its present monologism.

According to Blumler (1993), the public and public interests came to an interpretive standstill, thanks to the quasi-monopolistic privilege granted to PSB. The lack of competition in the context of the U.K., Blumler argues, brought BBC's discovery and search efforts on the needs and wants of the public to a halt. Hence, the full-blown public service model, based on the comprehensiveness ethic, Blumler (1993) asserts, "should be replaced by a partial, market-supplementing model" (p. 20). The moral fiber of the public and public interests envisaged by PSB, having been kept mummified over a half a century enduring large-scale political, economic, social, and cultural changes, might even be too archaic to be revamped. Hence, Blumler cites the Peacock Committee's report to communicate the imperative of adopting a partial, market-supplementing model in order to overcome the present torpidity and ineptitude of PSB in identifying the public and public interests. "A market, properly conceived, is not only a device to cater to consumers' known and static wants but also a 'discovery mechanism'

165

for finding out by trial and error what the consumer might be enticed to . . . and for trying out new and challenging ideas" (Peacock Committee "Report," as cited in Blumler, 1993, p. 20).

Increasingly, audience preferences—giving *what the audience wants*—is considered more appropriate than insisting upon public interests—giving *what the public is deemed needed*—in solving the estrangement of PBS with the public. For better or worse, such compassionate elitism is hard pressed to give in to the populism that bolsters the logic of consumer/market choice. Perturbed by the rise of market populism, some endeavor to reclaim the concepts of quality, education, information, and culture, which still receive a wide agreement (Minow, 1993, p. xii). Yet, agreement on what they actually mean and how they should be embodied has yet to be forged and filed through extensive and continuous consultation with the viewing subject. Without such accord or an adequate process of hammering out social consensus, PSB's lone adherence to the public interest and its blind faith in "quality and culture" can lead to a centralized model of the public sphere unsuited to the ethos of multicultural democracy. As Garnham (2000) claims, "what is needed is a decentralized model of multiple public spheres expressive of each distinct collective identity, culture or form of life" (p. 45).

Renewing Universalism in/of Broadcasting

PSB has many institutional and ideological quandaries to overcome: its paternalistic obsession with cultural harmony, its single-minded search for mechanical equality, its apprehension about individualization as the loss of sociality, its adherence to a uniform idea of universality as the only model of collectivity, all characteristics that had been fashioned during the height of the nation-state after WWII. Nevertheless, there is one form of universalism that PSB should strategically mobilize: the "outmoded" insistence on broadcasting as a public (shared) property. The pertinence of asserting broadcasting as a means of fostering shared experiences and consciousness becomes even

166

stronger in the field of digital media that is manifestly plagued by another form of universalism, privatization.

Although the ethos of privatization could serve as a powerful measure to deregulate the mind and system rigidly controlled by the state machinery, its uninhibited spread could harm even the benign tissues that breed communal consciousness. Public alarms have been expressed by scholars in and out of Japan against the potential of digital technology for having the information sphere transformed from an inviolable public matter to a privatized interest. Christopher Marsden, for example, rebukes the augmentation of exclusionary practices in information distribution through cryptography and other individualized transmissions, which is symptomatic of the changing nature of broadcasting from a public asset to a private property. He maintains,

> In contrast to broadcast public goods which are non-excludable and non-rivalrous, the privatization of information flows offers possibilities for private monopoly and sub-optimal exclusion of social groups and individuals. This is a justification for the strong European tradition of public service broadcasting, and the US provision of free-to-air terrestrial broadcasting (Marsden, 2000, p. 16).

Critics' anxiety about the unimpeded intrusion of info-commercialism and privatization norm converges on the concept of the digital divide. The term is commonly used to describe the disparity among various social demographics—different income brackets, education levels, racial/ethnic groups, etc.—regarding the ownership of and access to digital information devices. In the U.S context, the digital divide became one of the most important civil rights issues, as the information economy increasingly expands educational, social, financial and employment opportunities. According to a study conducted and released by the National Telecommunications and Information Administration, people with college degrees or higher are 10 times more likely to have Internet access at work as persons with only some high school education; households earning incomes over $75,000 are over 20 times more likely to have home Internet access than those at the lowest income levels; *the divide among races is found most striking.* Of

167

course, there has always been a divide between information haves and have-nots or frequent users and rare users of media technologies. Then, as asked by Michael Powell (2001), FCC Chairman, why is the digital divide so seriously debated when there is a "Mercedes divide"? While previous media played significant roles in shaping political, cultural climates of a society, they barely functioned as information infrastructure at a social level and a means of economic actions at individual levels. Digital media are, unlike their analog predecessors, tightly integrated into today's information capitalism. Hence, as Andy Carvin (2000) forecasts, "those who remain sequestered from the [digital] technology will be further segregated into the periphery of public life" (p. 2).

It is in this context where the "old-fashioned" universalist approach to the notion of the public and the value of broadcasting comes forward with compelling weight. Robert Phillis of the BBC perceptively asks whether PSB should produce something for all or be something that produces all that is demanded in the digital age of channel overabundance. He then claims that PSB should commit to enriching the lives of *everyone* by focusing on the needs and desires of the audiences, because the fundamental aim for public service broadcasters, available to all and paid for by all, must be to provide something of significant value to everyone. He maintains,

> In an age where technology is increasingly allowing individual programs to be delivered to individual homes for a price, this commitment to universality grows in importance; a willingness to provide serious news programs, support for the national culture, whether it be in dramatizing classic literature, coverage of great traditional sporting fixtures, or committing resources to covering other events which bring a nation together; willingness to give time to the reflection of a country's cultural diversity; the creation of opportunities for education, whether based around the examination or the classroom, or responding to the wish of older people to study at home (Phillis, 1997, pp. 1-2).

Nagaya (1998a), too, argues that the provision of vital televisual contents to "everyone" is a fundamental mission of broadcasting, for it is a "social and public asset formed through historical processes" (p. 5). He analogizes broadcasting to a "'park' needed in a community, and ideals in our minds" (1998a, p. 10). This view, of course, has

168

been confirmed time and again by many scholars across different countries, and the analogy of park in particular has been of well-worn idiom in characterizing public nature of broadcasting, irrespective of national specificity. In support of "public bandwidth" in the new digital age, for example, Ottenhoff argues that there should be publicly provided, non-profit and noncommercial lanes for public culture on the information superhighway. "Public service broadcasting is," maintains Ottenhoff (1997), "the electronic analogue of the public museum, library, school and park" (p. 17). But notice that Ottenhoff attributes the park metaphor to "public service broadcasting," not to broadcasting per se. Nagaya, in contrast, unambiguously addresses broadcasting in and of itself as a public asset, irrespective of distinction between "public" and "commercial."

Nagaya then puts forward counteractive measures to defend the public nature of broadcasting in the age where the digital multichannel environment is molded by the doctrines of privatization. Referencing Britain's law that prohibits the monopoly of popular "listed events" by fee-charging broadcasting, Nagaya promotes "quota-systems" to be imposed on all types of broadcasting for carrying out the obligation of delivering certain programs deemed essential for public interests. Additionally, Nagaya calls for the further expansion of the public service broadcasting concepts beyond television and radio to include other interactive and access-based media, such as the Internet, satellite, and cable. "Wherever media exist," he says, "the public sphere should be kept available for human rights and free-access communications, for the sake of democracy" (Nagaya, 1998a, p. 10). Can the key principles he puts forth, "universal time-differential accessibility, universal space-differential accessibility, and universal interests accessibility," be put into practice? Is Nagaya's audacious proposal simply a utopian, nostalgic wish, or something viable and well grounded within the backdrop of Japan's broadcasting system and applicable to other countries?

A number of facts indicate that it is not outside the realm of possibility to realize Nagaya's goals. Japan has consistently stressed the public nature of broadcasting, not just public service broadcasting personified by NHK. The tacit agreement on the public nature of broadcasting is extensive enough to comprise the scope of commercial broadcasting (at least some components of it). Although the torchbearer of public nature of broadcasting is undoubtedly NHK, the principle radiates afar even into some micro practices of commercial broadcasters. For instance, Tademasa Nakazawa (1997), Executive Director of TBS, a key commercial broadcaster based in Tokyo, comments that "the mass media will be all the more important as society becomes increasingly 'informationalized,' and public nature is the core of the mass media" (p. 9). This remark indicates that even some commercial broadcasters in Japan are of a kindred mindset as workers in NHK. It bears a striking resemblance with a commentary made in NHK's Broadcasting Culture and Research Institute quarterly report, which reads, "arrival of the multi-channel age means a rapid increase in the amount of information and programs available, and at the same time, a greater need for broadcasting service that can be shared by the entire society" (NHK Broadcasting Culture Research Institute, 1998, p. 11). Political figures and state officials are in accord by and large, as far as the priority of the public domain over the private sphere is concerned. Shintaro Ishihara, incumbent Tokyo city governor, recently spoke about the "civil minimum," people's basic right to obtain basic information and cultural resources to ensure their sound livelihood. Ishihara's notion of civil minimum is congruent with the inviolable tenet of universal access in broadcasting.

This is in no way to suggest that the social ambiance favorable to public affairs is unique to Japan. Nor is it true that Japan as a nation has an undivided consensus regarding the precedence of collective good over private interests, and public nature of broadcasting over the individuating nature of narrowcasting. In fact, discontent and defiance to the universal application of public nature of broadcasting have been steadily enunciated among scholars and professionals. Ota Makoto, for example, has argued for unfettering commercial broadcasters from the provisions to which NHK, as the public

170

broadcaster, is obliged. He asserts, "The rules and legal treatment for NHK's radio and television should differ from those for commercial broadcasting. It is necessary to set up for the commercial broadcasters new rules, different from NHK's, based on the freedom of expression and freedom of a business undertaking" (as cited in Hisao Komatsubara, 1989, p. 84). Notwithstanding, the degree by which Japan's institutional arrangements and social consciousness hold dear the public nature of broadcasting (not simply public service broadcaster) is remarkable.

Individual PSB in each country have developed different organizational structures, financial systems, and political objectives concordant with their own socio-economic surroundings and historical and cultural particularities. The individual distinctiveness surfaces even more evidently in times of great transformation and turbulence. In spite of national particularities, PSB as a whole was conceived with a common ideal of cultural and intellectual enlightenment of society and nurtured as a medium to uplift its audiences' quality of life and support an informed electorate. With this orientation, PSB has treasured the principles of universal service, diverse programs, and national-cultural enrichment (Avery, 1993; Tracey, 1998). When a judicious treatment is given to the harmonization of market mechanism and the public nature of broadcasting, it is not unworkable to promote the old universalism by which broadcast television is regarded as a public property even in a digital multichannel era.

The concepts of the "public" and "broadcasting" are strikingly isomorphic, in that both are pregnant with the ideal of universality and equality within the political and cultural boundary of the nation-state. Likewise, they are commonly embattled by the counter-universal/anti-uniform doctrines and institutions: broadcasting is challenged by narrowcasting; cable and satellite services are outgrowing terrestrial services; the concept of the public audience is battered by the idea of consumers; public interests are supplanted by audience preferences, etc. Ultimately, the decay of the values couched in the notions of the public and broadcasting amounts to the crisis of (national) universality espoused during the postwar construction of the nation-state. PSB is the locus where the rough challenges beset by new material environments—the primacy of digital technologies, an increase in commercial broadcast channels, and the normalization of deregulation—converge. However, the crisis of public service broadcasting should not be equated with the crisis of the public nature of broadcasting. Despite the insecure place of PSB, the relevance of the public nature of broadcasting remains unabated. In other words, the existing forms of PSB should not be assumed to be the mirror image or the finest materialization of the ideas imbued in the notions of the public, public interest, and public nature of broadcasting. The present instability of PSB in many countries is by no means a direct manifestation of the irrelevance of public nature of broadcasting, but an indicator of the imperative to reassert the public nature in and of broadcasting.

CHAPTER VII

CONCLUSION

ISDB and Interactive Television

In this dissertation I have discussed various dimensions of digital television and of the *digitalization* of television in Japan. But my discussion is limited in many respects, especially in its scope and subject matter. For instance, it barely touches upon the audience's re/actions toward the services provided through various channels of digital television—digital cable, CS, BS, and digital terrestrial services. How are they different from one another, and how are they differently perceived by the audience? How do digital television services alter or reinforce traditional viewing experiences? Does the introduction of digital television invite new methods of conducting audience research? What types of programs gain popularity, and what types are out of favor? Have any new genres evolved as a result of the launching of digital services?

The fact that I failed to address the actual use of digital television services is, I should emphasize, not expressive of an innate deficiency of political economic approaches to the above listed issues.[66] Arguably, it would be quite plausible to formulate political economic inquiries focused on the audience. As Japan's digital television shifts into new phases and areas, the next front line for the *digitalization* of television will be the realm of audience: namely the *digitalization* of the audience's attitudes, consciousness, viewing patterns, habits, desires, preferences, etc.

The *digitalization* of the audience's outlook, mindset, and demeanor is most likely to take place by way of interactive functions and programs. That is, the interactivity of digital television will be a carrier with which the political economy of the corporate-state

---

[66] Rather, much of the shortcomings stemmed from many practical reasons—restraints in budget and geographical accessibility, difficulty in obtaining relevant data/documents, shortage of preceding research both in English and Japanese, and so forth.

cartel penetrates into the quotidian routines of the audience. This campaign had already begun, as I discussed in chapter two, well before the launch of digital television in Japan. Interestingly, however, the current use of interactive television in Japan is remarkably "wholesome." Despite all the institutional and ideological maneuvers to mobilize interactive television as an economic device, Japan's commitment to the universal and public supply of information remains unaffected. Of course, the notion of "information" is no longer a safe zone immune from the reach of business; rather, it is the primary medium of realizing profit and the ultimate target of commodification in info-capitalism. Nevertheless, a close look at Japan's proposed interactive vision of digital television reveals that its foremost goal is to foster affordable, diversified information (news, weather, traffic, learning, hobbies, etc.) and to enhance the personal and flexible use of television.

Japan's interactive television follows the template set by the Integrated Services Digital Broadcasting (ISDB) plan, a blueprint for the nation's digital broadcasting system that provides multimedia-type services.[67] The NHK Broadcasting Culture and Research Institute (1997) describes ISDB as "a social system capable of providing multimedia-type broadcasting in an integrated manner and at low cost" (p. 21). What seems worth noting is that the institute defines ISDB as a "social" system. The term "social" here is used interchangeably with "broadcasting" in that it reaches the public as a whole. The emphasis on the social (broadcast) dimension is seen in other areas. Tatsuhiro Nagaya (1997b) states that TV, unlike the personal computer, is a broadcast mass medium, a medium shared by the public and used for social purposes:

> I believe that such evolution [of ISDB] will lead to the
> revitalization of TV in the digital age, as the node of all other
> electronic media and the first window of contact with information.

---

[67] Some of these services went into operation with the launch of terrestrial digital broadcasting in December 2003

Other media will develop around TV. With a decision by TV broadcasters to designate 'TV with a server' as the standard TV receiver for the digital age, TV will probably continue to play a role as a node for all media and the primary means of access to all sorts of information and entertainment. In the 21st century TV will revive as the basic infrastructure for the newly expanded distribution of information (p. 24).

Here, "TV with a server" refers to ISTV (Integrated Service Television), the household receiver of ISDB, engineered by NHK's Science and Technical Research Lab. ISTV also underlines the bi-focal charge of maintaining the social dimension of digital television as a mass broadcast medium and of improving individuality and flexibility for the user, as demanded by the increasingly diversifying configurations of Japanese society.

Akio Yanagimachi (1998a) defines ISTV as "the household receiver of digital broadcasting with a built-in server that can automatically record, update, store, and retrieve broadcast programs" (p. 12). The built-in home server of the ISTV, according to Yanagimachi, frees the user from the time and programming arrangement imposed by the provider in the analog broadcast system. Instead, it allows users to chose the most convenient time for viewing, elevating the degree of freedom in a similar and yet much more substantial way than TIVO does. Yanagimachi (1998b) uses an analogy of "program refrigeration" to explain the concept of the home server.

A refrigerator at home is always ready to offer cooled beer and snacks. How wonderful it would be if the same concept could be applied to broadcasting, allowing the audience to take out and see any program or news/information they need. The broadcasting version of a refrigerator![68] (p. 17).

Home server gives a "personal" dimension to TV. It is equipped with a "personal filter" or "agent software" that automatically identifies, remembers, and applies the usage habits of the viewer. In an interesting sort of way, it interacts with the user, while

---

[68] In the early part of the 1980s, those who involved in the ISTV project nicknamed it "*Hoso Shinkansen*," the broadcasting version of the *Shinkansen* bullet train. As the analogy denotes, the main preoccupation during this time was speed, not interactivity and individuality.

allowing the user to interact with the program provider. In addition to the built-in server, ISTV has other versatile functions that further ensures individuality and quasi-interactivity: an Anytime News function that enables users to watch the latest news and weather information anytime they like; an Electric Program Guide (EPG) that allows users to call up program categories to watch and make advance orders; Data/Info services that offer ancillary information such as recipes in cooking shows, synopses of dramas, records of athletes/sports teams, etc.[69]

Ironically, the current arrangement of Japan's interactive television is far from what has been campaigned for by the mainstream media and the MPT: the use of Internet, home-banking, e-mail, computer, and telecommunication devices, which are all aimed at boosting TV-based business. Of course, there are some technical obstacles to be cleared before the implementation of the full-blown T-commerce (TV-based commerce and business transaction). Still, the earlier emphasis on the economic dimension of interactive television—that I described in chapter two—has noticeably decreased. The present template and use of ISDB and ISTV exemplify the case in which the state's will to exploit interactive television for fulfilling economic imperatives is offset by the social will to defend TV as a public, broadcast medium. This reaffirms that that Japan's *digitalization* of television is an on-going process, open to further changes and efforts to change its future course. It also indicates that the *digitalization* of television is not a monolithic process dictated solely by the Japanese state's hegemonic plan; there are competing visions and objectives propounded by different social agents. The clash of economic interests and cultural concerns in Japan's interactive television is a revealing instance to be brought to bear on the general discussion of interactive television.

---

[69] For more detail, see p. 2, "Enriching Public Broadcasting: NHK Visions for the Digital Age," 1998, *Broadcasting Culture and Research*, No. 4.

Hypes and Hopes of Interactivity

Over the last fifty years, TV has undergone astounding transformations; the introduction of color TV, multi-channel capability, 24-hour services, convergence with VCR, cable, and satellite, and improvements in sound and picture quality. Contrary to the drastic alterations in the technological environment of television, no profound adjustment has occurred in either viewing experiences for the audience or the relationship between viewer and broadcaster. David Coockram and Christopher Rant (2002) hold, "while both choice and consumption have increased, the television experience is still ultimately passive, dominated by broadcaster schedules, with most consumers making relatively limited use of the channel choice available to them" (p. 1).

It is said, however, that the interactivity of digital television will prompt an irrevocable shift in the inveterate viewing experience and attitude of TV audience. Phillip Swann (2000), the founder of TV Online, prophesies that interactive television will transform once dull, passive experiences into something infinitely richer and more compelling. He claims that it will "scratch every itch and satisfy every desire" of the viewer and even give us a "greater sense of control and self-esteem" (p. 11). This upbeat prospect is not uniquely contemporary. In the 1980s, Denis McQuail (1987) predicted that then-emerging interactive media would present cultural and informational wealth at low cost, more choice and diversity, and greater control to the receiver/user:

> The new media seem to offer the potential of a shift on the balance
> of power away from the sender and towards the receiver, making
> much more content of all kinds accessible to users and choosers
> without dependence on the mediating and controlling systems of
> mass communication (p. 40).

Mark Poster shares McQuail's optimism. Poster (1997) announces that we have crossed a new threshold in media history with the arrival of interactive digital technologies, namely, a "second media age." These novel technologies, according to Poster, will nurture solidarity and multiplicity among audiences by enabling "a system of multiple producers-distributors-consumers, an entirely new configuration of

177

communication relations in which the boundaries between those terms collapse" (p. 3). With a global expansion of digital interactive media, he further postulates, the audience of the earlier period, condemned to alienating passivity and isolation, will enter a new social arena characterized by lateral camaraderie.

On the other hand, many scholars have raised serious doubts as to the fabled "interactivity" of interactive media, let alone its capability to change deep-seated practices of passive viewing. More than three decades ago, Raymond Williams (1974) commented on "pseudo-interactive" technologies in broadcasting. He portrayed the TV technologies introduced back then—cable system and a prototype of VOD (Video On Demand)—as simply "reactive" in nature since the range of choices was preset. Williams did not rule out the possibility that the use of "reactive" programs would enable many kinds of choice to be made quickly and accurately. Nevertheless, he remained incredulous toward the ill-considered notion that they would do much in correcting the power asymmetry between the sender and the receiver.

Even today, many continue to cast skeptical a gaze at what is now admired as "interactive television." Zygmunt Bauman (1998), for example, considers it a stone's throw from traditional one-way broadcast television: "the widely eulogized 'interactivity' of the new media is a gross exaggeration; one should rather speak of 'an interactive one-way' medium" (p. 53). For Bauman, the interactivity of the new media is a sheer publicity stunt by the suppliers, who seduce audiences to spend time and money choosing amongst the numerous packages they offer. Despite "a pretension to symmetry between the two sides of the screen," claims Bauman, "pure and unalloyed watching is their [audiences'] lot" (p. 53).

Indeed, today's interactive media boil down to either a sophisticated version of one-way broadcast media—dissemination of clustered, standardized messages—or a "selectively" interactive version supporting only purchase activities—Pay-Per-View, Near-Video-On-Demand, downloading video games, tele-education, and opinion polls of various forms. Noah Yasskin, CEO of Jupiter Communications, bluntly said, "Your TV set is not a big computer monitor. Interactivity on television is for simpler things—you're watching MTV and, click-click-click, the CD is in your house, and it's back to the show" (as cited in Swann, 2000, p. 2).

I share Bauman's disgust toward the marketing aggrandizement that interactive television will cure many cultural maladies caused by conventional one-way television. But at the same time, critiques of this kind often fail to provide languages and tools that would stimulate interventions into the positive social uses of interactive television. What must be admitted is that the interactivity of television was animated by the social aspiration to enhance the level of freedom, equality, and self-determination in mediated communications. It is this democratic yearning to overcome the drawbacks of one-way broadcast television that incubated the so-called "return path" or the channel for "talking back," which now we consider the foundation of interactive television. Regrettably, the aspiration has been temporarily hijacked and recast by info-capitalism, which reduces the meaning of two-way communication to business transactions, and confines the boundary of the user's participation to consumption. Some critics decry the fact that economic concern has become the de facto center of gravity. Chris Carlsson (1995) laments,

> The wide expansion of channels and bandwidth along with easy, cheap, two-way and conferencing capabilities could promote horizontal communication in ways that undercut the univocal voice of the dominant society. But the spectacle could also continue to absorb every social expression and movement into its underlying logic of buying and selling. (p. 242).

Yet, condemning interactive television for being held captive to commercialism is inane, if not invalid, and prone to cultural nihilism. While steering clear of hackneyed tribute, one should also resist the temptation of succumbing to demonology. Jesse Drew (1995) stresses that the advent of interactive media demands critical participation, not intoxicating admiration or paralyzing sarcasm:

> What is lacking, between the corporate hype and the jeremiads, is a perspective on the new media that combines criticism of nefarious

179

uses (commercial, governmental, military) with an understanding
of the democratic possibilities, in order to develop a theory of
communications technologies as tools for social progress (p. 75).

Drew maintains that the proliferation of interactive television by itself would not

prompt either a shift away from or a deepening of the centralized, uneven power structure

of television. Instead, Drew posits, "A popular movement for social change must take

advantage of the new technologies to further democratize the nation and to empower the

disenfranchised. It is not the technology that will revolutionize society, but a movement

of millions that must transform society" (p. 83). Drew's insistence on social activism

could provide an antidote to an undisciplined love affair with the erstwhile promise of

interactive television. At the same time, however, redeeming the innocent technology

from the "gruesome" hand of the military-corporate-state cartel could be a wistfully

romantic scenario. In addition, the supposed "innocence" or neutrality of interactive

television, open for any form of social articulations, appears equally chimerical.

Broadcast media, print or electronic, have consistently responded to the economic

needs of society since their onset. This enduring reality has fueled meaningful

discussions, actions, and contestations. The medium's conjugation with the market order

makes it a major site of social contradiction, where political struggle encounters de-

politicization, and enlightenment confronts cultural indoctrination; where economy bows

to culture, production narrates consumption, techniques of individuation lead to

socialization, and the private underwrites the public; where internal and external

challenges are created along two opposing axes of value—financial drives vs. communal

priorities, corporate initiatives vs. civic concerns, and consumer choices vs.

communicative rights.

It is important to admit that interactive media in general and interactive television

in particular are annexed to the broadcast, mass media system. As an extension of the

broadcast mass media system, interactive media carry on contradictions of the former,

rather than dissolving them. David Holmes (1997) maintains, in response to Poster's declaration of the second media age, "what is described as a second media age could more appropriately be termed a second media layer, something overlaid on TV or broadcast" (p. 33). Holmes suggests that interactive and diffusive modes of communication should not be seen as diametrical opposites. Instead, they complement each another in a concatenated circuit of social communication. Interactive media are a resident alien of the broadcast mass media system, an insider outside of the structure. But this continuity with broadcast mass media is not an unequivocal source of despair but can a sign of hope.

Broadcasting: Universal-Egalitarian vs. Universal-Totalitarian

In his book *Speaking into the Air*, John Peters (1999) perceptively renders the prominent trait of broadcasting as follows: "Electromagnetic signals radiate 'to whom it may concern'; they are no respecters of persons, and they rain on the just and the unjust" (p. 206). The indiscriminating nature of broadcasting has galvanized two contrasting vectors: the universality that safeguards social equality and communal bond on the one hand and the universality that tramples individuality and succumbs to the totalitarian spirit on the other hand. The innate ambivalence of broadcasting, the universal-egalitarian and the universal-totalitarian, animate and paralyze democratic ideals simultaneously.

However, the intrinsic duality of broadcasting Peters underscores has been largely overlooked. Instead, the antidemocratic tendency of broadcasting has been unduly overstated for decades. Much of the critique made of the broadcast's totalitarian propensity lapsed into earlier discussions about the nature of mass and mass media. To date, those who paint broadcast mass media evil overwhelm those who see and appreciate the dual tension of the authoritarian and the democratic embedded in mass media.

Prominent intellectuals of the 19th and early 20th centuries—Matthew Arnold, John Stuart Mill, Friedrich Nietzsche, Jose Ortega y Gassett, etc.—saw the rise of masses and mass society as the obliteration of cultural excellence. Similarly, the emergence of broadcast (as a form of social communication) was perceived as the eradication of individuality and the creation of cultural obedience. For example, Nietzsche (1990) regarded the rise of a free press and popular education as the decay of excellence. He commented on the deterioration of journalism and criticism as the natural result of quantitative increase: "[T]he journalist in the schoolroom, and the newspaper in society, art degenerated into the lowest kind of amusement and esthetic criticism into cement of a social group that was distracted, egoistic, and totally unoriginal" (p. 135).

Of course, voices of dissension were heard as well. Karl Marx (1975) was enthralled by the power of the press in promoting democracy and civil liberties:

> The free press is the ubiquitous vigilant eye of a people's soul, the embodiment of a people's faith in itself, the eloquent link that connects the individual with the state and the world .... It is the spiritual mirror in which a people can see itself, and self-examination is the first condition of wisdom. It is the spirit of the state, which can be delivered into every cottage, cheaper than coal gas. It is all-sided, ubiquitous, omniscient. It is the ideal world which always wells up out of the real world and flows back into it with every greater spiritual riches and renews its soul. (p. 165).

Debates on mass culture/media before and after World War II continued to abominate its universalization of "mass tastes," its homogeneity and narcotic self-indulgence. Together with Bernard Rosenberg and David Manning White, Dwight MacDonald (1957) berated mass culture as "a debased form of High Culture and thus becoming an instrument of political domination" (p. 60). Broadcasting in particular was begrudged as a cultural technique of fascism. It was treated as a machinery of hypnosis, hastening depoliticization of masses. Horkheimer and Adorno (1997) state, "[T]he majority of television shows today aim at producing . . . the very smugness, intellectual passivity, and gullibility that seek to fit in with totalitarian creeds, even if the explicit surface message of the shows may be antitotalitarian" (p. 222).

Adorno, and MacDonald's revulsion against mass media and their totalizing effect survive well into the present day. Many cultural studies cohorts, however, critique the "compassionate" radicals for overstating the victimhood of the masses as "the passive prey for whatever predators might be stalking the political jungle" (Bennett, 1982, p. 33). John Peters (1999) maintains, "The conventional concept of 'mass communication' captures only the abstract potential for alienation in large-scale message systems, not the multiple tactics of interpersonal appeal that have evolved to counter it. Early broadcasters saw 'mass society' looming and tried to stop it" (p. 217). He continues that dialogical components have grown powerfully even within a faceless one-way communication, and "the fostering of 'we-ness,' dialogical inclusion, and intimate address have remained at the core of broadcast discourse to this day" (p. 215). Whether this was a hegemonic pretense or democratic undertaking is a question Peters leaves unanswered. In my view, the broadcasters' effort to construct "we-ness" bears witness to the broadcast media's hollowness and alienating quality. At the same time, however, one cannot underestimate the fact it was the audience who made use of the "spurious" vector of communion to grope for and formulate their cultural associations with unknown, invisible multitudes. In the end, broadcasting is an entity of ambivalence, authoritarian and/or democratic, living only as a potential yet to be realized.

Enzensberger (1982) is one of the few who had a Benjaminian sensibility in recognizing the democratic potential of electronic media for turning aristocratic sanctity into democratic secularity. He praises the electronic media's potential for counter-hegemonic politics against bourgeois culture by "making possible mass participation in a social and socialized productive process" (p. 47). Later in the 1970s and 1980s, a number of academics began re/cognizing broadcast TV as an objectification of a general, collective will: Horace Newcomb (1976) called television a "medium of communion," while being critical of its equilibrium-seeking predisposition; Raymond Williams (1989) put forward the imagery of "many talking to many," as opposed to "a minority talking to majority"; and John Fiske (1987) argues that broadcast codes are the means by which a culture communicates with itself. Borrowing Basil Bernstein's idea, Fiske says,

"[Broadcast codes] are simple; they have an immediate appeal; and they do not require an 'education' to understand them. They are community-orientated, appealing to what people have in common and tending to link them to their society" (p. 73).

Denis McQuail (1997) has long argued that broadcast television has done much more good than harm: extending learning opportunities, enhancing rationality of the world, fostering outlooks towards transnational/cultural coexistence. He states that we cannot expect much more from television than the social and cultural environment in which it operates, although we can hope for some benefits along the way. Furthermore, he thinks that television is a relatively democratic medium, which, on balance, works against concentration and abuse of power, traditionalism, parochialism, and secretiveness.

No matter what is said about broadcast television, it is a form of public communication. Disdained for its uniformity, anonymity, one-sidedness, and passivity, it continues to serve as a powerful method of socialization, a property not afforded by most telecommunications tools. Broadcasting is an extension and relocation of public sphere, not diminution of it. Its capacity to reach out multitudes constitutes the central pillar of modern democracy. It is a vital instrument to national cohesion and supranational consciousness. Its tendency to encourage uniformity, passivity, and unidirectionality can be amended by the supplemental role of interactive television, as exemplified in the case of ISTV in Japan. But the positive overcoming of local and social divisions through broadcast communication, rather than universal collapsing of differences, remains a goal worth pursuing. The fact that today's interactive television resides within the boundary of broadcast television can be a source of hope, not despair.

BIBLIOGRAPHY

Adorno, Theodore W. & Horkheimer, Max. (1972). *Dialectic of Enlightenment*. New York: Continuum.

Advanced Information and Telecommunications Society Promotion Headquarters, Japan. (1998, November 9). *Basic Guidelines on the Promotion of an Advanced Information and Telecommunication Society*. (unofficial translation). Retrieved April 28, 2--5, from http://www.kantei.go.jp/foreign/990209guideline-aits.html

Advisory Committee on Public Interest Obligations of Digital Television Broadcasters, U.S.A. (1998). *Charting the Digital Broadcasting Future: Final Report of the Advisory Committee on Public Interest Obligations of Digital Television Broadcasters*. Washington, DC: U.S. Department of Commerce.

Akatsuka, Yuzo & Yoshida, Tsuneaki. (1999). *Systems for Infrastructure development: Japan's Experience*. Japan: International Cooperation Publishing.

Alasuutari, Pertti. (1999). Introduction: Three Phases of Reception Studies. In Pertti Alasuutari (Ed.), *Rethinking the Media Audience* (pp. 1-21). Thousand Oaks: Sage Publications.

Anderson, James, Brook, Chris & Cochran, Allan. (1995). *A Global World?: Re-ordering Political Space*. New York: Oxford University Press.

Ang, Ien. (1991). *Desperately Seeking the Audience*. New York: Routledge.

Avery, Robert K. (1993). Introduction. In Robert K. Avery (Ed.). *Public Service Broadcasting in a Multichannel Environment: The History and Survival of an Ideal* (pp. xiii-xix). New York: Longman.

Avery, Robert K. & Pepper, Robert. (1979). *The Politics of Interconnection: A History of Public Television at the National Level*. Washington, DC: National Association of Educational Broadcasters.

Bauman, Zigmund. (1998). *Globalization: The Human Consequences*. New York: Columbia University Press.

Bell, Daniel. (1999). *The Coming of Post-industrial Society: A Venture in Social Forecasting*. New York: Basic Books.

Bell, Desmond & McNeill, David. (1999). Multimedia and the Crisis Economy in Japan. *Media, Culture, and Society*, 21.6, 759-785.

Bennett, Tony. (1982). Theories of the Media, Theories of Society. In Michael Gurevitch et al. (Eds.). *Culture, Society, and the Media* (pp. 30-55). London: Methuen.

Besser, Howard. (1995). From Internet to Information Superhighway. In James Brook & Iain A. Boal (Ed.). *Resisting the Virtual Life: The Culture and Politics of Information* (pp. 59-70). San Francisco: City Lights.

Binkley, Joel. (1998, August 20). HDTV: High in Definition, High in Price. *New York Times*, G1.

Blakely, Robert J. (1971). *The People's Instrument: A Philosophy f Programming for Public Television*. Washington: Public Affairs Press.

Blumler, Jay. (1993). The British Approach to Public Service Broadcasting: From Confidence to Uncertainty. In Robert Avery (Ed.). *Public Service Broadcasting in a Multichannel Environment: The History and Survival of an Ideal* (pp. 1-28). New York: Longman.

Boyd, John. (2000, January 12). Some Hot Technologies for 2000. *The Japan Times*. Retrieved April 28, 2005, from http://www.japantimes.co.jp

Boyd-Barrett, Oliver. (1997). Global News Wholesalers as Agents of Globalization. In Annabelle Sreberny-Mohammadi, et al. (Ed.). *Media in Global Context: A Reader* (pp. 131-144). London: Arnold.

Boyd-Barrett, Oliver. (1998). Media Imperialism Reformulated. In D.K. Thussu (Ed.). *Electronic Empires: Global Media and Local Resistance* (pp. 157-176). London: Arnold.

Branscomb, Anne. (1976). A Crisis of Identity: Reflections on the Future of Public Broadcasting. In Douglass Cater (Ed.). *The Future of Public Broadcasting* (pp. 7-37). New York, Washington: Praeger Publishers.

Broadcasting Data. (2001, Summer). *Broadcasting Culture & Research*, 17, 4.

Broadcasting Data. (2001, Autumn). *Broadcasting Culture & Research*, 18, 4.

Brown, Les. (1971). *Television and the Business Behind the Box*. New York: Harcout, Brace, Jovanovich.

Brown, Les. (1979, June 22). WNYC-TV Studies Leasing Air Time. *New York Times*, Folder 623.

Building Japan's Information Infrastructure: Create New User Demands through Innovation that Brings 'Increasing Return.' (1993, April 16). *Nihon Keizai Shinbun*. Retrieved April 28, 2005, from http://www.anr.org/web/html/archive/old/html/output/95/bildjii_e.htm

Carlsson, Chris. (1995). The Shape of Truth to Come: New Media and Knowledge. In James Brooks & Iain A. Boal (Ed.). *Resisting the Virtual Life: The Culture and Politics of Information* (pp. 235-244). San Francisco: City Lights.

Carnegie Commission on the Future of Public Broadcasting. (1967). *Public Television: A Program for Action*. New York: Harper & Row.

Carnegie Commission on the Future of Public Broadcasting. (1979). *A Public Trust: The Report of the Carnegie Commission on the Future of Public Broadcasting*. New York: Bantam Books.

Carvin, Andy. (2000). Mind the Gap: The Digital Divide as the Civil Rights Issue of the New Millennium. Retrieved February 27, 2001, from http://www.infotoday.com/MMSchools/Jn00/carvin.htm

Castells, Manual. (1996). *The Information Age: Economy, Society and Culture: The Rise of the Network Society* (Vol. 1). Malden, MA: Blackwell Publishers.

Castells, Manual. (1998). *The Information Age: Economy, Society and Culture: End of Millennium* (Vol. 3). Malden, MA: Blackwell Publishers.

Crary, Jonathan. (1999). *Techniques of the Observer: On Vision and Modernity in the Nineteenth Century.* Cambridge: MIT Press.

Curran, James. (2000). Rethinking Media and Democracy. In James Curran and Michael Gurevitch (Eds.). *Mass Media and Society* (pp. 120-154). London: Arnold.

Dahlgren, Peter. (1997, March 14). The Public Nature of Broadcasting in the Digital Age. In *International Symposium: Public Nature of Broadcasting in the Digital Age* (pp. 17-20). Tokyo: NHK Broadcasting Culture Research Institute.

Day, James. (1995). *The Vanishing Vision: The Inside Story of Public Television.* Berkeley: University of California Press.

Deleuze, Gilles & Guattari, Felix. (1987). *A Thousand Plateau: Capitalism and Schizophrenia.* Minneapolis: University of Minnesota Press. (original work published 1980).

Dewey, John. (1954). *The Public and Its Problem.* Athens: Ohio University Press.

Dijk, Jan Van. (1999). *The Network Society: Social Aspects of New Media* (Leontine Spoorenberg Trans.). London: Sage Publications.

Discussion. (1997, March 14). *International Symposium: Public Nature of Broadcasting in the Digital Age* (pp. 31-51). Tokyo: NHK Broadcasting Culture Research Institute.

Doane, Donna. (1999). *Cooperation, Technology, and Japanese Development: Indigenous Knowledge, the Power of Networks, and the State.* Boulder: Westview.

Drew, Jesse. (1995). Media Activism and Radical Democracy. In James Brook & Iain A. Boal (Eds.). *Resisting the Virtual Life: The Culture and Politics of Information* (pp. 71-83). San Francisco: City Lights.

Ebisawa, Katsuji. (1998, New Year). Public Broadcasting in a Digital Age. *Broadcasting Culture & Research*, 2, 2.

Ebo, Bosah. (2001). *Cyberimperialism? Global relations in the new electronic frontier*, Westport, Connecticut, London: Praeger.

Electronics Giants Combine on Digital TV Tuners. (2000, October 24). *The Japan Times.* Retrieved April 28, 2005, from http://www.japantimes.co.jp

Ellis, John. (1982). *Visible fictions: Cinema, Television, Video.* New York: Routledge.

Enriching Public Broadcasting: NHK Visions for the Digital Age. (1998). *Broadcasting Culture & Research*, 3, 10-12.

Enzensberger, Hans M. (1982). Constituents of a Theory of the Media. *Critical Essays* (pp. 46-76). New York: Continuum.

Escobar, Arturo. (2000). Welcome to Cyberia: Notes on the Anthropology of Cyberculture. In David Bell & Barbara M. Kiennedy (Ed.). *The Cybercultures Reader* (pp. 56-76). New York: Routledge.

Faunce, William. (1968). *Problems of an Industrial Society*. New York: McGraw-Hill.

Featherstone, Mike. (1996). Localism, Globalism, and Cultural Identity. In Rob Wilson & Wimal Dissanayake (Eds.). *Global-Local: Cultural Production and the Transnational Imagery* (pp. 46-77). Durham: Duke University Press, 1996: 46-77.

Feldman, Tony. (1997). *An Introduction to Digital Media*. New York: Routledge.

Fisk, John. (1987). *Television Culture*. New York: Methuen.

Fonagy, Peter, Sandler, Joseph, & Person, Ethel, (Eds.). (1991). *Freud's "On Narcissism: An Introduction"*. New Haven: Yale University Press.

Ford, Glyn. (2000, February 2). High-tech Juggernaut is a Dangerous Ride. *The Japan Times*. Retrieved December 6, 2001, from http://www.japantimes.co.jp/cgi-bin/getarticle.p15?eo20000202a1.htm

Fornas, Johan. et al. (2002). *Digital Borderlands: Cultural Studies of Identity and Interactivity on the Internet*. (Digital Formations, Vol. 6). New York: Peter Lang Publishing.

Fujimoto, Masatomo. (1996). The Proposal to Split up Japan's NTT. *Advanced Materials*, 8(12), 957-958.

Fukuyama, Francis. (1992). *The End of History and the Last Man*. New York: The Free Press.

Full Text of Prime Minister's Speech to the Diet. (2000, September 22). *The Japan Times*. Retrieved December 5, 2001, from http://www.japantimes.co.jp/cgi-bin/getarticle.p15?nn20000922a4.htm

Garnham, Nicholas. (2000). The Role of the Public Sphere in the Information Society. In Christopher Marsenden (Ed.). *Regulating Global Information Society* (pp. 43-56). New York: Routledge.

Genther Yoshida, Phyllis & O'Neill-Brown, Patricia (1996, April). *Japanese Government S&T-Related Expenditures: Creation of a Favorable Climate for R & D*. Office of Technology Policy.

Gilder, George. (1992). *Life After Television*. New York and London: W. Norton & Company.

Gill, Stephen. (1997). Theorizing the Interregnum: the Double Movements and Global Politics in the 1990s. In Robert Cox & Bjorn Hettne (Eds.). *International Political Economy, Understanding Global Disorder* (pp. 65-99). London: Zed Books.

Ginneken, Jaap van. (1998). *Understanding Global News: A Critical Introduction*. London: Sage Publications.

Golding, Peter. & Harris, Phil. (Eds.). (1997). *Beyond Cultural Imperialism: Globalization, Communication and the New International Order*. London: Sage Publication.

Gordon, Andrew. (2003). *A Modern History of Japan—from Tokugawa Times to the Present*. Oxford: Oxford University Press.

Gore, A. (1996). Basic Principles for Building an Information Society. *International Information Communication and Education*, 15(2), 226-228.

Goto, Kazuhito. (1983). Japanese Project for Direct Broadcasting Satellite Service. *Studies of Broadcasting*, 19, 9-48.

Gunkel, David J. & Gunkel, Ann H. (1997). Virtual Geographies: The New Worlds of Cyberspace. *Critical Studies in Mass Communication*, 14, 123-137.

Hall, Peter (Ed.). (1986). *Governing the Economy: The Politics of State Intervention in Britain and France*. New York: Oxford University Press.

Ham, Peter van. (2001). The Rise of the Brand State: The Postmodern Policies of Image and Reputation. *Foreign Affairs*, 80(5), 2-6.

Hamelink, Cees. (1994). *The Politics of World Communication: A Human Rights Perspective*. London: Sage Publication.

Hanada, Tetsuro. (1999). Digital Broadcasting and the Future of the Public Sphere. *Studies of Broadcasting*, 34, 9-40.

Hart, Jeffrey. (1992). *Rival Capitalists: International Competitiveness in the United States, Japan and Western Europe*. Ithaca: Cornell University Press.

Hassan, Robert. (2000). The Space Economy of Convergence. *Convergence*, 6(4), 18-35.

Hein, Laura. (1990). *Fueling Growth: The Energy Revolution and Economic Policy in Postwar Japan*. Cambridge: Harvard University Press.

Her Majesty's Stationery Office. (1988). *Broadcasting in the '90s: Competition, Choice and Quality*. London: HMSO.

Hirao, Sachiko. (2000, September 7). Quest for Three Sacred Gadgets: Toshiba Transforms for IT Revolution. *The Japan Times* Retrieved December 6, 2001, from http://www.japantimes.co.jp/cgi-bin/getarticle.p15?nb20000907a2.htm

Hof, Robert D. (1998, July 6). How Sweet It Is (Again) for Chairman Bill. *Business Week*, p. 31.

Holmes, David. (1997). Virtual Identity: Communities of Broadcast, Communities of Interactivity. In David Holmes (Ed.). *Virtual Politics: Identity and Community in Cyberspace* (pp. 26-45). London: Sage Publication.

Hunt, Albert. (1981). *The Language of Television: Uses and Abuses*. London: Eyre Methuen.

Ichimura, Shinichi. (1998). *Political Economy of Japan and Asian Development*. Singapore: ISEAS.

Iida, Masao. (1999). The Digital Broadcasting Debate: How to Harmonize Public and Commercial Services. *Studies of Broadcasting*, 34, 81-103.

Imai, Takashi. (2000, July 21). Stimulus Policy Should Continue. *The Japan Times*. Retrieved April 28, 2005, from http://www.japantimes.co.jp/cgi-bin/getarticle.pl5?nb20000721c1.htm

Information Economy Committee of the Industrial Structure Council, Japan. (2001). *Policy Panning for Implementing National Strategies on Information Technology: Second Draft Proposal*. Tokyo: General Policy Division, Information and Communications Policy Bureau.

Ingersoll, Bruce. (1998, April 16). Internet Spurs U.S. Growth Cuts Inflation. *Wall Street Journal*, p. A3.

Innis, Harold. (1950). *Empire of Communications*. Oxford: Oxford University Press.

Ishii, Yoshinaga. (1985). The New Media and Public Broadcasting Service. *Studies of Broadcasting*, 21, 7-26.

Ishihara, Shintaro. (1991). *The Japan That Can Say No: Why Japan Will Be First Among Equals*. New York: Simon & Schuster.

Ito, Masami. (1978). *Broadcasting in Japan*. London and Boston: Routledge & Kegan Paul.

Ito, Yoichi. (1980). The 'Johoka Shakai' Approach to the Study of Communication in Japan. *Keio communication Review*, 1, 13-40.

Ito, Yoichi. (1991). Johoka as a Driving Force of Social Change. *Keio Communication Review*, 13, 33-59.

Iwabuchi, Koichi. (2000). To Globalize, Regionalize, or Localize Us, That Is the Questions: Japan's Response to Media Globalization. In Georgette Wang, Jan Servaes, & Anura Goonasekera (Eds.). *The New Communication Landscape: Demystifying Media Globalization* (pp. 142-159). New York: Routledge.

Japan's TV Leaps High: Scenario for 2000 and 2001, A Big Jump toward the Century of Digital-Casting. (2001). *Broadcasting Research & Culture*, 15, 2-3.

Johnson, Chalmers. (1982). *MITI and the Japanese Miracle: The Growth of Industrial Policy, 1925-1975*. Stanford: Stanford University Press.

Kaifu, Kazuo. (1997). Internationalization, Market Deregulation and Digitization: Restructuring Japan's Broadcasting Industry. *Broadcasting Culture & Research*, 1, 5-9.

Kaifu, Kazuo. (1998). Digitization of Japan's Satellite Broadcasting. *Broadcasting Culture & Research*, 3, 7-9.

Kajimoto, Tetsushi. (2000, April 17). Business Must Sink or Swim with the Net. *The Japan Times*. Retrieved December 6, 2001, from http://www.japantimes.co.jp/cgi-bin/getarticle.p15?nb20000417a2.htm

Kanayama, Tsutomu. (1999, August 7). Japanese Television Broadcast Policy-Making Analysis: From Analog to Digital 1987-1997. *The Association for Education in Journalism and Mass Communication (AEJMC) Annual Convention*. New Orleans, LA.

Kash, Don (1989). *Perpetual Innovation: The New World of Competition*. New York: Basic Books.

Kato, Hidetoshi. (1978). *Communication Politics in Japan*. Paris: UNESCO.

Kazmierczak, Marcus. (2000, December 2). The Interactive TV/Web? *MKAZ.COM*. Retrieved July 30, 2001, from http://www.mkaz.com/ebeab /webtv2.html

Keidanren (Japan Federation of Economic Organizations). (2000, February 8). *Policy Recommendations and Priority Requests to the Japanese Government on the Promotion of Regulatory Reform*. Retrieved May 6, 2005, from http://www.keidanren.or.jp/english/policy/2000/003.html

Kimura, Mikio. (1998). The Japanese Broadcasting Visions for 2005-2010: Industry Spending Simulation to the Beginning for the 21st Century. *Broadcasting Culture & Research*, 2, 18-20.

Kitahara, Michio. (1991). *The Tragedy of Evolution: The Human Animal Confronts Modern Society*. New York: Praeger.

Kobayashi, Kouichi. (1985). New Media in Japan Today. *Studies of Broadcasting*, 21, 7-28.

Komatsubara, Hisao. (1989). New Broadcasting Technologies and the Press in Japan. *Studies of Broadcasting*, 25, 77-89. (1989).

Krasner, Stephen. (2001). *Problematic Sovereignty: Contested Rules and Political Possibilities*

Kroker, Arthur & Keoker, Marilouise. (2000). Code Warriors: Bunkering in and Dumbing Down. In David Bell & Barbara M. Kennedy (Eds.). *The Cybercultures Reader* (pp. 96-103). New York: Routledge.

Kudo, Akira. (1998). *Japanese-German Business Relations: Cooperation and Rivalry in the Interwar Period*. New York: Routledge.

Lash, Scott. (2002). *Critique of Information*. London: Sage Publication. Check with oppa if this is right one.

Lehtonen, Mikko. (2000). *The Cultural Analysis of Texts*. London: Sage Publication.

Lim, C.W. (2000, April 26). S. Korea Shows Murdoch Who Has The Force. *Seoul (AFP)*. Retrieved August 3, 2002, from http://www.spacedaily.com/news/murdoch-00d.html

Lippmann, Walter. (1997). *Public Opinion*. New York: Simon Schuster.

191

Lister, Dovey, et al. (2003). *New Media: A Critical Introduction*. London & New York: Routledge.

Lyon, David. (1995). The Roots of the Information Society Idea. In Nick Heap et al. (Eds.). *Information Technology and Society: A Reader* (pp. 54-73). Thousand Oaks: Sage Publication.

MacDonald, Dwight. (1957). A Theory of Mass Culture. In Bernard Rosenberg & David Manning White (Eds.). *Mass Culture: Popular Arts in America* (pp. 59-73). New York: Free Press.

Mackay, Hughie. (1995). Theorizing the IT/Society Relationship. In Nick Heal, et al. (Eds.). *Information Technology and Society: A Reader* (pp. 41-53). Thousand Oaks: Sage Publication.

Magnetic Media Information Services. (2003, July 10). *What's News for July 10, 2003*. Retrieved April 28, 2005, from http://www.mmislueck.com/Archives/071003.htm

Manabe, Tomohito. (2001). Digital Broadcasting: Creating 21st Century Broadcasting Dreams. *Broadcasting Culture and Research*, 15, 5-7.

Mann, Michael. (1997). Has Globalization Ended the Rise and Rise of the Nation-State? *Review of International Political Economy*, 4, 472-496.

Marsden, Christopher. (2000). ICTs, Globalization and Regulation. In Christopher Marsden (Ed.). *Regulating the Global Information Society* (pp. 1-40). London and New York: Routledge.

Martin, Jay. (1997). *Dialectic Imagination: History of the Frankfurt School and the Institute of Social Research, 1923-1950*. Berkeley: University of California Press.

Maruyama, Yoshiki & Takahashi, Yasuo. (2004, October 14). *Current State of Digital Broadcasting of Japan*. Tokyo: Digital Broadcasting Expert Group (DiBEG). Retrieved April 28, 2005, from http://www.dibeg.org/PressR/seminar_in_thailand2004/presentation2.pdf

Marx, Karl & Engels, Friedrich. (1975). *Collected Works Vol. 1 1835-1843*. New York: International Publishers.

Mason, Mark. (1992). *American Multinationals and Japan: Political Economy of Japanese Capital Controls, 1899-1980*. Cambridge: Harvard University Press.

Masuda, Yoneji. (1980). *The Information Society as a Post-Industrial Society*. Tokyo, Japan: Institute for the Information Society.

Masuda Yoneji. (1981). *The Information Society as Post-Industrial Society*. Washington: D.C.: World Future Society.

Masuda, Yoneji. (1985). Computopia. In Tom Forester (Ed.). *The Information Technology Revolution* (pp. 620-634). Oxford: Blackwell.

Mathiesen, Thomas. (1997). The Viewer Society: Michel Foucault's 'Panopticon' Revisited. *Theoretical Criminology*, 1(2), 215-234.

McChesney, Robert. (2000). So Much for the Magic of Technology and the Free Market: The World Wide Web and the Corporate Media System. In Andrew Herman & Thomas Swiss (Eds.). *The World Wide Web and Contemporary Cultural Theory* (pp. 5-35). New York: Routledge.

McQuail, Denis. (1987). *Mass Communication Theory: An Introduction*. London: Sage Publication.

McQuail, Denis. (1997). After Fire—Television: The Past Half Century in Broadcasting, Its Impact on our Civilization. *Studies of Broadcasting*, 33, 7-36.

Miles, Ian. (1988). *Home Informatics: Information Technology and the Transformation of Everyday Life*. London: Pinter.

Mill, John Stuart. (1996). *On Liberty and the Subjection of Women*. Hertfordshire: Worsworth.

Millard, Steve. (1976). Specialized Audiences: A Scaled-down Dream? In Douglas Carter (Ed.). *The Future of Public Broadcasting* (pp. 185-199). New York: Praeger Publishers.

Ministry of Posts and Telecommunications, Japan. (1998, June 8). Outlining the Orientation of Info-Communications Policies for the Cyber Society. *MPT News*, 9(5), 3.

Ministry of Posts and Telecommunications, Japan. (1999, November 1). *Press Release*. Tokyo: Ministry of Posts and Telecommunications, Japan.

Ministry of Public Management, Home Affairs, Posts and Telecommunications, Japan. (2001). *White Paper: Information and Communications in Japan*. Tokyo, Japan: General Policy Division, Information and Communications Policy Bureau.

Ministry of Public Management, Home Affairs, Posts and Telecommunications, Japan. (2002). *Major Aspects of Japan's Broadcasting Policy*. Tokyo, Japan: Ministry of Public Management, Home Affairs, Posts and Telecommunications.

Minow, Newton. (1993). Introduction. In Robert Avery (Ed.). *Public Service Broadcasting in a Multichannel Environment: The History and Survival of an Ideal* (pp. xi-xii). New York: Longman.

Mitsuya, Keiko & Nakano, Sachiko. (2001). Job-Holders Working Longer Hours in the Economic Downturn: From the Survey on Japanese Time Use, 2000. *Broadcasting Culture & Research*, 18, 5-20.

Miyoshi, Susumu. (2001). Expectations Regarding ECOM—Toward a True IT Revolution. *Ecom Journal*, 4. Retrieved May 2, 2005, from http://www.ecom.jp/ecom_e/latest/ecomjournal_no4/kikou1_e04.htm

Mohammadi, Ali. (1997). *International Communication and Globalization*. London: Sage.

Moore, Richard O. (1976, Fall). Public Television Programming and the Future: A Radical Approach. *Television Quarterly*, 8(3), 5-17.

193

Moores, Shaun. (1993). *Interpreting Audience: The Ethnography of Media Consumption*. London: Sage Publication.

Morley, David. (1994). Between the Public and the Private: The Domestic Uses of Information and Communication Technologies. In Jon Cruz & Justin Lewis (Eds.). *Viewing, Reading, Listening: Audience and Cultural Reception* (pp. 101-123). Boulder: Westview Press.

Morley, David & Robbins, Kevin. (1995). *Spaces of Identity: Global Media, Electronic Landscapes and Cultural Boundaries*. London: Routledge.

Murakami, Yasusuke. (1987). The Japanese Model of Political Economy. In Kozo Yamamura and Yasukichi Yasuda (Eds.). *The Political Economy of Japan vol.1: The Domestic Transformation*. (pp. 33-90) Stanford: Stanford University Press.

Nagaya, Tatsuhito. (1997a, March 14). Digital Technology and Expansion of Market Principles. In *International Symposium: Public Nature of Broadcasting in the Digital Age* (pp. 21-28). Tokyo: NHK Broadcasting Culture Research Institute.

Nagaya, Tatsuhito. (1997b). Integrated Services Television: Digital Age TV with a Build-in Home Server: ISTV and Users' Selections. *Broadcasting Culture & Research*, 1, 20-24.

Nagaya, Tatsuhito. (1998a). Digital Technology and the Expansion of Market Principles: The Impact of Changing Technology of the Concepts and Nature of Public Service Broadcasting. *Broadcasting Culture & Research*, 2, 5-10.

Nagaya, Tatsuhito. (1998b). 500,000 Hi-Vision TV Sets Shipped, Plus 720,000 M-N Converter Receivers. *Broadcasting Culture & Research*, 2, 1.

Nagaya, Tatsuhito. (2001). The Curtain Rises on the Digital Century: Broadcasting Reborn Phase Three: From Radio and TV to Digital-Casting. *Broadcasting Culture and Research*, 15, 1-3.

Nakamura, Akemi. (2000, November 30). Interactive TV Era to Begin Friday. *The Japan Times*. Retrieved April 28, 2005, from http://www.japantimes.co.jp

Nakasa, Hideo. (1978). Effects on the Change in Telecommunication Policy. *Studies of Broadcasting*, 14, 63-85.

Nakatani, Iwao. (2000, January 18). Here Comes Japan's E-boom. *The Japan Times*. Retrieved December 6, 2001, from http://www.japantimes.co.jp/cgi-bin/getarticle.p15?eo20000118a1.htm

Nakazawa, Tademasa. (1997, March 14). The Public Nature of Broadcasting. In *International Symposium: Public Nature of Broadcasting in the Digital Age* (pp. 13-16). Tokyo: NHK Broadcasting Culture Research Institute.

Narveson, Jan. (1999). Globalism and the Obsolescence of the State: New Support for Old Doubts. In Yeager Hudson (Ed.). *Globalism and the Obsolescence of the State*. (3-20). Lewiston: Edwin Mellen Press.

National Telecommunications and Information Administration. (2000). Falling Through the Net: A Survery of the 'Have-Nots' in Rural and Urban America. In Benjamin Compaine (Ed.). *The Digital Divide: Facing a Crisis or Creating a Myth?* (pp. 7-15). Cambridge: MIT Press.

Newcomb, Horace. (2000). Television and the Present Climate of Criticism. In Horace Newcomb (Ed.). *Television: The Critical View* 6th ed. (pp. 1-11). New York: Oxford University Press.

NHK. (2002). *The Evolution of TV: A Brief History of TV Technology in Japan.* Retrieved April 28, 2005, from http://www.nhk.or.jp/strl/aboutstrl/evolution-of-tv-en/index-e.html

NHK Broadcasting Culture & Research Institute. (1998). Enriching Public Broadcasting: NHK Visions for the Digital Age. *Broadcasting Culture & Research*, 3, 10-12.

NHK Broadcasting Culture & Research Institute. (2001a, New Year). Japan's TV Leaps High: Scenario for 2000 and 2001, a Big Jump Toward the Century of Digital-Casting. *Broadcasting Culture & Research*, 15, 2-3.

HNK Broadcasting Culture & Research Institute. (2001b, Early Summer). Good Start to Digital HDTV Broadcasts: Customers Satisfied with Digital HDTV Receivers. *Broadcasting Culture & Research*, 16, 1.

NHK Broadcasting Culture & Research Institute. (2001c, Summer). Broadcasting Data. *Broadcasting Culture & Research*, 17, 4.

NHK Broadcasting Culture & Research Institute. (2001d, Autumn). Broadcasting Data. *Broadcasting Culture & Research*, 18, 4.

NHK International Public Relations. (2001a). *NHK Update*, 61. Retrieved April 28, 2005, from http://www.nhk.or.jp/pr/english/update/61/update.htm

NHK International Public Relations. (2001b). *NHK Update*, 62. Retrieved April 28, 2005, from http://www.nhk.or.jp/pr/english/update/62/update.htm

NHK International Public Relations. (2003). *NHK Update*, 68. Retrieved April 28, 2005, from http://www.nhk.or.jp/pr/english/update/pdf/update68.pdf

NHK International Public Relations. (2004). *NHK Update*, 69. Retrieved April 28, 2005, from http://www.nhk.or.jp/pr/english/update/pdf/update69.pdf

NHK Science and Technical Research Laboratories. (1993). *High Definition Television: Hi-Vision Technology.* New York: Van Nostrand Reinhold.

NHK Science and Technical Research Laboratories. (2002, June). *Newsletter*, 35. Retrieved April 28, 2005, from http://www.nhk.or.jp/strl/publica/dayori-new/en/oh-0201e.html

Nietzsche, Friedrich. (1956). *The Birth of Tragedy and The Genealogy of Morals.* (Francis Golffing Trans.). Doubleday: Anchor Books. (original work published 1870-1871, 1887).

Nihei, Wataru & Suzuki, Yuji (2004, July 1). Trends in Digital Terrestrial Broadcasting and the Prospects for a Partnership between the Broadcasting and Telecommunications Sectors. *The NHK Monthly Report on Broadcast Research*. Retrieved April 28, 2005, from http://www.nhk.or.jp/bunken/english/book/book_indexbk0407.html

Noam, Eli. (1987). The Public Telecommunications Network: A Concept in Transition. *Journal of Communication*, 37(1), 30-48.

Noble, David F. (1984). *Forces of Production: A Social History of Industrial Automation*. New York: Knopf.

Nordenstreng, Kaarle. (2001). Epilogue. In Nancy Morris & Silvio Waisbord (Eds.). *Media and Globalization: Why the State Matters* (pp. 155-160). New York: Rowman & Littlefield Publishers.

Odagiri, Hiroyuki & Goto, Akira. (1996). *Technology and Industrial Development in Japan: Building Capabilities by Learning, Innovation, and Public Policy*. Oxford: Clarendon Press.

Ohgami, Takashi. (1998). How Will Terrestrial Stations Respond to Digitization of DBS and Terrestrial Broadcasting? *Broadcasting Culture & Research*, 3, 5-6.

Okimoto, Daniel. (1986). Regime Characteristics of Japanese Industrial Policy. In Hugh Patrick (Ed.). *Japan's High Technology Industries: Lessons and Limitations of Industrial Policy* (pp. 35-95). Seattle: University of Washington Press.

Okimoto, Daniel. (1989). *Between MITI and the Market Place: Japanese Industrial Policy for High Technology*. Stanford: Stanford University Press.

Ong, Aihwa. (1999). *Flexible Citizenship: The Cultural Logics of Transnationality*. Durham: Duke University Press.

Ottenhoff, Robert. (1997, March 14). The Public Nature of Broadcasting in the Digital Age. In *International Symposium: Public Nature of Broadcasting in the Digital Age* (pp. 5-11). Tokyo: NHK Broadcasting Culture Research Institute.

Owen, Bruce. (1999). *The Internet Challenge to Television*. Cambridge: Harvard University Press.

Peters, John Durham. (1999). *Speaking into the Air: A History of the Idea of Communication*. Chicago: University of Chicago Press.

Phillis, Robert. (1997, March 14). Public Service Broadcasting in a Digital Age. In *International Symposium: Public Nature of Broadcasting in the Digital Age* (pp. 1-4). Tokyo: NHK Broadcasting Culture Research Institute.

Polanyi, Karl. (1957). *The Great Transformation: The Political and Economic Origins of Our Time*. Boston: Beacon Press.

Porter, Michael, Takeuchi, Hirotaka, & Sakakibara, Mariko. (2000). *Can Japan Compete?* London: Macmillan.

Postman, Neil. (1985). *Amusing Ourselves to Death: Public Discourse in the Age of Show Business.* New York: Viking Penguin Inc.

Powell, Michael. (2001). What Digital Divide? Retrieved September 5, 2002, from http://www.beyond55.com/digital_cdivide_debunked.htm

Preston, Paschal & Kerr, Aphra. (2001). Digital Media, Nation-State, and Local Cultures: The Case of Multimedia 'Content' Production. *Media, Culture, and Society*, 23(1), 109-131.

Public Broadcasting and Its Roles in the Digital Age. (1998). *Broadcasting Culture & Research*, 3, 2.

Raboy, Marc. (1997, March 14). The Public Oblitations of Broadcasting in the Digital Age. In *International Symposium: Public Nature of Broadcasting in the Digital Age* (pp. 13-16). Tokyo: NHK Broadcasting Culture Research Institute.

Rogers, Everett M. (1986). *Communication Technology: The New Media in Society.* New York: Free Press.

Rosenau, James. (1995). Governance in the Twenty-first Century. *Global Governance*, 1(1), 13-43.

Rosovsky, Henry (1972). What Are the Lessons of Japanese Economic History? A.J. Youngson (Ed.). *Economic Development in the Long-Run* (pp. 229-244). London: Allen & Unwin.

Rowland, Willard D. Jr. (1976). Public Involvement: The Anatomy of a Myth. In Douglas Carter (Ed.). *The Future of Public Broadcasting* (pp. 109-137). New York, Washington & London: Praeger Publishers.

Rowland, Willard D. Jr. & Tracey, Michael. (1990). Worldwide Challenges to Public Service Broadcasting. *Journal of Communication*, 40(2), 8-27.

Samuels, Richard J. (1994). *Rich Nation, Strong Army: National Security and the Technological Transformation of Japan.* Ithaca: Cornell University Press.

SARJAM Communications Ltd. (no date). *Satellite Magazine Japan.* Retrieved May 21, 2003, from http://www.sarjam.com/satel.html

Schiller, Herbert I. (1995). The Global Information Highway: Project for an Ungovernable World. In James Brook & Iain A. Boal (Eds.). *Resisting the Virtual Life: The Culture and Politics of Information* (pp. 17-33). San Francisco: City Lights.

Schiller, Herbert I. (1998). Striving for Communication Dominance: A Half-Century Review. In Daya K. Thussu (Ed.). *Electronic Empires: Global Media and Local Resistance* (pp. 17-26). New York: Arnold.

Shimizu, Mikio. (1983). 30 Years of Japanese TV in Figure and Tables. *Studies of Broadcasting*, 19, 120-144.

Shimizu, Mikio. (1985). Chronology of Events Involving New Media in Japan (1976-1984). *Studies Of Broadcasting*, 21, 121-132.

Shiono, Hiroshi. (1978). The Development of Broadcasting Technology and Related Laws in Japan. *Studies of Broadcasting*, 14, 7-36.

Shiono, Hiroshi. (1985). The Development of the System of the Telecommunications Law in Japan. *Studies of Broadcasting*, 21, 29-48.

Silverstone, Roger. (1994). *Television and Everyday Life*. London: Routledge.

Silverstone, Roger, Hirsche, Eric, & Morley, David. (1992). Information and Communication Technologies and the Moral Economy of the Household. Roger Silverstone & Eric Hirsch (Eds.). *Consuming Technologies: Media and Information in Domestic Space* (pp. 15-31). New York: Routledge.

Simon, Roger. (1985). *Gramsci's Political Thought: An Introduction by Roger Simon*. London: Lawrence and Wishart.

Sklair, Leslie. (1997). Classifying the Global System. In Annabelle Sreberny-Mohammadi et al. (Eds.). *Media in Global Context: A Reader* (pp. 37-47). London: Arnold.

Sky Perfect Communications Ltd. (2003a, August 29). *Press Release: Notice Regarding Change in Major Stockholders and the Ratio of Foreigners' Stockholding*. Retrieved October 16, 2003, from http://www.skyperfectv.co.jp/skycom/e/press/02-02/20030829_2e.html

Sky Perfect Communications Ltd. (2003b). *Annual Report 2003*. Tokyo: Sky Perfect Communications Ltd.

Smith, Anthony. (1973). *The Shadow in the Cave*. Urbana: University of Illinois Press.

Stimulus Policy Should Continue: Imai. (2000, July 21). *The Japan Times*. Retrieved April 28, 2005, from http://www.japantimes.co.jp

Straubhaar, Joseph D. (1997). Distinguishing the Global, Regional and National Levels of World Television. In Annabelle Sreberny-Mohammadi, et al. (Eds.). *Media in Global Context: A Reader* (pp. 284-298). London: Arnold.

Study Group on Convergence and Developments in Telecommunications and Broadcasting (1998, June 8). Outlining the Orientation of Info-communications Policies for the Cyber Society. *MPT News*, 9(5), 3.

Sussman, Gerald. (1997). *Communication, Technology, and Politics in the Information Age*. London: Sage.

Suzuki, Masabumi. (1999). *Toward Constructive International Trade Dispute Resolution: Lessons from Recent U.S.-Japan Disputes on Restrictive Practices*. Center for Northeast Asian Policy Studies (CNAPS), Foreign Policy Studies, The Brookings Institution. Retrieved April 28, 2005, from http://www.brookings.edu/fp/cnaps/papers/1999_suzuki.htm

Swann, Phillip. (2000). *TV Dot Com: The Future of Interactive Television*. New York: TV Books L.L.C.

Swyngedouw, Erik. (1997). Neither Global nor Local. In Kevin Cox (Ed.). *Spaces of Globalization: Reasserting the Power of the Local* (pp. 137-166). New York: Guilford Press.

Szuprowicz, Bohdan O. (1995). *Miltimedia Networking*. New York: McGraw-Hill.

Tachikawa, Keiji. (1983). Information Network System: New Telecommunications Converged with Computers. *Studies of Broadcasting*, 19, 49-70.

Tamura, Minoru. (1987). The Information Environment around the Japanese People. *Studies of Broadcasting*, 23, 7-26.

Telecommunication Council, Japan. (1997). *Vision 21 for Info-Communications*. Tokyo: Ministry of Posts and Telecommunications.

Telecommunication Council, Japan. (2000). *Info-Communications Vision for the 21st Century: IT Japan for All*. Tokyo: Ministry of Posts and Telecommunications.

Thompson, John B. (1995). *The Media and the Modernity: A Social Theory of the Media*. Cambridge: Polity Press.

Todreas, Timothy. (1999). *Value Creation and Branding in Television's Digital Era*. Westport: Quorum Books.

Toffler, Alvin. (1990). *Powershift: Knowledge, Wealth, and Violence at the Edge of the 21st Century*. New York: Bantam Books.

Tomita, Tetsuo. (1978). The Information and Communications Policy in Japan. *Studies of Broadcasting*, 14, 37-61.

Touraine A. (1969). *The Postindustrial Society*. London: Wildwood House.

Tracey, Michael. (1998). *The Decline and Fall of Public Service Broadcasting*. New York: Oxford University Press.

Ujiie, Seiichiro. (1998, New Year). The Challenges of Digital Broadcasting. *Broadcasting Culture & Research*, 2, 3.

United Nations Conference on Trade and Development, E-Commerce and Development Report 2001. Retrieved April 28, 2005, from http://r0.unctad.org/ecommerce/docs/edr01_en/enr01_en.pdf

U.S. Subcommittee on Telecommunications and the Internet of the Committee on Energy and Commerce House of Representatives. (2001, March 15). *Digital Television: A Private Sector Perspective on the Transition*. (Serial No. 107-20). Washington, DC: U.S. Government Printing Office.

Van der Pijl, Kees. (1998). *Transnational Classes and International Relations*. New York: Routledge.

Van der Pijl, Kees. (1989). Ruling Classes, Hegemony and the State System: Theoretical and Historical Considerations. *International Journal of Political Economy*, 193, 7-35.

Van Tassel, Joan. (2001). *Digital TV over Broadband: Harvesting Bandwidth*. Boston: Focal Press.

Vincent, Richard. (2001, March 16). Transnational Media and the Survival of Democracy. *The Freedom of Information Day Conference*. Honolulu Community-Media Council. Honolulu.

Vogel, Ezra. (1979). *Japan as Number One: Lessons for America*. Cambridge: Harvard University Press.

Waisbord, Silvio & Morris, Nancy. (Eds.). (2001). *Media and Globalization: Why the State Matters*. Lanham: Rowman & Littlefield Publishers.

Wallerstein, Immanuel. (1999). States? Sovereignty? The Dilemmas of Capitalists in an Age of Transition. In David Smith, Dorothy Solinger, & Steven Topik (Eds.). *States and Sovereignty in the Global Economy* (pp. 20-33). New York: Routledge.

Wang, Georgette. (Ed.). (2000). *The New Communication Landscape: Demystifying Media Globalization*. New York: Routledge.

West, Joel, Dedrick, Jason, & Kraemer, Kenneth L. (1996). Back to the Future: Japan's NII Plans. Retrieved April 28, 2005, from http://ksgwww.harvard.edu/ipp/GIIconf/westpap.html

Williams, Raymond. (1975). *Television: Technology and Cultural Form*. New York: Shocken Books.

Williams, Raymond. (1989). *Resources of Hope: Culture, Democracy, Socialism*. (edited by Robin Gale). New York: Verso.

Winner, Langdon. (1985). Do Artifacts Have Politics? In Donald Mackenzie & Judy Wajcman (Eds.). *The Social Shaping of Technology: How the Regrigerator Got Its Hum* (pp. 26-38). Philadelphia: Open University Press.

Woodall, Brian. (1996). *Japan Under Construction: Corruption, Politics, and Public Works*. Berkeley: University of California Press.

Yamada, Takashi. (2001, New Year). Digital Broadcasting: Creating 21st Century Broadcasting Dreams. *Broadcasting Culture and Research*, 15, 5.

Yamamoto, Tadashi. (1999). Foreword. In Tadashi Yamamoto (Ed.). *Deciding the Public Good: Governance and Civil Society in Japan* (pp. 7-9). Tokyo: Japan Center for Educational Exchange.

Yamashita, Shoichi (Ed.). (1991). *Transfer of Japanese Technology and Management to the ASEAN Countries*. Tokyo, Japan: University of Tokyo Press.

Yanagimachi, Aiko. (1998a). A Brief History of the Technological Development of ISDB/ISTV. *Broadcasting Culture & Research*, 4, 10-16.

Yanagimachi, Aiko. (1998b). Home Server Technology. *Broadcasting Culture & Research*, 4, 17-22.

Yasuma, Sosuke, Kodaira, Sachiko, & Hara, Yumiko. (1993). A Study on the Internationalization of TV Programs. *Study of Broadcasting*, 29, 125-150.

Yoshida, Shinichi. (1999). Rethinking the Public Interest in Japan: Civil Society in the Making. In Tadashi Yamamoto (Ed.). *Deciding the Public Good: Governance and Civil Society in Japan* (pp. 13-50). Tokyo: Japan Center for Educational Exchange.

Yoshimi, Shunya. (1999). "Made in Japan": The Cultural Politics of "Home Electrification" in Postwar Japan. *Media, Culture & Society*, 21(2), 149-173.

Wissenschaftlicher Buchverlag bietet

kostenfreie

Publikation

von

wissenschaftlichen Arbeiten

Diplomarbeiten, Magisterarbeiten, Master und Bachelor Theses
sowie Dissertationen, Habilitationen und wissenschaftliche Monographien

Sie verfügen über eine wissenschaftliche Abschlußarbeit zu aktuellen oder zeitlosen
Fragestellungen, die hohen inhaltlichen und formalen Ansprüchen genügt,
und haben **Interesse an einer honorarvergüteten Publikation**?

Dann senden Sie bitte erste Informationen über Ihre Arbeit per Email
an info@vdm-verlag.de. Unser Außenlektorat meldet sich umgehend bei Ihnen.

VDM Verlag Dr. Müller Aktiengesellschaft & Co. KG
Dudweiler Landstraße 125a
D - 66123 Saarbrücken

www.vdm-verlag.de

www.ingramcontent.com/pod-product-compliance
Lightning Source LLC
LaVergne TN
LVHW022311060326
832902LV00020B/3399